31

DAYS TO

HAPPINESS

31
DAYS TO
HAPPINESS

How to Find What Really Matters in Life

DAVID JEREMIAH

W PUBLISHING GROUP

AN IMPRINT OF THOMAS NELSON

Published in Nashville, Tennessee, by W Publishing Group, an imprint of Thomas Nelson.

Published in association with Yates & Yates, www.yates2.com.

Thomas Nelson titles may be purchased in bulk for educational, business, fundraising, or sales promotional use. For information, please e-mail SpecialMarkets@ thomasnelson.com.

Unless otherwise noted, Scripture quotations are taken from the New King James Version®. © 1982 by Thomas Nelson. Used by permission. All rights reserved.

Scripture quotations marked TLB are from *The Living Bible*. © 1971. Used by permission of Tyndale House Publishers, Inc., Wheaton, Illinois 60189. All rights reserved.

Scripture quotations marked NLT are from Holy Bible, New Living Translation. © 1996. Used by permission of Tyndale House Publishers, Inc., Wheaton, Illinois 60189. All rights reserved.

Scripture quotations marked NET are from NET Bible®, New English Translation. © 1996–2006 by Biblical Studies Press L.L.C. from http://www.bible.org. All rights reserved. Used by permission.

Scripture quotations marked NIV are taken from the Holy Bible, New International Version®, NIV®. © 1973, 1978, 1984 by Biblica, Inc.™ Used by permission of Zondervan. All rights reserved worldwide.

ISBN 978-0-7852-2484-6 (trade paper)
ISBN 1-59145-234-1 (international trade paper)

Library of Congress Cataloging-in-Publication Data

Jeremiah, David.
    Searching for heaven on Earth : how to find what really matters in life / by David Jeremiah
        p. cm.
    ISBN 1-59145-066-7
    1. Bible. O. T. Ecclesiastes—Criticism, interpretation, etc. I.   Title.
BS1475.52.J47   2004
223'.807—dc22

                                                                  2004015126

Printed in the United States of America
18 19 20 21 22 LSC 5 4 3 2 1

*Dedicated to
the faculty, staff, and students
of Christian Heritage College
in El Cajon, California*

Contents

Acknowledgments

Whenever I see the word *acknowledgment,* it seems so proper and so cold. I do not want to acknowledge the following people. I want to express my profound gratitude to each of them. I want to say "thank you."

To William Kruidenier and Rob Morgan for their research and their many helpful suggestions.

To Rob Suggs, my favorite editor, who always makes me sound better than I deserve. Rob, what a gift God has given you!

To Dianne Stark and Lois Spain, who have read and reread this manuscript with the purpose of making it grammatically correct.

To Diane Sutherland, my administrative assistant, who protects my time and makes it possible for me to have the hours needed for such a challenging assignment.

To Helen Barnhart. Helen, where would we all be without you? You managed this project from the beginning to the end, coordinating our efforts with the publisher, tracking down references, reading and rereading each draft, and so much more.

To my wonderful friends Byron Williamson and Joey Paul. You have made this book everything I dreamed it could be.

To Sealy Yates and the entire Yates and Yates literary team. Sealy, without you, I might have given up writing years ago. Thank you for your constant encouragement and motivation.

To my son, David Michael, who manages the expanding ministry of Turning Point so that I can have time to study and think and write.

To Paul Joiner, the most creative person I have ever known, for your ideas and suggestions.

To Barbara Boucher, who faithfully administers my office at Shadow Mountain Community Church.

To the senior leadership team of Shadow Mountain Community Church. You manage the day-to-day ministry of this congregation so that I might have the time to put these life-changing principles into written form.

To my wonderful wife, Donna, who allows me the late nights and long days that inevitably become part of a book project. Her belief in me keeps me excited about the wonderful opportunities God has given us to touch the lives of people through writing.

Most of all, to my wonderful Lord and Savior, Jesus Christ! This book is ultimately about You, for You are the End of the search for true happiness, finding heaven on earth.

—David Jeremiah
Oceanside, California

Preface

L et me come right at you with a tough question.

Is happiness still within our reach? Can there be a full life in an empty generation?

To put the question another way, is there some isolated corner, some hidden alcove, some distant hill where one can find a genuine touch of heaven on earth?

No trite answers will do. This particular question is too urgently important to most of us. Where is that elusive doorway, or perhaps just a keyhole, where we can catch a fleeting glimpse of the Eden we know in our hearts this earth should be?

Maybe perfect joy is just another myth—an empty reverie composed of wishes and what-ifs. Maybe we just haven't found the treasure map that would show us where to find what really matters in life.

Or maybe we have simply been looking in the wrong places. Could it be that a dusty old composition tucked into a book, found in your own home, has a message you and I have missed for too long?

Consider Ecclesiastes: thousands of years old, obscure, deep in the middle of your Bible, rarely disturbed by formal preacher or casual reader in these loud and crowded days. Oh, and one more thing about this book—it was penned by the wisest man on earth:

Solomon. Remember him? Sure, we are comfortable among his pithy aphorisms found in the book just preceding this one—the one we know as Proverbs.

But Ecclesiastes . . . apart from a few "greatest hits" pulled from its pages, you might well make it all the way through life without a single visit to Ecclesiastes.

You are likely to be startled, though, by this book's starkly modern insights into the human condition. Its message is as contemporary as a postmodern university textbook, a celebrity interview, or even a teenage suicide note. It is like an urgent "E-mail" (*E* for Ecclesiastes) written an hour ago.

It is not the *proverbial* Solomon but a weary and despairing one who cries out into the emptiness his questions of passion and pathos: Why do I feel so empty? Why do the good guys so often lose? Why do the shadows of death block out the light of life?

From the loneliness of a crowded palace, he gives voice to his own afflictions—echoed by Courtney Love, who from the palaces of pop culture has sung: "It's the emptiness that follows you down. It's the ache inside when it all burns out."[1]

Solomon hits this year's nerve. He isolates the very places where you and I have ached lately with the probing finger of a skilled doctor who says, "Does it hurt . . . *right here?*"

Solomon explores the questions: What was it that pushed you and me into the wrong pursuits? The unwise relationships? The destructive habits? How can we climb out of it now, or is it too late?

His eyes fall upon the shadows that blanket our hearts, and he describes the problems and regrets that travel uncomfortably with us, like shackles upon feet that long to run free.

Listen to the hard-wrought titles of Solomon: anointed monarch, visionary architect, cherished son of David. Yes, he is all of these things. But in the final analysis, he is one more wounded human specimen in the Great Physician's waiting room, where the rest of us sit for months or years or decades.

Yet we need to know this Solomon, for by the grace and wonder of God, his wounds are mingled with wisdom. His pain is colored by perception. And not *in spite of* but *because of* his suffering— supplemented at the outset by a special gift from God—Solomon becomes known as *the wisest man on the face of the earth.* We could do much worse for faculty in the school of life.

Listen, then, to the voice of wisdom and experience; the voice that, if you are willing to listen, will speak directly into the flesh and bones and blood cells of your life. Prepare for age-old secrets to renew and re-create you in heart, mind, body, and spirit, that you might recover the joy you have lost.

This is not only Solomon's voice; a deeper, quieter, yet more powerful voice breaks through his weariness and desperation. This One longs to bless your life with wisdom and to bring you to the crest of a hill where you can catch a glimpse of what seems impossible: heaven on earth.

Introduction

Ecclesiastes 1:1–3

In the wide world of poetry, the name of John Berryman soared among the elite of his century. He seemed to have made every conquest a poet might crave. He was a beloved university professor. A Pulitzer Prize sat upon his shelf, given for *77 Dream Songs*, his boldly innovative collection of 1965. Widespread acclaim brought him fame, friends, and followers. He had seemingly found the pot of gold at the end of the rainbow.

But one frozen January day in 1972, he came to the final stanza. The poet walked across a bridge in Minnesota, waved to a stranger, and leaped to his death in the icy Mississippi River.

Why?

"At fifty-five, half famous and effective," he had written, "I still feel rotten about myself." And in one of his poems, Berryman wrote: "After all has been said, and all *has* been said, man is a huddle of need."[1]

Do you ever feel that way? Rotten about yourself? A *huddle of need*?

One survey asked 7,948 students at forty-eight colleges what they considered "very important" to them. The study, conducted by scientists from Johns Hopkins University, reported that 16 percent of the students answered "making a lot of money." We can't be too surprised. Even so, a whopping 75 percent said that their first goal was "finding a purpose and meaning to my life."[2]

Psychologist Carl Jung, in his book *Modern Man in Search of a Soul*, wrote, "About a third of my cases are suffering from no clinically definable neurosis, but from the senselessness and emptiness of their lives. This can be described as the general neurosis of our time."[3] Jung wrote those words in the early part of the twentieth century, but with every passing year and decade their truth has become even more glaring.

Holocaust survivor Viktor Frankl produced an influential volume called *Man's Search for Meaning*, in which he wrote, "The existential vacuum is a widespread phenomenon of the twentieth century."[4]

That sense of a humanity-wide vacuum has followed us into the twenty-first century. Rick Warren's book *The Purpose Driven Life* has been a *New York Times* bestseller because it isolates this need so well. Within every single one of us lies an intense desire to understand the *why* of our existence.

In his introduction Warren describes a survey conducted by Dr. Hugh Moorhead, philosophy professor at Northeastern Illinois University. Moorhead wrote to 250 famous philosophers, scientists, writers, and intellectuals, asking a simple question: "What is the meaning of life?" Some offered their best guesses; others admitted they just made up a response; still others honestly admitted they were clueless. Several of the intellectuals even asked Moorhead to write back and tell them if he had discovered the purpose of life![5]

The conclusion is unsettling: in our time, the wise men are running low on wisdom.

Maybe this is why we look around at too many of our young people, expecting to see joy and humor and infectious energy, only to find instead substance abuse, promiscuity, and suicide.

Someone once gave me a copy of an anonymous suicide note from a college student that said:

To anyone in the world who cares: Who am I? Why am I living? Life has become stupid and purposeless. Nothing makes sense anymore. The questions I had when I came to college are still unanswered and now I am convinced there are no answers. There can only be pain and guilt and despair here in this world. My fear of death and the unknown is far less terrifying than the prospect of the unbearable frustration, futility, and hopelessness of continued existence.

Wisest of the Wise

None of this is new. The times may be changing, but human nature is not. We can't feel a single shred of emotion that hasn't already been felt a million times over. The wisest of the wise have shared fully in our plaintive cry to the cosmos, including the wisest of them all—King Solomon. Successful though he was, luxuriously wealthy though he was, surrounded by great men and beautiful wives and concubines though he was, and exceedingly blessed by God though he was—Solomon still felt all that you and I feel today.

The book of Ecclesiastes is an inner road map of his quest—a testament to his search for meaning. It stands unique within the Bible as a classic of real-world, everyday philosophy, seen through the eyes of the most powerful, influential, and educated man in the world at the time.

Solomon was the king of Israel. We find his story, both private and political, within eleven remarkable chapters in the book we call 1 Kings. At the time of his birth to David and Bathsheba, the Lord gave him a special name: *Jedidiah*, meaning "beloved of the Lord." So it was from the very beginning that an air of greatness and destiny hung about this prince.

Imagine the incredible day of Solomon's ascension to Israel's throne, in the reflected glory of his father's wild popularity and unprecedented achievements. God asked the newly crowned Solomon to make a request (1 Kings 3:5).

Can you imagine being granted such a privilege? What would you have chosen, once you caught your breath and reflected upon the staggering possibilities? Solomon had the choice of a thousand lifetimes . . . and he chose the gift of wisdom.

The Lord was pleased. Most of His children, He observed, would have opted for lengthy years or unlimited riches. It took wisdom to ask for wisdom; Solomon understood that this one precious gift is the key that opens the door to every other rightful desire.

That wisdom was granted, and Solomon enjoyed a gilded life for many years. Every decision seemed to be a sound and perceptive one. His people loved him. And the greatest legacy of all, his crowning achievement, was building the Jerusalem temple—a wonderful dwelling place for God and His people. In seeing this project through, he fulfilled the dream of his earthly and heavenly fathers.

During Solomon's reign, the nation of Israel reached its golden age. It became the empire that had always been within its capability—a light unto the ancient world. Rulers from many countries, including the queen of Sheba, made pilgrimages to Jerusalem to pay homage to Solomon.

How wonderful if we could pronounce a "happily ever after" ending on Solomon's life and the golden age of Israel. It was not to be, not for man or for nation. Solomon's vast wealth, his fame, and especially his sensual appetites tainted his special standing before God. Wealth, power, and pleasure can be dangerous even in the hands of the wisest;

these things long not to be mastered, but to master. Solomon compromised himself before the Lord who had given him enough foresight to know better. The drifting came slowly, deceptively, but the further he moved from Lord and Creator, the greater became his emptiness, frustration, and confusion.

The course of Solomon's life—and perhaps something recognizably yours—can be traced in the three biblical books that were his legacy.

In the morning of his life came the Song of Solomon, a prose rhapsody of passionate romance.

In the noontime of his life came Proverbs, a book of heavenly rules for earthly living on the Main Streets of the world.

Finally, in the evening of his life came Ecclesiastes, a regretful retrospective. In the disillusioned autumn of his years, Solomon revisited the wreckage of a wasted life. The proverbial pithiness purged, he made one final stab at redemption: an attempt to block others from his own perilous downhill road to destruction.

"It's what you learn *after* you know it all that really counts," John Wooden once said. If Ecclesiastes were a movie, the posters might read, "Solomon is back—*and this time it's personal.*"

Ecclesiastes is indeed a personal book. Solomon personally presided over a forty-year season of peace. Free of the consuming rigors of military command, he had time to think and write.

He had personally accumulated the wealth of an empire. The riches of the world were at his disposal, as well as the counsel of kings across the Mediterranean world.

Above all, Solomon had navigated life as the most intelligent and well-educated man of his time. He writes: "I communed with my heart, saying, 'Look, I have attained greatness, and have gained more wisdom than all who were before me in Jerusalem. My heart has understood great wisdom and knowledge.' And I set my heart to know wisdom" (Ecclesiastes 1:16–17).

The traditional name of this book, *Ecclesiastes,* and the author's title in verse 1, "Preacher," both come from the same Hebrew term: *qohelet.* This term described one who convened an assembly of wise men and served as its principal spokesman. Solomon chose this as his pen name for Ecclesiastes. Perhaps instead of the "Preacher," we might call Solomon the "Searcher" or the "Quester."

Empty at the Top

The words of the Preacher, the son of David, king in Jerusalem.

"Vanity of vanities," says the Preacher;
"Vanity of vanities, all is vanity."

What profit has a man from all his labor
In which he toils under the sun?
—ECCLESIASTES 1:1–3

Solomon begins his book with his conclusion: "The words of the Preacher, the son of David, king in Jerusalem. 'Vanity of vanities,' says the Preacher; 'Vanity of vanities, all is vanity'" (Ecclesiastes 1:1–2).

Immediately we stumble across that word *vanity.* Let's make a closer acquaintance of this word, for it will cross our path more than thirty times in this book. Today we connect vanity with egotism—with that man or woman who is overly self-involved. Vanity is always based on an illusion. A woman once told her pastor, "When I confess my sins, I confess the sin of vanity most of all. Every morning, I admire myself in the mirror for half an hour."

To this the pastor replied, "My dear, that isn't the sin of vanity. You're suffering from the sin of imagination."

As Solomon uses the word in his ancient Hebrew text, he refers to emptiness, to that which is transitory and has little meaning. In this case, vanity is akin to a vapor that lasts only a moment before quickly vanishing, leaving nothing behind. Imagine getting to the top only to find that it's all smoke, illusion, vapor, nothingness, emptiness.

Jack Higgins, famous author of such bestsellers as *The Eagle Has Landed*, says the one thing he knows now that he wishes he had known as a small boy is this: "When you get to the top, there's nothing there."[6]

Solomon climbed the same ladder and made the same discovery. *There's nothing here; all is vanity.* His repetition of the word *vanity* was a Hebrew poetic device that intensified meaning. He was saying, "Life is utterly, absolutely, totally meaningless."

Jewish statesman Abba Eban tells of meeting Sir Edmund Hillary, the first man to climb Mount Everest. Eban asked Hillary precisely what he felt when he reached the peak. Hillary replied that there was an immediate rush of triumphal ecstasy—for a fleeting moment. It was quickly replaced by a sense of desolation. Where could he go from here? What mountains remained to climb?[7]

Interestingly, another Everest climber expressed a similar sentiment. In May 1996, journalist Jon Krakauer was part of an expedition that reached the top of Everest. Twelve of his companions were killed in the highly publicized descent, a story that Krakauer records in his chilling book *Into Thin Air*. But he begins his account by describing his feelings on May 10, 1996, as he reached the highest spot on earth:

> Straddling the top of the world, one foot in China and the other in Nepal, I cleared the ice from my oxygen mask, hunched a shoulder against the wind and stared absently down at the vastness of Tibet. . . . I'd been fantasizing about this moment, and the release of emotion that would accompany it, for many months. But now

that I was finally here, actually standing on the summit of Everest, I just couldn't summon the energy to care. . . . I snapped four quick photos . . . then turned and headed down. My watch read 1:17 p.m. All told, I'd spent less than five minutes on the roof of the world.[8]

Solomon spent forty years on the roof of history, only to feel the same bland puzzle of anticlimax. Not only is it empty at the top, but it's empty at the bottom—and everywhere in between. Life, in and of itself, is a cluster of electrons silently coursing through their appointed atomic revolutions; cells dividing and redividing; nature recycling its rituals ad infinitum. *Emptiness. Vanity.* As Peggy Lee used to sing, "Is that all there is?"[9]

I think you know exactly what I am talking about. What did you find at the Everest of your own life? Perhaps you received the promotion, won the lottery, made the dream vacation, got the book published—all for the thorny crown of unexpected despondency. It is that horrifying emptiness, not the first gray hair nor the unwelcomed birthday, that is the real culprit draining our youthful adrenaline. It is the vacuum of success, not the fullness of failure, that deflates in the end.

Dreams come true, not free; and part of that price is realizing that alas, one more time, that elusive joy has escaped our clutches. And deep within the quiet of the soul, something suggests that one more time we have looked in the wrong place. If heaven is to be found on earth, no mountain could be high enough, no ocean could provide the necessary depth. The search must continue somewhere else.

Come, then, and join the search. Climb with Solomon to the roof of the world and take in the panoramic view. Then climb down again and walk with him down the boulevards of life.

Our journey of discovery together is designed to require one brief month. Take one chapter at a time, one short reading per day. This is, after all, not a quick stroll but a crucial pilgrimage. You may never set

out on a journey of greater import. You will want to stop and smell a
rose or two, take in a deeper truth, sit and reflect before moving on to
the next short chapter and tall truth. Get to know Solomon—king,
philosopher, philanderer, elder sage—as you have never known him.

Then one month hence we will rest like children, free and unbur-
dened, with the weight of the world off our shoulders—for we will
have found at last the object of every quest, the true North Star of
every journey, the never-dimming light of our fondest dreams.

1

Will the Circle Be Unbroken?

Ecclesiastes 1:4–7

The Sobibor Nazi concentration camp was set in the scenic woods near the Bug River, which separates Poland and Russia. The natural beauty of the setting stood in stark contrast to the stench and horror of the camp, where torture and death awaited every man, woman, and child who arrived there.

On October 14, 1943, Jewish slave laborers in Sobibor surprised their captors by using their shovels and pickaxes as weapons in a well-planned attack. Some of the Jewish prisoners cut the electricity to the fence and used captured pistols and rifles to shoot their way past German guards. Hundreds of others stormed through the barbed wire and minefields to the potential safety of the nearby forest.

Of the seven hundred prisoners who took part in the escape, three hundred made it to the forest. Of those, less than one hundred are known to have survived. The remainder were hunted down by the Germans and executed.

One of the survivors was a man named Thomas Blatt—or Toivi,

as he was known in his native Poland. Toivi was fifteen years old when his family was herded into Sobibor. His parents were executed in the gas chamber, but Toivi, young and healthy, was a prime candidate for slave labor. In the confusion of the escape, Toivi attempted to crawl through a hole in the barbed-wire fence but was trampled by prisoners who stormed the fence. As a result, he was one of the last to make it out of the camp.

Toivi and two companions set off on a nightmare journey through the dense woods. By day they rested beneath the camouflage of brush and branch; by night they fought their way through a black expanse of tree and foliage. They were driven both by youthful vigor and fear, by determination and desperation. Most significantly, they were propelled by that elusive thing they had now reclaimed: *hope.*

What they needed and craved was a guide—someone who could read the stars, who knew north from south and east from west. These were city boys lacking in outdoor skills.

After four nights of stumbling through the cold forest, the three boys saw a building silhouetted against the dark sky in the distance. Could it mean sanctuary? Perhaps a woodsman to help them toward safety? With hope and growing gratitude, they hurried forward.

As they got closer, they noticed that the building they had seen was a tower—a familiar tower. It was part of the Sobibor concentration camp! The three boys had made one giant circle through the woods and ended up exactly where they started.

Terrified, horrified, they backed into the waiting arms of the forest once more. But only Toivi lived to recount their awful experience.[1]

Have you ever felt like Toivi and his friends? We spin our wheels. We throw ourselves forward, pushing toward some goal that seems like the meaning of life itself. Then we discover we might as well have run the marathon on a treadmill—we have gone nowhere. We are right back where we started.

Solomon understood the bleak despair that follows that

realization. He begins his journal with the ultimate conclusion of his search for meaning: "What profit has a man from all his labor in which he toils under the sun?" (Ecclesiastes 1:3).

Notice the phrase "under the sun." This is another of those characteristic phrases to be encountered nearly everywhere in this book—twenty-nine times, in this case. "Under the sun" implies an earthbound view of things. Solomon was not speaking from any pious eternal perspective. Remember, he had drifted away from his Lord over the years—day by day, inch by inch, worldly entanglement by worldly entanglement.

In this chilly season of Solomon's life, he comprehended the folly of a personal journey that lasted decades and went nowhere. There was not a great deal of self-righteous zeal to be found within him anymore. And with all the wealth, all the wives, and all the world before him— including an awe-inspiring temple on his personal résumé—there was nothing left in the world to bring him satisfaction. Oh, there were the fleeting pleasures of everyday life, the little things. But he well knew that none of those could deliver peace to his embattled soul.

To illustrate his conclusion, the Searcher presents several arguments about life "under the sun." In verses 4–7, his thoughts journey to four things:

1. The course of life (v. 4)
2. The circle of the sun (v. 5)
3. The circuit of the winds (v. 6)
4. The cycle of the water (v. 7)

By the way, notice that Solomon was a man for all seasons—part philosopher, part astronomer, part meteorologist, and part hydrologist. We are not embroidering the truth by declaring him the wisest and best-educated man of his time.

The Course of Life

One generation passes away, and another generation comes;
But the earth abides forever.

—Ecclesiastes 1:4

Solomon's view is gloomy. "Generations come and go, but nothing really changes" (1:4 NLT). We could well imagine Solomon sitting at his breakfast table with the newspaper open, reading the birth announcements on one page and the obituaries on the next. Generations pass in parade. There is a deathbed in one room, a crib next door. History is a running drama of millennial length; the earth abides, but the actors play their parts and move on.

Solomon returns often to the subject of death. Remember, he is in the twilight of life and his spirits have withered. No wonder! When life is built without a spiritual foundation, death is a killer on the prowl, peering in the window.

Bertrand Russell shares this same sense of despair when he writes in his autobiography, "We stand on the shore of an ocean, crying to the night and the emptiness; sometimes a voice answers out of the darkness. But it is the voice of one drowning, and in a moment the silence returns."[2]

Rabbi Harold Kushner tells of a man who came to him for counseling. After the usual chatter that precedes such appointments, the man told Kushner why he had come.

"Two weeks ago," said the man, "for the first time in my life I went to the funeral of a man my own age. I didn't know him well, we worked together, talked to each other from time to time, had kids about the same age. He died suddenly over the weekend. . . . It could just as easily have been me. That was two weeks ago. They have already replaced him at the office. I hear his wife is moving out of state to live with her parents. Two weeks ago he was working fifty feet away from me, and now it's as if he never existed. It's like a rock falling into a pool of water, and then the water is the same as it was before, but the rock isn't there anymore. Rabbi, I've hardly slept at all since then. I can't stop thinking that it could happen to me, and a few days later I will be forgotten as if I had never lived. Shouldn't a man's life be more than that?"[3]

In the midst of his search, that could have been Solomon speaking—and it could be any number of moderns who have failed to find meaning in the day-to-day repetitions of their own lives. We get up, go to work, come home, watch TV, go to bed—only to repeat until retirement. Then we die. Or at least that is how a lot of people view life.

Solomon is saying, "On the surface, life looks like a gerbil running on a wheel. What's the point?" That is how it can look if you do not have eyes to see beneath the surface.

The Circle of the Sun

The sun also rises, and the sun goes down,
And hastens to the place where it arose.

—ECCLESIASTES 1:5

We can excuse Solomon for not knowing that the sun does not revolve around the earth. Had he known, he would have just said the same thing in a different way: "This planet of ours circles the sun. Fall, winter, spring, summer—then we take it from the top and start again. One more birthday party for everyone, and *so what?* What's the big deal?" The science is irrelevant; the philosophy is a deadly killer.

5

Solomon's phrase "the sun also rises" speaks of the silent, uncaring machine that life and nature can appear to be. He seems bewildered by comparing the unblinking consistency of the cosmic machine to the inconsistency of the human machine. For him, every golden sunset represents another short day gone from his ephemeral life. The sun does not slow down; time cannot be stopped, and death marches toward us relentlessly like a conquering army. We can run, but we cannot hide.

It is intriguing that Ernest Hemingway chose these words, *The Sun Also Rises*, as the title of his first best-selling novel. He wrote of "lost generation" Americans and Brits after the First World War, and his book conveys the despair that characterized his life and writings. Years later, shortly before his suicide, the great writer confessed, "I live in a vacuum that is as lonely as a radio tube when the batteries are dead and there is no current to plug into."[4] C. Douglas Caffey posted this poem on the website of the International War Veterans' Poetry Archives:

The morning wears
A fresh white rose,
Gleaming white on white
From head to toes!

Noonday, the rose
Begins to wilt,
And splotches show
Like a patch-work quilt!

At eventide
The rose is dead!
Its fragrance lies
In silent bed![5]

To be sure, not an encouraging outlook. But remember, Solomon's pessimism comes from his disconnect with God. When we see only what is under the sun and never what is behind it, we are left with that empty, churning cosmic machine, a great production line running to eternity and producing exactly nothing.

The Circuit of the Winds

The wind goes toward the south,
And turns around to the north;
The wind whirls about continually,
And comes again on its circuit.

—ECCLESIASTES 1:6

Solomon the meteorologist is as impressive as Solomon the poet. He anticipates what is now known about the world's great wind circuits and the global circulation of the atmosphere. There is no evidence that ancient "scientists" understood anything about wind, clouds, and the great cyclical jet streams of the earth. But Solomon, with his special, God-given wisdom, knew some of these things and expressed them in words that are poetically poignant while being scientifically accurate.

Solomon seems fascinated by the wind. We can picture him pondering life, huddled on the roof of his palace, watching the clouds driven by strong eastern currents while his robe blows in the dust. He refers to the wind once in Song of Solomon, six times in Proverbs, and fourteen times in Ecclesiastes, where the references deeply move us because the wind becomes a symbol of his despair.

There is something about the wind that speaks to the soul. Jesus spoke of it as blowing "where it wishes, and you hear the sound of it, but cannot tell where it comes from and where it goes" (John 3:8).

In that case, Jesus was speaking about the mystery and marvel of the Christian life.

But for Solomon the wind represented the invisible brevity of life. As Margaret Mitchell would later express in the title of her great novel *Gone with the Wind*, sooner or later everything in life—even our most cherished relationships and possessions—vanishes with the wind.

Remember this haunting pop song of some years ago? This is exactly what Solomon was saying:

> Dust in the wind, all they are is dust in the wind.
> Same old song, just a drop of water in an endless sea.
> All we do, crumbles to the ground, though we refuse to see.
> Don't hang on, nothing lasts forever but the earth and sky.
> It slips away, and all your money won't another minute buy.
>
> Dust in the wind, all we are is dust in the wind;
> Dust in the wind, everything is dust in the wind.[6]

The Cycle of Water

> All the rivers run into the sea,
> Yet the sea is not full;
> To the place from which the rivers come,
> There they return again.
>
> —ECCLESIASTES 1:7

As vivid as are his word-paintings, Solomon is not satisfied with the canvas. He proceeds to give us another illustration: the cycle of water: "All the rivers run into the sea, yet the sea is not full; to the place from which the rivers come, there they return again" (Ecclesiastes 1:7).

Again, how did he know that? This is an example of what some Bible scholars call "prescience"—scientific statements in Scripture that far exceed the general knowledge of the time. Solomon describes the earth's amazing hydrologic cycle. Experts tell us that at any given time, 97 percent of all the water on earth is in the oceans; only .0001 percent is in the atmosphere, available for rain. The cooperation of the sun and the wind makes possible the evaporation and movement of moisture, and this keeps the water circulating. But the sea never changes. The rivers and waters pour into the seas, but the seas remain the same. Amazed at this, Solomon uses it as a picture of the remarkable, endless monotony of life without God.

A psychologist named William Moulton Marston asked three thousand individuals, "What have you to live for?" The answers shocked him. He found that 94 percent were not living at all; they were simply enduring the present while waiting for something in the future. They were waiting for something to happen—waiting for children to grow up and leave home, waiting for next year when things would be better—or at least different—waiting for the chance to take a trip, waiting for tomorrow. *Waiting . . . waiting.* For them, life had deteriorated to a cycle with little meaning in and of itself.[7]

We all feel it. We all have an enduring sense that the universe got it wrong, that things are exactly the reverse of what they should be. Shouldn't the ignorant machine of nature be temporary, and *we* be permanent? We just know this somehow; as Solomon will soon tell us, we have eternity set in our hearts (3:11). We refuse to see ourselves as temporal creatures. We are made for everlasting life, and the clock we live on should run down while we go on forever.

But under-the-sun thinking keeps us from making the leap—from finding out that our intuition is exactly correct. The truth cannot be found under the sun but in the One who set it in motion and presides over it.

On the other hand, over-the-rainbow thinking is equally deceptive. Baseless optimism is one more dead-end street. We are to live not *under* or *over*—but *above*. The Bible says, "If then you were raised with Christ, seek those things which are above, where Christ is, sitting at the right hand of God. Set your mind on things above, not on things on the earth. For you died, and your life is hidden with Christ in God" (Colossians 3:1–3).

We live under the sun, but our destiny is beyond its rising and setting. In 1890, Anna Price wrote "Above the Trembling Elements," a beautiful hymn that provides a fine tonic for the gloominess of Solomon in these first seven verses of Ecclesiastes.

> Above the trembling elements,
> Above life's restless sea,
> Dear Savior, lift my spirit up,
> O lift me up to Thee!

> Great calmness there, sweet patience, too,
> Upon Thy face I see;
> I would be calm and patient, Lord,
> O lift me up to Thee! . . .

> And when my eyes close for the last,
> Still this my prayer shall be:
> Dear Savior, lift my spirit up,
> And lift me up to Thee!

2

Bored to Death

Ecclesiastes 1:8–11

Popular novelist Kathe Koja has claimed to spin her tales from threads of bleak nothingness. She speaks of a "black hole [that] is at the heart of every novel . . . the emptiness we each carry close to our hearts, the emptiness of being alive in a world that doesn't care. And the way we fill that Freudian hole, well, that's the novel."

When asked during an interview about her statement, Koja replied:

> Everyone is cored by that existential void, the deep hole in the heart that cries for radiance; our entire consumer culture is predicated on the belief that, if you stuff enough things down that hole, you can finally satisfy it into silence. That has never been the case. Nor does creativity, sex, art, or even love fill that hole.[1]

Solomon would have agreed. In Ecclesiastes 1:1–7 he tells us that life is futile; now in verses 8–11, he is going to tell us that it is also frustrating. Who hasn't heard stories about the old days of military training when recruits were told to dig a hole the first half of the day, then refill it in the second half? The point of such an exercise was to find the recruits' frustration threshold. How much futility could they endure before becoming frustrated enough to blow their top at the drill sergeant?

The natural outgrowth of futility is frustration—or worse. All around us in our world we see frustrated people—road rage on the freeways, shooting sprees in corporate offices, hopelessness in the hearts of individuals. In his observations, Solomon moves from the evidence of futility to the evidence of frustration when God is removed from the picture.

Nothing Is Fulfilling

All things are full of labor;
Man cannot express it.
The eye is not satisfied with seeing,
Nor the ear filled with hearing.

—ECCLESIASTES 1:8

Life is frustrating, Solomon tells us, because nothing satisfies. "Everything is wearisome beyond description. No matter how much we see, we are never satisfied. No matter how much we hear, we are not content" (1:8 NLT).

The ultimate put-down in today's society is to say we are experiencing boredom, yet everyone seems afflicted by it. This verse explains why. Nothing new "under the sun" satisfies. We can never see enough or hear enough to bring satisfaction. Everything ultimately brings weariness and boredom, forcing us to seek diversion constantly.

Our entire entertainment industry rests on this premise. Billions of dollars are spent annually around the world on producing and purchasing entertainment. Some people track their year, not on the basis of the months or seasons, but on sports: baseball in the summer, football in the fall, basketball and hockey in the winter, NASCAR in the spring. Where do you go when you conclude there is nothing truly meaningful in life? Back to the stadium, where at least there are games with consistent rules, rewards, and penalties.

Michael Crichton's thriller *Timeline* has an interesting take on this subject. A character named Robert Doniger is the CEO of an enormous and highly secretive technology company. Near the end of the book, Doniger addresses a group of people in his company's auditorium:

> In other centuries, human beings wanted to be saved, or improved, or freed, or educated. But in our century, they want to be entertained. The great fear is not of disease or death, but of boredom. A sense of time on our hands, a sense of nothing to do. A sense that we are not amused. But where will this mania for entertainment end?[2]

Where indeed? The implications are rather unsettling.

In his profound book *Man's Search for Meaning*, Viktor Frankl wrote that phenomenally large numbers of modern men and women suffer from an existential vacuum that manifests itself mainly in a state of boredom.

> Now we can understand Schopenhauer when he said that mankind was apparently doomed to vacillate eternally between the two extremes of distress and boredom. In actual fact, boredom is now causing, and certainly bringing to psychiatrists, more problems to

solve than distress. And these problems are growing increasingly crucial.[3]

In 1958, American writer Barnaby Conrad was badly gored in a bullfight in Spain. Eva Gabor and Noel Coward were overheard talking about the incident in a New York restaurant. "Noel, dahling," said Eva, "have you heard the news about poor Bahnaby? He vas terribly gored in Spain."

"He was *what*?" asked Coward in alarm.

"He vas gored!"

"Thank heavens. I thought you said he was bored."[4]

There is a bit of wisdom there. Ultimate boredom—the fate of those who can look only under the sun for meaning—may be the worst fate of all.

Nothing Is Fresh

That which has been is what will be,
That which is done is what will be done,
And there is nothing new under the sun.
Is there anything of which it may be said,
"See, this is new"?
It has already been in ancient times before us.
There is no remembrance of former things,
Nor will there be any remembrance of things that are to come
By those who will come after.

—ECCLESIASTES 1:9–11

Solomon gives us another reason for today's widespread frustration: nothing is fresh.

History merely repeats itself. It has all been done before. Nothing under the sun is truly new. Sometimes people say, "Here is something new!" But actually it is old; nothing is ever truly new. We don't remember what happened in the past, and in future generations, no one will remember what we are doing now (Ecclesiastes 1:9–11, NLT).

We look at the world that is around us—what we can see and feel and hear under the sun—and we realize there is nothing new. It is as it ever was. The deist school of theology sets up the visual image this way: God is the great watchmaker who built a beautiful watch (the universe), and then just walked away, abandoning it to run forever. Nothing is new, just the same old tick-tick-ticking.

Rudyard Kipling expressed the sentiments of Solomon when he wrote these lines:

> The craft that we call modern,
>   The crimes that we call new;
> John Bunyan had 'em typed and filed
>   In Sixteen Eighty-two.[5]

When Chris Ross filed his last column for the *Jacksonville Daily Progress*, this is part of what he had to say:

> If I've learned anything in my days at the Progress, it's there really isn't anything new under the sun. One of the first things people said when I'd tell them what I did, was usually, "Wow, I bet that's interesting. Something new every day." And I'd smile and say, "Yeah, it beats getting a real job," or something. But the longer I worked as a reporter, the more I realized I'm doing the same stories over and over. Some of the names and places and even motives would change, but essentially it was the same old thing.[6]

So as Solomon files the first chapter of his investigative study, his conclusion is that life under the sun, with its mechanical repetition, is all vanity. Nothing is satisfying, and nothing is new, and nothing is remembered. There is no profit under the sun.

Solomon had lost the sense of meaning—his reason to get out of his plush palace bed in the morning. He had the wealth and fame and power to do whatever he wanted, yet he could find nothing that was worth wanting.

We could compare him to a spider in an old European fable. It descended one day on a single thread from a barn's lofty rafters and alighted near the corner of a window. From there it wove its web. This corner of the barn was very busy and soon the spider waxed fat and prospered. One day as he surveyed his web, he noticed the strand that reached up into the unseen. He had forgotten its significance and, thinking it a stray thread, he snapped it. Instantly, his whole world collapsed around him.

Solomon had lost the silken thread that held his whole world aloft. He had forsaken the God of his youth. So far afield had the web led him that he had forgotten his godly dependence entirely.

Solomon would later summarize the central question of his book this way: "For who knows what is good for man in life, all the days of his vain life which he passes like a shadow? Who can tell a man what will happen after him under the sun?" (6:12).

There is only one Person who knows. Remember Solomon's powerful insight that still lies ahead of us: "He has put eternity in their hearts" (3:11). That *E* for eternity is engraved permanently within you, and it will not let you be content as an earthbound creature. As one hymnist wrote, "I want to live above the world. . . . Lord, lead me onto higher ground."[7]

God has made us in such a way that until we return home to the arms of our Father, we will be like the prodigal son, a miserable and misplaced heir to a lost kingdom.

Howard Mumma was a Methodist pastor who, during several summers in the 1950s, served as a guest minister at the American Church in Paris. One Sunday after the service, he noticed a small crowd of admirers gathered around a man in a dark suit. The man was Albert Camus, a famous existentialist author whose books centered on the theme of the absurdity of the human condition. Camus had begun attending the church's services to listen to the organist, and he had continued attending to listen to Mumma's sermons.

Camus's novels, *The Plague* and *The Stranger*, and essays such as "The Myth of Sisyphus," were the talk of the intellectual community, and he won the 1957 Nobel Prize for literature.

Mumma and Camus became friends in spite of the gulf that separated their beliefs and their notoriety. For the most part, their discussions centered around Camus's questions of religious belief. Mumma kept the content of their conversations private for forty years. But Camus passed away in 1960, and Mumma, at the age of ninety-two, finally went on the record about his discourses with the nihilist philosopher. In one conversation Camus told Mumma:

> The reason I have been coming to church is because I am seeking. I'm almost on a pilgrimage—seeking something to fill the void that I am experiencing—and no one else knows. Certainly the public and the readers of my novels, while they see that void, are not finding the answers in what they are reading. But deep down you are right. I am searching for something that the world is not giving me. . . . In a sense we are all products of a mundane world, a world without spirit. The world in which we live and the lives which we live are decidedly empty. . . . Since I have been coming to church,

I have been thinking a great deal about the idea of a transcendent, something that is other than this world. It is something that you do not hear much about today, but I am finding it.

One of the basic teachings that I learned from French existentialist Jean-Paul Sartre is that man is alone. We are solitary centers of the universe. Perhaps we ourselves are the only ones who have ever asked the great questions of life. Perhaps, since Nazism, we are also the ones who have loved and lost and who are, therefore, fearful of life. I certainly don't have it, but it is there. On Sunday mornings, I hear that the answer is God.

You have made it very clear to me, Howard, that we are not the only ones in this world. There is something that is invisible. We may not hear the voice, but there is some way in which we can become aware that we are not the only ones in the world and that there is help for all of us.[8]

These are not the words of a man who is making a profession of faith in Jesus Christ, but they are highly significant nonetheless—note Camus's words "but I am finding it." Like the cracks and groans of a glacier under a warming sun, they are the words of a man whose worldview was shifting. Camus had built a career out of the idea that life is absurd and meaningless, but after living with that philosophy for several decades, he wasn't so sure anymore. He was willing to admit that he had found only spiritual quicksand in the landscape of meaninglessness—and to consider that there was a God who might satisfy his thirst for meaning after all.

Another philosopher lived centuries earlier. Blaise Pascal was without equal, a brilliant French thinker, scientist, mathematician, and inventor. As a boy in Paris his remarkable grasp of mathematics led to his involvement with the Academy of Science, where he mingled with the greatest intellectuals of his day. At fifteen he was writing books and developing theorems that left his professors shaking their heads. As a teenager he invented history's first digital calculating machine; other discoveries led to the invention of the barometer, the vacuum pump, the air compressor, the syringe, and the hydraulic press.

But as a young man Pascal had trouble with the spiritual equations of life, and he soon grew disillusioned with the pleasures of his fashionable society. Everything seemed boring to him. Nothing was fresh or fulfilling.

One night Pascal picked up a Bible and turned to John 17. As he began reading, verse 3 blazed out like a spark and seemed to set the room on fire: "And this is eternal life, that they may know You, the only true God, and Jesus Christ whom You have sent." His soul instantly took wing, and he was in the permanent embrace of Jesus Christ. Taking pen and parchment, he began quickly writing snatches of his thoughts:

> In the year of Grace, 1654
> On Monday, 23rd of November
> Fire
> God of Abraham, God of Isaac, God of Jacob,
> not of the philosophers and scholars.
> Certitude. Certitude, Feeling, Joy. Peace.
> Joy, joy, joy, tears of joy.
> This is eternal life, that they may know You, the Only true God,
> and Jesus Christ whom You have sent.
> Jesus Christ. Let me never be separated from Him.

Pascal spent the rest of his life proclaiming the greatness of God. That scrap of parchment was found after his death sewed into the lining of his coat, that it might ever be close to his heart.

It was this same Pascal who echoed the words of Ecclesiastes: "There is a God-shaped vacuum in the heart of every man that cannot be filled by any created thing, but by God alone made known through Jesus Christ."[9] Anything else would be the equivalent of forcing a square peg into a round hole. None but Christ can fill that hole, though men spend their lives trying every other possibility in vain. But the moment the rightful Lord of your soul fills its vacuum, there will be a fullness such as you never knew could be possible under the sun.

And just as your heart is perfectly and joyfully filled, so will everything seem to be around you. The trees will seem to be raising their branches in heavenly praise. You will hear the very rocks cry out His glories. You will have emerged from the dark web of destruction to the light of heaven on earth.

3

Trivial Pursuits

Ecclesiastes 1:12–2:11

On one edition of the CBS television show *NFL Today*, Deion Sanders and Dan Marino found themselves arguing on the air. The bone of contention was Lawrence Taylor's book, *LT: Over the Edge*—a controversial account of Taylor's years in the National Football League.

"When I was on the field, I was Superman," Taylor had described in his book. "It was almost like I operated on a higher plane. . . . But when I came off the field, something happened. LT became Lawrence Taylor, and Lawrence Taylor was completely clueless. Like Clark Kent on crack."[1]

Taylor admitted he had often been out of control, addicted to cocaine and a hard-partying lifestyle that led to a bitter divorce, numerous arrests, financial ruin, broken health, and deep depression. He went on to describe the excesses of other NFL players.

As Sanders and Marino discussed the book on the air, Marino

expressed surprise at some of the revelations in Taylor's book and indicated that such things did not happen when he was a quarterback. When Sanders scoffed at Marino's incredulity, Marino took offense. "Why are you saying I'm naive?" he retorted.

Deion replied:

Don't tell me you don't know what goes on in the NFL. You don't know guys get high and guys do everything under the sun? Twenty-year-old or thirty-year-old guys with millions of dollars—that equals destruction. So you can't sit up here and tell me that you were immune to that stuff.[2]

I found it interesting that Sanders reached back three thousand years for Solomon's phrase to describe the lives of modern athletes. Whether athlete or emperor, you can try everything "under the sun," but none of it will fill an empty life. *None of it.*

To drive home his point, Solomon recounts some of his own experiences under the sun.

Searching for Meaning in Wisdom

I, the Preacher, was king over Israel in Jerusalem. And I set my heart to seek and search out by wisdom concerning all that is done under heaven; this burdensome task God has given to the sons of man, by which they may be exercised. I have seen all the works that are done under the sun; and indeed, all is vanity and grasping for the wind.

What is crooked cannot be made straight,
And what is lacking cannot be numbered.

I communed with my heart, saying, "Look, I have attained
greatness, and have gained more wisdom than all who
were before me in Jerusalem. My heart has understood
great wisdom and knowledge." And I set my heart to know
wisdom and to know madness and folly. I perceived that this
also is grasping for the wind.

For in much wisdom is much grief,
And he who increases knowledge increases sorrow.
—ECCLESIASTES 1:12–18

Solomon ends the first chapter of Ecclesiastes by describing the
futility of searching for fulfillment through learning. Was the king
soured on education? Not a bit. He was the best-educated man of
his generation. His wisdom was legendary; he had pursued wisdom
wherever it could be found. Yet to his surprise, the more he learned,
the emptier he felt.

He's not alone. Several years ago, in his monthly letter from
Focus on the Family ministry, Dr. James Dobson told the story of
Karen Cheng, age seventeen, from Fremont, California. She achieved
a perfect score of 800 on both sections of the SAT test. She also got
a perfect 8,000 on the rigorous University of California acceptance
index. Never before had anyone accomplished this staggering intellectual feat.

Karen, a straight-A student at Mission San Jose High School,
described herself as a typical teenager who munches on junk food and
talks for hours on the telephone. She even claimed to be a procrastina-
tor who did not do her homework until the last minute.

Karen's teachers told a different story. They called her "Wonder
Woman" because of her unquenchable thirst for knowledge and her
uncanny ability to retain whatever she read. But when a reporter asked

her, "What is the meaning of life?" Karen's reply was surprising. "I have no idea," she answered. "I would like to know myself."[3]

T. S. Eliot once dryly remarked, "All our knowledge brings us nearer to our ignorance."[4] In other words, the more we learn, the smaller we feel.

Solomon was confused. He pursued education, wisdom, and knowledge as no one before him had done. And the fuller his mastery of these fields, the emptier they seemed. "I perceived that this also is grasping for the wind," he concluded wearily. "For in much wisdom is much grief, and he who increases knowledge increases sorrow" (Ecclesiastes 1:17–18).

Consider the sum total of all our knowledge, all our progress, all our technology. Has any of it really made the experience of life richer? Yes, we are thankful to God for medical advances and jet travel. Most of us have more information on the hard drives of our computers than entire nations once possessed in their ancient libraries.

Yet there have never been so many unhappy people, so many illiterate, so many hungry and diseased and disowned. All our accumulated knowledge of history cannot keep us from terrorism and war and discord on every continent.

This, of course, is a global crisis. *The Star*, published in Johannesburg, South Africa, reported on a survey conducted among South African students. There were alarming increases in the levels of substance abuse and sexual expression. Did these freedoms bring happiness? The newspaper reported: "The survey also gave an indication of the mental health of many teenagers, showing that many had feelings of emptiness, depression, and hopelessness about their future. About 25 percent of the pupils have felt 'sad,' resulting in 19 percent considering suicide."[5]

For all its benefits, education and intellectual attainment can only speak to us about life under the sun. The rest of the story is found in

God's revealed Word. When we neglect or reject the revealed truth of Scripture, even our most brilliant scientists and professors are little more than mice scurrying around inside a piano, analyzing all the hammers and strings, willfully ignorant of the musical score sitting on the stand above the keys.

To paraphrase a quaint old North Carolina evangelist, Vance Havner, it is exceedingly odd that scholars master whole libraries seeking wisdom, while the janitor nearby has enjoyed it for years.[6]

Christian apologist Josh McDowell, speaking on college campuses in the 1960s and '70s, often reminded audiences that if education was the key to life, then universities would be the most moral, ethical, and spiritual centers in any nation. Education would equate to contentment. We all know that's not the case.

Paul had his era's equivalent of a wall full of Ivy League master's degrees. Yet Jesus, the Lord of life, was a self-taught peasant. The meaning of life is something discovered elsewhere.

Education is a wonderful thing, an earthly treasure to be sought. But we must realize that Western civilization has set the value of it too high. As Paul explained clearly in 1 Corinthians 13:2, knowledge minus soul amounts to a great deal of nothing. And as he said in verse 13, spiritual character trumps all other gifts every time. As America learned in the first few years of the twenty-first century, knowledge and power in corporate offices can simply lead to more creative ways to rebel against goodness and reason.

Searching for Meaning in Wild Living

I said in my heart, "Come now, I will test you with mirth; therefore enjoy pleasure"; but surely, this also was vanity. I said of laughter—"Madness!"; and of mirth, "What does it accomplish?" I searched in my heart how to gratify my flesh with wine, while guiding my heart with wisdom, and how to lay hold on folly, till I might see what was good for the sons of men to do under heaven all the days of their lives.

—Ecclesiastes 2:1–3

Forward into the second chapter of Ecclesiastes comes the weary king, prolonging his quest for meaning. Education proved fruitless, but perhaps he'll find what he seeks in reckless abandon. These verses sound like a report from one of our tabloids or celebrity magazines.

Solomon began with amusement: "Come now, I will test you with mirth" (Ecclesiastes 2:1). You can almost visualize the scene. His palace in Jerusalem probably resembled a tenth-century-BC version of Caesar's Palace in Las Vegas—bright lights, big city, bells and baubles everywhere. But no meaning . . . no peace . . . no happiness. The mornings-after all looked the same.

The possibilities for sensual pleasure were nearly endless in Solomon's world. And who had better access to those possibilities than the king? He had a palace and all its servants at his fingertips. He had rooms full of wives and concubines. And still he found no fullness. The emptiness of it brought him to a wise realization: "Even in laughter the heart may sorrow, and the end of mirth may be grief" (Proverbs 14:13). For many, laughter only breaks the monotony of crying, and pleasure is only an intermission to pain. Solomon was trying to be happy, but he was failing.

So many today can empathize with Solomon. They have been down the road of pleasure and found that it led nowhere but to destruction.

When amusement failed to satisfy him, Solomon turned to alcohol. "I searched in my heart how to gratify my flesh with wine," he said, "while guiding my heart with wisdom" (Ecclesiastes 2:3).

It is not that Solomon became an alcoholic; he apparently avoided being drunk. He says he was able to keep his heart with wisdom. He kept his senses about him so he could record his observations on the effects of the wine. But as he sampled the tastes of the drink before him, he found that the pleasure was fleeting and artificial. His answer was certainly not in a bottle.

The bottomless budgets of the liquor industry make drinking seem very attractive today. A wineglass or beer bottle becomes a ticket to social acceptance for our young people, and soon they feel naked without it. Campus parties and social life revolve completely around drinking and intoxication, as if these were the most glorious of pursuits, the focus of life itself. Meanwhile, the mounting tragedies of drunk driving and dissipated lives are ignored, because who can shout over the message of movies, songs, and TV commercials that glorify the emptiness?

Solomon knew the truth. Alcohol was perhaps the emptiest of pursuits.

Searching for Meaning in Work

I made my works great, I built myself houses, and planted
myself vineyards. I made myself gardens and orchards, and I
planted all kinds of fruit trees in them. I made myself water
pools from which to water the growing trees of the grove.

—ECCLESIASTES 2:4–6

Wisdom and wild living failed, so off to work. Perhaps through accomplishment he could find the meaning of life. Solomon turned to his genius for building. He put up houses and planted vineyards. He planted gardens and orchards and made pools to water them.

The history of that period confirms that Solomon was one of the greatest builders of any era. How could he have thought the selfish, temporal pleasures of amusement or alcohol would amount to anything? Surely the answer was in leaving a legacy—a solid monument for future generations that would say, "This was Solomon and here are his great works."

Building a monument is a glorious thing. But in these three verses Solomon refers to himself no fewer than ten times. Instead of doing all this building for God, or for the people of Jerusalem, he was doing it for himself. Why? What was he trying to prove?

Is work a valid place to find ultimate meaning in life? Certainly many of us think so, judging from the schedules we keep. But David Henderson, in his book *Culture Shift*, suggests there may be something more subtle behind our frantic activity levels:

> Our lives, like our Daytimers, are busy, busy, busy, full of things to do and places to go and people to see. Many of us, convinced that the opposite of an empty life is a full schedule, remain content to press on and ignore the deeper questions. Perhaps it is out of fear that we stuff our lives to the walls—fear that, were we to stop and ask the big questions, we would discover there are no satisfying answers after all.[7]

When I was growing up, my father was the president of Cedarville College near Columbus, Ohio. He invested fifty years of his life as president and then chancellor of that school. More recently, Dr. Paul Dixon, a dear friend of mine, served as Cedarville president. When Dr. Dixon retired, I watched him go through the challenges of turning over all he had done for twenty-five years to another man.

A member of the college staff remarked to me, "Do you know that during Dr. Dixon's presidency, one hundred million dollars' worth of buildings were constructed on this campus?"

I was surprised, but as I walked across campus I realized it was true. Dr. Dixon was a great leader and a great builder. Were those building projects meaningful? Absolutely. Will they serve young people and educate them? Without question. But I know—and Dr. Dixon knows—that none of those buildings have vested his life with lasting meaning.

Buildings are attractive and useful, but ultimately they are no more than masses of brick plastered together. Students enjoy them for four or five years; the faculty will use them during their teaching careers. But eventually everyone who walks into those buildings will walk out again, and someday not one brick will still be standing. Solomon's great temple as well as all of his buildings, perfect in every detail, are in ruins.

Ecclesiastes teaches us that our work and our projects are generally worthwhile, but if we look to them as sources of ultimate meaning we will invariably be disappointed. Remember what we have already noted: eternity is the northward compass point of our hearts (Ecclesiastes 3:11). That means we can never be satisfied with temporal-based work. We could fill the earth with skyscrapers; we could spend every hour of our lives in toil—and the emptiness would abide. Ultimate satisfaction has one exclusive source.

Ernest Hemingway was the archetypal twentieth-century man. He filled many books with reflections of his worldwide adventures. He might be found sipping champagne in Paris, hunting grizzly bears in Alaska, watching bullfights in Spain, or fishing for tarpon in the Florida Keys. He lived the fullest life imaginable—under the sun. Yet the time closed in upon him when he chose to take his own life. Discovered many years later, his reportedly suicide note read, "Life is just one damn thing after another."

We want so badly to believe that we earn our own tickets in life. We want to believe that our proud individual accomplishments will lend us distinction and significance. After all, that would imply that we are in total control, that we are the "captains of our souls," as the poet put it. But only a brief search through history is required to call the roll of those who have walked in greatness yet died in despair.

Old Testament commentator Derek Kidner makes this observation: "What spoils the pleasures of life for us is our hunger to get out of them more than they can ever deliver. Getting eternal and ultimate meaning out of temporal and temporary pursuits is destined to fail."[8]

Searching for Meaning in Wealth

I acquired male and female servants, and had servants
born in my house. Yes, I had greater possessions of herds
and flocks than all who were in Jerusalem before me. I
also gathered for myself silver and gold and the special
treasures of kings and of the provinces. I acquired male and
female singers, the delights of the sons of men, and musical
instruments of all kinds.

So I became great and excelled more than all who were
before me in Jerusalem. Also my wisdom remained with me.

Whatever my eyes desired I did not keep from them.
I did not withhold my heart from any pleasure,
For my heart rejoiced in all my labor;
And this was my reward from all my labor.
Then I looked on all the works that my hands had done
And on the labor in which I had toiled;
And indeed all was vanity and grasping for the wind.
There was no profit under the sun.

—ECCLESIASTES 2:7–11

What nation would you guess to have the happiest citizens? It's probably not one that you would think. According to a 2003 report on CNN, an analysis of more than sixty-five countries by the World Values Survey suggested a higher "happiness index" in Nigeria than any other country. Mexico followed, then Venezuela, El Salvador, and Puerto Rico.

The United States came in sixteenth, Australia twentieth, and Great Britain twenty-fourth. This survey, conducted by an international network of social scientists, showed that happiness has little to do with wealth or income. In fact, the researchers included this surprising sentence in their report: "Survey after survey has shown that the desire for material goods, which has increased hand in hand with average income, *is a happiness suppressant*" (emphasis added).[9]

In other words, the more we have what we want, the more we want what we don't have. We try stuffing runaway materialism into the empty pockets of our souls, but the pockets have holes in them and we never achieve a feeling of real, existential satisfaction. Jesus summed it up this way: "One's life does not consist in the abundance of the things he possesses" (Luke 12:15).

The immensity of Solomon's wealth is beyond adequate description. But we'll give it a try anyway.

In 1 Kings 10:14, we find that "the weight of gold that came to Solomon yearly was six hundred and sixty-six talents of gold." In current dollars, Solomon's annual income of gold was nearly $304 million—"besides that from the traveling merchants, from the income of traders, from all the kings of Arabia, and from the governors of the country" (1 Kings 10:15).

There were many other sources of income; silver was so abundant that it wasn't even counted (1 Kings 10:21). Therefore, we might safely round the $304 million up to $500 million—a half-billion dollars of annual income—without fear of overstatement. There are people in the world today whose lifetime net worth is counted in the billions (much of it in the form of paper, not hard assets as was Solomon's). But in this age of wealth, there are very few whose annual income approaches Solomon's. The writer of 1 Kings sums up by saying, "King Solomon surpassed all the kings of the earth in riches" (10:23). It's easy to see why.

If we had walked into Solomon's palace during that golden age of Israel's history, we would have seen precious stones from Africa, spices from Arabia, almond and sandalwood from India, ivory from India and Africa, and cedars from Lebanon. Solomon had forty thousand stalls for his chariot horses and twelve thousand horsemen.

His awe-inspiring palace left the nation breathless. Gold was found everywhere in its design; stairways beautifully ornamented; pillars and posts, curtains and courtyards all made of rare and costly materials. A nearly infinite array of servants populated it, dressed in gorgeous clothes. Rich cuisine, costly uniforms, and expensive animals were imported from around the world. It was a building worthy of a king whose wisdom and splendor eclipsed that of all the rulers on earth. Solomon rightly claimed that he was greater and wealthier than any of his predecessors in Jerusalem.

But in the end, it was "meaningless—utterly meaningless." Solomon, in today's language, would have said, "I had it all; I had it my way, and I climbed to the highest peaks of human achievement. But the one thing I sought was never within my grasp."

Solomon made a timeless error in his quest for meaning: he sought it in things and experiences. He searched in wisdom, in wild living, in work, in wealth—all in vain. The object of his search was, in fact, unavailable under the sun.

Centuries later another wise man, C. S. Lewis, corrected the assumption that ultimate meaning can be found in anything in this world:

The books or the music in which we thought the beauty was located will betray us if we trust to them; it was not in them, it came through them, and what came through them was longing. These things—the beauty, the memory of our own past—are good images of what we really desire; but if they are mistaken for the thing itself, they turn into dumb idols, breaking the hearts of their worshippers. For they are not the thing itself; they are only the scent of a flower we have not found, the echo of a tune we have not heard, news from a country we have not visited.[10]

4

Careening Careers

Ecclesiastes 2:12–23

T ennis champion Hana Mandlikova was once asked how she
felt about defeating great players like Martina Navratilova
and Chris Evert Lloyd. She replied, "Any big win means
that all the suffering, practicing, and traveling are worth it. I feel like
I own the world."

When asked how long that feeling lasts, she replied, "About two
minutes."[1]

We live in a world searching for fleeting, momentary flashes of
satisfaction. British environmentalist and keen social critic Derek
Ratcliffe wrote a compelling analysis of the Western television audi-
ence and its viewing habits. He spoke of

> the mindless, shallow hedonism that seems to be the way our soci-
> ety is heading: a restless search for instant gratifications, trivial
> and ephemeral pleasures that leave no lasting satisfaction, let alone
> fulfillment. TV appears to me to be feeding rather than following
> this trend, although its bosses will always say they are giving the

public what it wants . . . a decadent media culture of soap operas, docusoaps, quizgames, police action, cooking shows, home make-overs . . . football, pornography and other expressions of the current intellectual and aesthetic development of modern western society.[2]

Some of us get off the couch and go to work. We know that we cannot satisfy the soul with nonstop entertainment, but we expect a good dose of the Christian work ethic to fill the bill.

Not so fast, warns Solomon.

Our Work Does Not Satisfy Us

Then I looked on all the works that my hands had done
And on the labor in which I had toiled;
And indeed all was vanity and grasping for the wind.
There was no profit under the sun.

Then I turned myself to consider wisdom and madness
and folly;
For what can the man do who succeeds the king?—
Only what he has already done.

—ECCLESIASTES 2:11–12

Few have more professional accomplishments than Solomon had. He excelled as a politician, a public leader, an educator, a zoologist, a biologist, and an economist. You name it, he did it. But when he took a step back from his work, viewed it objectively, and evaluated it, he was disappointed. It left him without any sense of permanent happiness. "There was no profit under the sun," he complained.

We plunge into our careers with the adrenaline of a diver off the high board, dreaming of influence and impact—of "making a splash." We want to be the best in the game. We want to be recognized as pacesetters. As one of Europe's best soccer players, Germany's Oliver Kahn, said, "At times . . . I think to myself that this is the worst job in the world. I remember what I felt like after losing the 1999 Champions League final against Manchester United. I felt empty and I almost had a nervous breakdown."[3]

It is not just well-known athletes who are disillusioned. Listen to an ordinary person: "I'm a single parent, working full time—so juggling work, home and my social life placed me on a treadmill that left me unfulfilled, drained and powerless. I could not see how else to live my life."[4]

U.S. News and World Report devoted its cover story to this subject several years ago, saying:

> Today, work dominates Americans' lives as never before, as workers pile on hours at a rate not seen since the Industrial Revolution. Many workers are left feeling insecure, unfulfilled, and underappreciated. . . . It's no wonder surveys of today's workers show a steady decline in job satisfaction. . . . People are feeling crushed.[5]

The magazine goes on to comment that intrusive cell phones, whirring faxes, and the relentless pursuit of e-mail have blurred the lines between work and home. Home is no longer a refuge but an extension of the office. Work just does not satisfy life's deepest needs. It did not do so in Solomon's day, it has not since, and it never will.

Our Work Does Not Separate Us

Then I saw that wisdom excels folly
As light excels darkness.

The wise man's eyes are in his head,
But the fool walks in darkness.
Yet I myself perceived
That the same event happens to them all.

So I said in my heart,
"As it happens to the fool,
It also happens to me,
And why was I then more wise?"
Then I said in my heart,
"This also is vanity."
For there is no more remembrance of the wise than of the
    fool forever,
Since all that now is will be forgotten in the days to
    come.
And how does a wise man die?
As the fool!

—ECCLESIASTES 2:13–16

Now Solomon astonishes us with his conclusion. He claims that when we see things only as they are "under the sun," we discover that our work neither satisfies nor separates us; it reduces us all to the same level. Imagine for yourself a life of relentless, bone-wearying work. The man in the next cubicle puts in a career of lazy underachievement. The two of you die on the same day and are laid out in the same funeral home. No stranger could view both bodies and identify which was the go-getter and which was the slacker.

Job says, "Naked I came from my mother's womb, and naked shall I return there" (Job 1:21).

Harry Ironside once wrote, "Death is the great leveler of all men. Whether rich or poor, wise or foolish, powerful or weak, renowned or obscure—no one can rise above it, cheat it, or escape its eventual claim on his life."

The seventeenth-century British playwright James Shirley put it graphically in his famous poem "Death the Leveler."

> Death lays his icy hand on kings:
>> Scepter and Crown
>> Must tumble down,
> And in the dust be equal made
> With the poor crookèd scythe and spade.[6]

Our Work Does Not Succeed Us

Therefore I hated life because the work that was done under the sun was distressing to me, for all is vanity and grasping for the wind.

Then I hated all my labor in which I had toiled under the sun, because I must leave it to the man who will come after me. And who knows whether he will be wise or a fool? Yet he will rule over all my labor in which I toiled and in which I have shown myself wise under the sun. This also is vanity. Therefore I turned my heart and despaired of all the labor in which I had toiled under the sun. For there is a man whose labor is with wisdom, knowledge, and skill; yet he must leave his heritage to a man who has not labored for it. This also is vanity and a great evil. For what has man for all his labor, and for the striving of his heart with which he has toiled under the sun? For all his days are sorrowful, and his work burdensome; even in the night his heart takes no rest. This also is vanity.

—ECCLESIASTES 2:17–23

You may not appreciate hearing it, but Solomon is simply saying aloud what we all know to be true. Build what you want; save what you might; put it in the bank; liquefy it into stocks and bonds; drop it into real estate; place it anywhere you choose. You only control your wealth for a season, and then it's out of your hands completely. As you draw your last breath, you withdraw your grip on all that you have labored to build under the sun. It's a matter for others now.

Solomon is not telling us to forsake our children or to deny them a reasonable inheritance. The same man writes, "A good man leaves an inheritance to his children's children" (Proverbs 13:22). Providing for our loved ones after our deaths is part of our Christian stewardship.

No, his message here is that the accumulation of wealth doesn't produce anything that endures through time and eternity. Leaving our loved ones too much might be worse than leaving them too little.

French novelist Gaston Leroux, creator of *The Phantom of the Opera*, was almost destroyed in this way. When his father died suddenly, leaving him with a fortune of almost one million francs, Gaston abandoned his career and relaxed into a dissipated existence of gambling and pleasure in colorful Paris society. Within a year he had squandered his inheritance—another sadder but wiser prodigal.

Solomon is warning us that accumulating mountains of money becomes meaningless to us within two seconds of death. In fact, the very reality of death strips our possessions of lasting significance.

In his book *Reasonable Faith*, the brilliant apologist William Lane Craig describes the ultimate implications of that truth. He speaks from the perspective of the nonbeliever, who might say:

> I realize I am going to die and forever cease to exist. My life is just a momentary transition out of oblivion into oblivion. And the universe, too, faces death. Scientists tell us that the universe

is expanding, and everything in it is growing farther and farther apart. As it does, it grows colder and colder, and its energy is used up. Eventually all the stars will burn out and all matter will collapse into dead stars and black holes. . . . Mankind is a doomed race in a dying universe. Because the human race will eventually cease to exist, it makes no ultimate difference whether it ever did exist. Mankind is thus no more significant than a swarm of mosquitoes or a barnyard of pigs, for their end is all the same. The same blind cosmic process that coughed them up in the first place will eventually swallow them all again.[7]

Who cares if we leave behind a dollar or two on the road to oblivion? Who cares if we leave millions of dollars for our children? It might merely hasten their spiritual destruction.

That is why Paul tells us to set our affections on things above, not on things below (Colossians 3:1–4). That is why Jesus tells us to lay up treasures for ourselves in heaven, not on earth (Matthew 6:19–20). That is why Paul writes these words to Timothy:

> Command those who are rich in this present age not to be haughty, nor to trust in uncertain riches but in the living God, who gives us richly all things to enjoy. Let them do good, that they be rich in good works, ready to give, willing to share, storing up for themselves a good foundation for the time to come, that they may lay hold on eternal life. (1 Timothy 6:17–19)

What Is the Answer?

Some time ago, an aspiring television star was given a shot at a network series. He went to the NBC studios, saw his name on a parking space, found the crew treating him like royalty, and admired the star on his dressing room door. The series pilot was shot in five days, but television executives rejected it. When the young actor left, no one said good-bye, the name was gone from his parking space, and his dressing room was locked.

"All the success was like smoke," he said. "I couldn't get a handle on it, like cotton candy, once it was in my mouth it was gone."[8]

Our culture is a cotton-candy world—sugary and seductive—a pink swirl of empty calories. Today you might be the "flavor of the month," with Hollywood or Wall Street at your command. Tomorrow your pockets may be as empty as your soul.

Enjoyment Is a Gift from God

Nothing is better for a man than that he should eat and drink, and that his soul should enjoy good in his labor. This also, I saw, was from the hand of God. For who can eat, or who can have enjoyment, more than I?

—ECCLESIASTES 2:24–25

Solomon could have settled into a spirit of cynicism about life under the sun. He could have lived out his days in silent despair. But he remembered something wonderful from his youth. He recalled when life was simpler, when he had much less and enjoyed it much more. Particularly, he remembered the message of two fathers: one who taught him of heaven, the other who taught him of earth.

The last few words of Ecclesiastes 2:25 are key. The New International Version, the New American Standard Version, and other modern translations get it right. For example, the New Living Translation renders verse 25 this way: "For who can eat or enjoy anything apart from him?" That is Solomon's conclusion: God is the essence of the positive life, and every moment of it is a gift from Him.

Eight times in this book we will hear this sentiment—a kind of upbeat refrain for the dirgelike verses of Ecclesiastes. And let's not miss the relief of this thought: even under the sun, even with what is missing, what we do have is still the gift of God. The wisdom, the work, and the pleasure of a good meal are no more than appetizers, but they are good appetizers.

We can enjoy our good homes and families, the pleasure of our recreation, the chilled swim, and the grilled steak. We can feel good in connecting with our work. These things will never give us the one great pleasure that lies at the center of life, but they will complement it. They will cluster around the great shining star of godly contentment like lesser lights that point to the greatness of what is at the center.

We can smile as we watch Solomon dismantle the idea that God is in His heaven peering through the clouds to catch people having fun, so that He might put a stop to it. The God of Ecclesiastes is nothing like that; He is the Joygiver, the dispenser of pleasurable pursuits. Christ, the Bread of Life, leaves a little trail of good things like bread crumbs in the forest, leading straight to joy that is eternal: intimate fellowship with Him. Only in the aftertaste of that fellowship do these lesser tastes become truly pleasurable to us.

How important it is, then, to keep God in the middle of our bank accounts, our possessions, and our portfolios. Picture your hands out in front of you, cupped together, palms up. In your open hands are all the things He has entrusted to you—money, cars, a home, furniture, everything. All of this is His gift (James 1:17). We are the stewards, and faithfulness is our charge. That means our hands must never close over the gifts, but remain open so that He may use them as required—and refill our hands.

The human impulse, of course, is to "clutch and clench"—to close our fists protectively. We then find ourselves facing limited resources. How can God fill us when there is no opening? And as long as we cannot loosen our grip, we cannot enjoy what is there.

With open hearts and open hands, however, we understand that God lacks no resources and neither will we. The more of Him we discover and enjoy, the more we find available. Our hands joyfully open wider, and He gives from His infinitely generous heart. It is not the gifts that bring the joy, but He Himself; the gifts are simply His creative expression in telling us how much He loves us. And we agree with David: "You will show me the path of life; in Your presence is fullness of joy; at Your right hand are pleasures forevermore" (Psalm 16:11).

Enlightenment Is a Gift from God

For God gives wisdom and knowledge and joy to a man
who is good in His sight; but to the sinner He gives the
work of gathering and collecting, that he may give to him
who is good before God. This also is vanity and grasping for
the wind.

—ECCLESIASTES 2:26

God not only gives us true enjoyment, but He gives us true enlightenment. We grow in the wisdom of using His daily blessings.

There are people who have spent decades building spacious homes, but God inhabits none of the rooms because the houses are clutched, clenched, hoarded—investments in material and financial value. These homes seem beautiful at first glance, but they come to feel empty and soulless.

There are others with spacious homes that have been opened, like their owners' hands, to the glory of God. The people who live here host Bible studies. They entertain missionaries. God inhabits every room, because they have invested it spiritually. And the joy under this roof is like a beautiful wallpaper that runs through every hall, a soft and delightful music that warms the soul.

Solomon is drawing on something he learned earlier in his life . . . that wisdom and knowledge come from God. Notice the similarity between verse 26 and Proverbs 2:6.

> For God gives wisdom and knowledge and joy to a man who is good in His sight; but to the sinner He gives the work of gathering and collecting, that he may give to him who is good before God. (Ecclesiastes 2:26)

> For the LORD gives wisdom;
> From His mouth come knowledge and understanding. (Proverbs 2:6)

Would you rather be the first in line for wisdom and knowledge and joy, or would you rather be handed the heavy tools of "gathering and collecting" in service of the knowledge-and-joy-getters? It's entirely your choice. If you decide to serve God, those wonderful gifts of wisdom and knowledge and joy come with the deal. Otherwise, life is an unending round of heavy lifting.

This same interesting hierarchical arrangement is found in Proverbs 13:22: "The wealth of the sinner is stored up for the righteous." God's eye is on all the wealth of this world, and He says that the wealth of the sinner is being gathered and stored up to accomplish His purposes in due time.

Those who know God intimately will attest to the fact that life is filled with wonderful blessings from above at every turn. He wants us to know how to use His blessings, so He includes wisdom in the overflow.

Many years ago there was a woman named Clara Tear Williams who became a circuit-riding Methodist preacher, an unusual role for a nineteenth-century woman. When a friend asked Williams for a poem to include in his book of poetry, this is what she gave him. It summarizes Solomon's message in this part of Ecclesiastes:

All my life I had a longing
For a drink from some clear spring,
That I hoped would quench the burning
Of the thirst I felt within.

Hallelujah! I have found Him
Whom my soul so long has craved!
Jesus satisfies my longings,
Through His blood I now am saved.[9]

Every longing is satisfied. Our deep thirst is quenched. And from there, life is a cavalcade of blessings—the old items of drudgery transformed, even as we have been transformed, to new and joyful gifts every morning from now to eternity.

5

Impressions About Life

Ecclesiastes 3:1–8

It is said that on Veteran's Day, November 11, 1963, President John F. Kennedy visited Arlington Cemetery to pay his respects to America's fallen heroes. Gazing over the rolling Virginia hillside from Arlington House, he remarked, "It is so beautiful that I could stay here forever." Two weeks later he returned in a flag-draped coffin to be buried beneath an eternal flame.

Kennedy's favorite passage from the Bible was Solomon's poem in Ecclesiastes 3:1–8, which begins: "To everything there is a season, a time for every purpose under heaven: A time to be born, and a time to die."

Also in 1963, the nation was singing that same ancient passage of Scripture to a contemporary beat. Folk singer Pete Seeger adapted the words as the song "Turn, Turn, Turn," and the Byrds' rendition later sailed to the top of the charts.

Seeger stayed fairly close to Solomon's poetry in his adaptation—until the song's last line. He had come to Solomon's words, "a time

of war, and a time of peace." This, of course, was a time of peace—
at least to the young generation that listened to the Byrds. The folk
music scene was busy providing the soundtrack for the antiwar movement, so Peter Seeger tweaked Solomon's poetry a bit. The new line
was, "A time of peace, I swear it's not too late."[1]

What is it about Ecclesiastes 3 that fascinated a troubled generation and its charismatic young president? Why has this passage
endured the ages as one of the oldest philosophical poems in our literary canon? It's certainly among the most pensive passages of God's
Word, a beautiful meditation that casts a near-hypnotic spell over
readers of any generation.

In its setting in Ecclesiastes, it follows as the next step in Solomon's
unfolding logic about the futility of living the under-the-sun life.

The author was the wisest and wealthiest man who ever lived,
and this book is a chronicle of his lifelong quest for true happiness and
joy. We have already seen in the first two chapters of Ecclesiastes how
Solomon tried wealth, wisdom, work, and wild living. At the end of his
wide-ranging experiments, he concluded that everything was an empty
exercise in vanity. It was like trying to capture the wind in his hands.

As we come to the third chapter, we find Solomon facing an even
bigger challenge, a "problem with God."

I know all about the "problem with God." A few years ago I
encountered a life-threatening cancer and a life-changing adventure. I
would not have chosen cancer as a path to spiritual growth, nor would
I wish such fear and pain on anyone. On the other hand, I do not see
my illness as a random event, some miscellaneous accident of health.
And I do not believe there was a moment when God was absent from
the physical, emotional, and spiritual crisis I endured.

In fact, I found Him everywhere during that time. I found Him
as never before. I glimpsed His face among the doctors and nurses
who cared for me so skillfully. I saw Him there in shining power

among the family of my church, and intimately among the family circle of my wife and children. He met me in the private chapel of my soul, where with each passing day I felt deeper in His grace and comfort. At one bend of the road after another, I found my Lord more present and more powerful. I wrote about my experiences in a book titled *A Bend in the Road*.[2]

Knowing there must be pain and suffering for us all, I dearly wish everyone could travel the road I did. I wish every human soul could see the face of God in the fear and turmoil. So many walk a very different path; they experience only His absence.

I was asked to participate in a debate with an individual who had shared my particular disease. He believed in God but had come to radically different conclusions than I had about God and the troubles of life. The debate was sponsored by the internationally recognized Scripps Clinic located in San Diego, California, a leading provider of health care for cancer patients. The individual I debated was a Jewish rabbi, a disciple of Rabbi Harold Kushner, the author of *When Bad Things Happen to Good People*.

Rabbi Kushner's book generated much interest when it was published in 1981, and again when it was rereleased on its twentieth anniversary. As a young theology student, Kushner had many questions about Job and his experience of suffering. But when his own three-year-old son contracted a rare disease that took his life at a young age, Kushner penned his conclusions about God and suffering in order to provide answers to others in similar circumstances.

Kushner's conclusion was a popularization of an ancient theological conundrum: How can God be both perfectly good and perfectly powerful? The suffering in the world suggests that if He is God, He is not good; or that if He is good, He is not God. In other words, there must be something lacking in either His love or His strength, or He would cure every little pain.

Rabbi Kushner worked through the old enigma. He concluded that God is all-loving but not all-powerful. He cares deeply about the people He created, but after creating the world He backed away and allowed it to run without His interference—again, the cosmic watchmaker who abandons his workmanship.

Kushner decided that we navigate the waters of an ocean that God does not control. That is, if you were to pray to God in your need, He would have to answer, "Sorry, that's not My job." The message of his book is supposed to offer hope and comfort to those who hurt. I have never heard it explained how that is so because we are told we live within a kind of fence God will not enter.[3]

The rabbi I debated held Kushner's view. He admitted that he did not pray for God's healing intervention in his life; if God was not involved with him getting sick, why should God get involved with making him well?

Solomon had a different view entirely. In chapter 3 of Ecclesiastes, he concludes that God is sovereign and in control, regardless of the imponderables that remain. Here Solomon sees God as being present inside the fence with us but not helpful enough. The king wants to know why God does not improve the standard of life, do something about the aging process, show more favoritism to His children, and perhaps discontinue the program of human pain.

In his poem recorded in Ecclesiastes 3:1–8, Solomon presents fourteen couplets and twenty-eight statements. There are fourteen negative statements and fourteen positive ones, and they fall into three separate categories. The first describes the influence of time on our bodies, the second focuses on our souls, and the last deals with our spirits.

That is, after all, the way you and I are made. We are human beings with bodies, minds, and souls.

And Solomon's main thought? Well, it doesn't take a Hebrew

scholar to notice that the word *time* occurs twenty-nine times in these verses. We rarely turn our backs on the time. You and I probably have a dozen clocks and four or five calendars in our homes. Many of us carry a timepiece attached to our wrist, and time indicators are built into our smartphones, computer screens, and tablets. Every major corporation in America tries to teach its employees time-management skills.

When Don Regan became chief of staff for President Ronald Reagan, he was staggered by the immensity of managing the president's schedule. "It is a sobering experience to realize," he said, "that you have been entrusted with managing the time of the most powerful man in the world." Regan wrote in his memoirs:

> A president has no more than eight years (and he may be granted half that time or even less) to keep the promises he had made to the people. Therefore it is true of the President as it is true of few other men that he hasn't a minute to waste. Every meeting, every conversation, every ceremony must have a purpose, and it must take place in the time allotted to it. What a president might fail to do for lack of time can have profound consequences.[4]

Remember that Solomon was the greatest leader of his day, a head of state to whom all of Israel and much of the known world looked for guidance. He pondered carefully the allocation of time, and he was aware of how quickly it passed.

Time and Your Physical Life

To everything there is a season,
A time for every purpose under heaven:

A time to be born,
  And a time to die;
A time to plant,
  And a time to pluck what is planted;
A time to kill,
  And a time to heal;
A time to break down,
  And a time to build up.

—ECCLESIASTES 3:1–3

Solomon begins his contemplation with a sobering observation: birth and death both have their appointed times.

When my grandson, Ryland, was born, I flew to Baltimore for the event. As I peered through the nursery window at this beautiful new citizen of the world, it struck me that only a corridor away, some other citizen was being dispatched. Some family had gathered for the agony of farewell. It is not a lengthy walk between the nursery and the intensive care unit. We spend our own time making that trek between entrance and exit, womb and tomb.

Meanwhile, there is a time to plant and a time to harvest. Solomon refers to the food supply because he knows that God sets the boundaries of the seasons. Just as a composer of beautiful music builds certain rhythms and repetitions into his songs, so God has built certain rhythms into His world. The steady repetition of the seasons provides comfort and a workable cadence to life.

We are a bit discomforted to read that there is a time to kill as well as a time to heal. Yet our bodies are in the process of dying every moment. Scientists tell us that every seven years we replenish all the cells within our bodies. There is an ongoing maintenance department in the human machine that is constantly changing out the old for the new. And it is governed by time.

Cancer cells, infection cells, or simply worn-out cells must be killed—so even killing has its time, and we are grateful. There must be a time to kill so we might also have a time to heal.

And what of "a time to break down, and a time to build up"? We build up in our early years, and we start breaking down as we get older—painful but true. Someone said we know we are getting older when the type gets smaller, the steps get higher, the voices get softer, the muscles get weaker, and our medicine chest gets larger.

How old is old? You are old at twenty-one if you are a female gymnast. Your performance will peak in your mid- to late teens. You are over the hill at thirty if you are a professional tennis player. Do you think of forty as old? For Michael Jordan, reaching forty meant his years as an NBA star were behind him.

I was enjoying a birthday when David Todd, my six-year-old grandson, crunched the numbers on my age. He said, "If Poppy was a dog's age, he'd be dead!" He was right. Time is relative for God's creatures, but it rules their itineraries.

There is a time for breaking down, but God is there. He is as powerful as He is loving, regardless of what the rabbi said; and you have the opportunity to experience His power all the more effectively and vividly when you turn to Him in the breakdowns of life.

Time and Your Emotional Life

A time to weep,
　And a time to laugh;
A time to mourn,
　And a time to dance;
A time to cast away stones,

And a time to gather stones;
A time to embrace,
And a time to refrain from embracing.

—ECCLESIASTES 3:4–5

Time is also involved with the operations of the soul, the seat of human emotions. There's a time to cry, when tears flow freely; there are also times for laughter. Hopefully, the latter outnumber the former, for in another passage Solomon prescribes cheerfulness as good medicine for the soul (Proverbs 17:22). Yet tears are a part of life. The Bible says, "Jesus wept. . . . He groaned in the spirit and was troubled" (John 11:35, 33). Job states, "My eyes pour out tears to God" (Job 16:20). The psalmist asks God to store his tears in a heavenly bottle, for they are precious (Psalm 56:8). And Psalm 126:5 promises, "Those who sow in tears shall reap in joy."

Your tears are God's jewels; they are precious to Him. The greater your suffering, the greater His ministry and grace for you. We need to laugh, but sometimes we must also cry. The Lord is near us in both sadness and gladness. One day, He'll wipe away every tear from our eyes and the days of crying will be forgotten. But for now, there's a time to laugh and a time to weep.

There is a time to mourn and a time to dance. There is a time to hug, and there are times when hugging is inappropriate. God has given us a wide spectrum of emotions, and sometimes we feel we are at the mercy of our anger or depression or grief. It helps to know that each emotion is simply playing the part allotted to its own special time. We need a blue sky and green meadows; we need clouds that are willowy white. In the same way, we need our full spectrum of God-given emotions, for they are the emblems of our humanity. They mark us as children of a God who also has anger, grief, and laughter.

Time and Your Spiritual Life

A time to gain,
 And a time to lose;
A time to keep,
 And a time to throw away;
A time to tear,
 And a time to sew;
A time to keep silence,
 And a time to speak;
A time to love,
 And a time to hate;
A time of war,
 And a time of peace.

      —Ecclesiastes 3:6–8

The last three verses have to do with inner decisions—the deep commitments of our lives. Sometimes we gain; sometimes we lose—money, weight, hair, loved ones, privileges, rights, responsibilities, joys, possessions.

Sometimes we store things in our garages, and sometimes we clean out our garages. We collect and we throw away.

Even large corporations do this. In periods of expansion, they swallow smaller companies; then when they need to raise cash to retire debt or enter new markets, they sell off part of what they have accumulated. Unfortunately, at the personal level we seem far more interested in accumulating than in throwing away. We need to recognize the spiritual value of both, that there is a time and a season to get rid of stuff.

Sometimes we need to speak up. Other times we need to keep our mouths shut. Solomon knew there was a "time to keep silence, and a time to speak." The assets and liabilities of words show up repeatedly in Solomon's proverbs. The father in Proverbs continually admonishes his children to pay attention to words of wisdom and instruction (Proverbs 2:1; 3:1; 4:1, 10, 20; 5:1, 7; 7:1, 24), but he also warns against talking too much (17:27) and becoming ensnared by one's own words (6:2).

The more we talk, the more likely we are to sin (Proverbs 10:19); the fire of gossip dies out as soon as the talk ceases (26:20). In short, words can contain life or death; it is up to us to choose them carefully (18:21). There is no greater wisdom than knowing the seasons of the tongue—when it is time to speak and when it is time to keep silent (26:4–5).

There is a time for love and even a time to hate. A time to hate? Yes, of course. Even Jesus hated. He hated sin. He hated its mastery over human souls. He hated the wake of its destruction. We need to learn how to hate that which is evil without hating the people who are evil. We may hate the act of abortion, but we have compassion on both the aborted and the aborting. We may hate the ravages of alcohol, but we love those who struggle with alcoholism, and we want to do whatever we can to help them.

The passage ends by reminding us that while we all long for a peaceful world, there is even a time when war is morally necessary. "A time of war, and a time of peace" (v. 8).

Peter Muhlenberg was an Anglican pastor in Virginia. In 1774, he was elected to the Virginia legislature and was present at St. John's Church in Richmond when Patrick Henry proclaimed, "Give me liberty or give me death!" Peter was so moved that he promptly joined George Washington's army.

On a bitterly sad Sunday morning, he resigned from his church and preached his farewell sermon. He read Ecclesiastes 3:1: "To everything there is a season, a time for every purpose under heaven."

Looking up, he said, "There is a time to preach and a time to pray, but there is also a time to fight, and that time has now come." Then he suddenly flung off his ministerial robe to reveal underneath the uniform of a militia colonel.

He recruited other men in his church, and they became known as the German Regiment under his command. It's because of men like Peter Muhlenberg that America has been the home of the brave and the land of the free for more than two hundred years.[5]

What Solomon is teaching us in Ecclesiastes 3:1–8 is that all of life unfolds under the appointment of providence. Birth and death, sowing and harvest, joys and sorrows, acquiring and losing, speech and silence, war and peace—everything has its appointed time from God. He is sovereign, but He is always faithful.

Our lives need to reflect His divine pacing. We need the cadence of His call, the rhythm of His wisdom running through our moments, our days, and our years. Through all the seasons of life, through all the undulating circumstances of the passing years, God remains both loving and powerful. As the old Methodist hymn puts it:

> Summer and winter, and springtime and harvest,
> Sun, moon, and stars in their courses above
> Join with all nature in manifold witness
> To Thy great faithfulness, mercy, and love.[6]

6

Insights About God

Ecclesiastes 3:9–11

When all is said and done, what is the point of all I have said and done?

It sounds fatalistic. It sounds anything in the world but biblical. If you spoke up and said it at church, you might well get a lecture. But you are not Solomon; he is the king, and he can ask questions like that.

And he really wants an answer. Does all this effort make a difference? After the times and seasons and feelings have played themselves out in me—what is left?

In the king's words, "What profit has the worker from that in which he labors?" (3:9).

He poses a fair question. If God controls the peaks and the valleys of life, if *He* has it all covered, then what is the point of *my* work? Why should I even bother to punch in on time when tomorrow morning rolls around?

I have known friends to spend twenty years building a secure home for their families, only to see it quickly evaporate through some disaster or financial crisis. Were all those years a total waste?

The *Times* of London carried a profile of Philip Guston, the Canadian American abstract-expressionist painter who died in 1980. The article was titled "Exposing a Futile Existence." It was a profile of a man who managed, through his art, to show the meaninglessness of every little thing people do.

The art reviewer described Guston as a man who, being expelled from school, "went on to smoke three packets of untipped Camels a day, and eat and drink so much, and who somehow succeeded in making noble, even heroic art about these excesses." To Guston, life was empty—have another smoke.

The *Times* writer added this despairing line: "Most modern lives do, indeed, unravel and then stop, like a stair-carpet being unrolled."[1]

That is rather vivid, isn't it? It's simply the more modern version of Macbeth's famous soliloquy:

> To-morrow, and to-morrow, and to-morrow,
> Creeps in this petty pace from day to day,
> To the last syllable of recorded time. . . .
> Life's but a walking shadow, a poor player,
> That struts and frets his hour upon the stage,
> And then is heard no more; it is a tale
> Told by an idiot, full of sound and fury,
> Signifying nothing.[2]

God's Plan Is Good

What profit has the worker from that in which he labors? I have seen the God-given task with which the sons of men

are to be occupied. He has made everything beautiful in
its time.

—ECCLESIASTES 3:9–11

Solomon faces this attitude of futility and despair head-on, and
the middle of chapter 3 gives us three answers to ponder.

In verse 10, Solomon says our busywork can obscure the true
meaning of life unless we stop and take a close look. In so doing, we
realize that God's plan is good. The truth is, "He has made everything beautiful in its time" (3:11). If we allow the meaning of this
statement to sink in, we will realize that *everything* is beautiful in
God's sight; *everything* in life has a purpose.

Life is not empty and random and godless, but full and precisely
aligned and God-ordained. It's not that your most important work is
meaningless; it's that your most trivial movements are also significant.

Ruth Bell Graham used to have an inscription over her kitchen
sink: "Divine service conducted here three times a day." She understood that whatever we do—even washing a dirty pot—is worthwhile
if done in God's will and for Christ's glory.

One man who understood this well was Nicholas Herman, otherwise known in history as Brother Lawrence. He was born in Lorraine,
France, in 1605, but little is known of his early life. He reached his
teen years at the onset of the Thirty Years' War. He fought for the
French army, was seriously wounded, and was lame for the rest of his
life. Converted at eighteen, he went to work as a footman for a local
official in the treasury.

Nicholas, however, had a nagging fear of living an insignificant
life. At the age of fifty, he joined a Carmelite monastery in Paris where
he was dubbed Brother Lawrence and assigned to the kitchen. It was
a task that struck him as insulting and humbling. For the next several
years, he went about his chores, miserable but dutiful.

Then one day he began thinking about his attitude. He started reminding himself that God's presence continually permeated him. Even the most menial tasks, if undertaken for God's glory, are holy. And that means the heat of a kitchen, the sweat of the unplowed field, even the stench of the gutter are holy ground because God goes there with us.

Many years passed. Brother Lawrence's countenance and demeanor gradually changed, until others began asking him a reason for his radiance. His thoughtful message began to have a profound influence on those around him, and it was preserved in the little book titled *The Practice of the Presence of God*. Thus the simple message of a simple kitchen hand has had a worldwide impact, because Lawrence understood the full implications of God's invisible presence.[3]

What profit has the worker? Much profit, if our tasks are God-given and Christ-centered. The real question is, "Am I doing what God wants me to do? Am I in the place, above all others, that He wants me to occupy?"

Solomon goes on in verse 11 to add this beautiful sentence: "He has made everything beautiful in its time." Everything that happens in our lives has a purpose. God makes it beautiful in its time. This verse is the Old Testament counterpart of Romans 8:28: "We know that all things work together for good to those who love God, to those who are the called according to His purpose."

In our churches we used to sing a chorus based on this verse:

> In His time, in His time,
> He makes all things beautiful in His time.
> Lord, please show me every day,
> As You're teaching me Your way
> That You'll do just what You say in Your time.[4]

We have no problem connecting with that truth in the nice moments. What sets the true saint apart is his ability to apply it during moments of unpleasantness. When young couples fall in love and get married, they are convinced that God has made everything beautiful in His time. But ten years later, when little children are underfoot, bills are due, a job has been lost, and a medical scare has been diagnosed—we wonder what happened to all that beauty. Marriage has lost a little luster, parenthood is less glorious, and homebuilding is more sweat than sweet.

Men and women leave their marriages in times like these simply because they are unaware of God's presence in the rugged times as well as the smooth. Our challenge is to recognize that everything has a time, a season, a reason, and to trust God to bring sense and unity on His schedule. Then not only will the beauty be there, but it will be far more beautiful for the hard polishing.

When I was sick with cancer, people would ask me, "Pastor, why did you get cancer? You're a godly man, serving the Lord in full-time ministry." It is true that I am a pastor. But on a deeper level I am just another human being. And human beings get cancer. The game of Monopoly offers a "Get out of jail free" card, but God offers no such card to Christians. We must take the rain with the sun, the dark with the light, and know that God is painting a beautiful picture that requires all the tones, all the colors, all the depths of suffering as well as joy.

Years ago British media expert Malcolm Muggeridge, who became a committed follower of Christ, wrote the following in his book, *A Twentieth Century Testimony:*

> Contrary to what might be expected, I look back on experiences that at the time seemed especially desolating and painful with particular satisfaction. Indeed, I can say with complete truthfulness

that everything that has truly enhanced and enlightened my existence has been through affliction and not through happiness, whether pursued or attained. In other words, if it ever were to be possible to eliminate affliction from our earthly existence by means of some drug or other medical mumbo jumbo, as Aldous Huxley envisaged in Brave New World, the result would not be to make life delectable, but to make it too banal and trivial to be endurable. This, of course, is what the Cross signifies. And it is the Cross, more than anything else, that has called me inexorably to Christ.[5]

In other words, if life were like drawing a picture, and your pencil included a nice eraser, you might rub away all the darker marks in the picture. In the end there would be no real picture at all, for it is what happens at those junctions between light and darkness that tells the final story.

Civil War–era devotional writer E. M. Bounds wrote many great books on the subject of prayer. He also penned this little poem:

> Why should I fear tomorrow? The Lord directs my way.
> Why should I trouble borrow? I live but for today.
> Whenever I am weary, in God I find my rest,
> And when my path seems dreary, I know it's for the best.

In his autobiographical book, *A Turtle on a Fencepost,* business leader Allan Emery tells of accompanying his friend and mentor Ken Hansen to visit a hospitalized employee. The patient lay very still, his eyes conveying anguish. His operation had taken eight hours, and recovery would be long and uncertain.

"Alex," said Ken quietly, "you know I have had a number of serious operations. I know the pain of trying to talk. I think I know the questions you are asking. There are two verses I want to give you—Genesis 42:36 and Romans 8:28. We have the option of these two attitudes. We need the perspective of the latter."

Hansen turned to the passages, read them, then prayed and left. Allan Emery never forgot those two verses, nor should we.[6]

The choice is this: to be beat up or to be upbeat. To say with Jacob in Genesis 42:36: *All these things are against me.* Or to say with Paul in Romans 8:28: *All things work together for good to those who love God.*

The perspective you choose will color your life completely and thoroughly—will it be gentle tones of grace and providence, or harsh slashes of despair and emptiness?

Missionary Hudson Taylor sometimes quoted this Frederick W. Faber poem when afflictions came his way:

> Ill that God blesses is our good,
> And unblest good is ill.
> And all is right that seems most wrong,
> If it be His sweet will.[7]

This is where faith comes into play, of course. We walk by faith, not by sight. If our faith works only when everything is rosy and upbeat, it's not worth very much. Faith kicks in when the roof falls in. We keep up our spirits and fortify ourselves by trusting in God's presence and promises despite the dismal circumstances.

We have to understand that God's plan is good, and that includes even the negative things that come into our lives. I know we are left with some serious questions: What about the Holocaust? What about 9/11? What about genocide in Bosnia? I can't answer all those questions. But I can say this: *When you stand back and view the great cavalcade of human experience from the divine perspective, God's fingerprints cover everything—the places of misery and tragedy most of all.*

In Tommy Nelson's book on Ecclesiastes, he shares an object

lesson he used in his church. He had his pianist come to the piano. He asked her to play "Jesus Loves Me" using only the white keys on the piano—the "do-re-mi" notes of the diatonic scale. Then he asked her to play it again, adding the black keys—the sharps and flats. Then he asked his congregation, "Which version did you prefer?" There was no contest; it took "light music" and "dark music," major and minor, sharps and flats to make a melody.[8]

If you do not learn to trust God, you will do one of two things: You will invent a god who has no basis in fact, as my friend the rabbi did. Or you will believe in the true God but live in a constant state of agitation because He does not act the way you think He should or explain to you what you think you deserve to know.

We must trust God to be God.

God's Purpose Is Clear

Also He has put eternity in their hearts.

—ECCLESIASTES 3:11

A missionary-scholar named Don Richardson wrote an award-winning book called *Eternity in Their Hearts*, based on Ecclesiastes 3:11. He presented more than twenty-five examples of missionaries all over the world who had discovered cultures completely cut off from Christianity in which vestiges of truth about God existed.

The people were looking for God, indeed were *hungry* for God, since knowledge about Him had been passed down in their culture for generations. Leading them to Christ required little more than explaining how the God they had been searching for had come to earth in the person of Christ to save them from their sins. Richardson set forth the idea that every human being has eternity in his heart, that winning people to Christ is a matter of discovering what piece or part of eternity they were familiar with and connecting the dots to Christ.

God has put something in our hearts—a taste or longing for eternity that cannot be discovered through the experiences of life. There will always be a longing within us for something more than we have experienced until we know God personally.

And even after we come to know Christ, there will still be an ache, for the Bible says the whole creation is groaning, waiting for the day of redemption (Romans 8:22). Planet Earth was not fitted to carry a curse of sin, and we were not created to live with a sin nature. We will never find ultimate satisfaction in this life because we were made for eternity.

C. S. Lewis, in his classic *Mere Christianity*, said it this way:

Creatures are not born with desires unless satisfaction for those desires exists. A baby feels hunger; well there is such a thing as food. A duckling wants to swim; well there is such a thing as water. Men feel sexual desire; well there is such a thing as sex. If I find in myself a desire which no experience in this world can satisfy, the most probable explanation is that I was made for another world. If none of my earthly pleasures satisfy it, that does not prove that the universe is a fraud. Probably, earthly pleasures were never meant to satisfy it, but only to arouse it, to suggest the real thing.[9]

I wonder if Saint Augustine had Ecclesiastes 3:11 in mind when he wrote, "Thou hast made us for thyself, restless is our heart until it comes to rest in thee."[10] That says it as succinctly as it could be said. The unrest we see in our world and in our own hearts tells us we have not found our rest completely in God. And we will not experience that rest completely until we enter the realm for which we were created—eternity.

Once again C. S. Lewis's words help us: "Our Heavenly Father has provided many delightful inns for us along our journey, but He takes great care to see that we do not mistake any of them for home."[11]

As we make these stops along the road, we can only wonder about the mansions He is preparing for us.

His Program Is Mysterious

Except that no one can find out the work that God does
from beginning to end.

—ECCLESIASTES 3:11

God's plan is good; His purpose clear. But the last part of verse 11 tells us that His program is mysterious. Nobody can figure it out.

If you have picked up this book thinking that I have answers to all of life's imponderable mysteries and miseries, I must apologize. I am not God, and I cannot understand it all. I try to figure it out just as you do, and I often wish God would be more forthcoming with the answers. The evangelist Vance Havner used to say, "God writes over some of our days: 'Will Explain Later.'"

The word *why* occurs 430 times in the Bible—and you and I have asked it that many times or more. Catherine Marshall, the eloquent writer and wife of former US Senate chaplain Peter Marshall, wrote about her anguish over the death of a beloved grandchild. For quite a while Catherine felt anger and depression toward God for allowing such a thing, when she had earnestly prayed and trusted for the child's healing.

Then one day she was reading through Isaiah 53, a poignant passage about the suffering of the Messiah.

I had read this passage many times before, even since Amy Catherine's death, but it had not affected me as it did now, particularly the tenth verse. God made His own Son suffer, but it was a "good plan." More than "good." It was perfect, as only something from God could be. It was terribly important to the future of the human race that Jesus Christ have His dark night experience on the cross. Yet what a desperately dark night it had to be for Him to have cried out, "My God, my God, why hast thou forsaken me?"

Catherine concluded:

When life hands us situations we cannot understand, we have one or two choices. We can wallow in misery, separated from God. Or we can tell Him, "I need You and Your presence in my life more than I need understanding. I choose You, Lord. I trust You to give me understanding and an answer to all of my whys, only if and when You choose."[12]

God is God, and He does not owe us every answer to every question on demand. Someday we will understand, but right now we live by faith and peer through a glass darkly. It is like looking through the back window in the foggy morning mist. You cannot make out every detail of the fields and trees, but you have faith that things will clear up, and the world will be beautiful—all the lovelier, somehow, after a good rain or fog.

7

Read the Instructions

Ecclesiastes 3:12–15

Several years ago, there was a bestseller titled *Life's Little Instruction Book*. The title said it all. We all want profound insights about living, given in bite-sized chunks that we can digest. It was Solomon who invented this form of teaching, and these verses in Ecclesiastes 3 could be considered the original *Life's Little Instruction Book*. Having given us his impressions about life (verses 1–8) and his insights about God (verses 9–11), Solomon ends this section by sharing some instructions about living (verses 12–15).

Watch out: These verses are heavy loads in small packages. It's best to take them one at a time.

Don't Forfeit Enjoyment Because of What You Can't Understand

I know that nothing is better for them than to rejoice, and to do good in their lives.

—ECCLESIASTES 3:12

You enter the world's greatest amusement park. You have the whole day to spend there. Which amazing roller coaster will you ride first?

None! You sit on the bench, pull out a laptop computer, and dedicate yourself to computing the precise mechanical configurations of every attraction. You figure that mastery of the nuts and bolts will enhance the roller-coaster experience.

Eight hours later, it is time to go home. The laptop is humming . . . but you have not experienced a single thrill.

That is what happens in life when we become preoccupied with looking over God's shoulder. You will never understand even a small portion of His program, so you might as well enjoy a larger portion of His provisions. If He tried to explain the science of providential mechanics, it would be like you trying to explain your job to a flea. Better to let the flea find a dog and do what it does best.

Life—the awesome gift of God—should not be afflicted by the paralysis of analysis. We will be either frozen in fear over what comes next or so confused over the meaning of it all that we will not notice the joy leaking out through the seams of everyday living.

There comes a time to "lighten up" a bit, as people sometimes say. Do we take God, His Word, and His laws any less seriously? Not at all. We simply acknowledge the boundaries defined by His greatness and our smallness.

He cannot be put into any convenient box of our design. As Archie Bunker once said (with painfully mangled theology), "That's how He got to be God." Besides, poking too far into the matter is how we got to be in *our* present state.

The Eternal One says in Isaiah 55:9, "For as the heavens are higher than the earth, so are My ways higher than your ways, and My thoughts than your thoughts."

"God moves in a mysterious way His wonders to perform," hymnist William Cowper wrote.[1] Some people want to master every corner of the God question before they make a commitment to believe in Him, and they miss the heart of the issue—the issue of the heart.

Jesus says, "I have come that they may have life, and that they may have it more abundantly" (John 10:10). In telling us that, Jesus uses a great old Bible word to describe the way God wants to bless our lives. He *abundantly* pardons our sins (Isaiah 55:7). His grace is exceedingly *abundant* (1 Timothy 1:14).

Psalm 37:11 promises us an abundance of peace. The apostle Paul says that out of the abundance of God's grace and righteousness, we can reign in life through Jesus Christ (Romans 5:17). We have abundant labors in His kingdom (2 Corinthians 11:23), but also abundant joy (Philippians 1:26) and abundant mercy (1 Peter 1:3).

I think when most Christians approach the end of life, they are going to wish they had served God more faithfully. But I think they will have another regret—that they did not fully take advantage of the wonderful abundance in life that Christ offers us.

God enjoys our enjoyment. He filled the world with good things for a reason. Go to a football game. Spend time with your family. Take a vacation. Pursue an enjoyable hobby. Relax in the sauna. Do a little something for yourself every day, and thank God for the blessings He has abundantly poured into your life.

Author Jim McGuiggan has observed:

> Some saints can't enjoy a meal because the world is starving. They can't joyfully thank God for their clothing and shelter because the world is naked and homeless. . . . They can't enjoy an evening at home with their families because they feel they ought to be out "saving souls." They can't spend an hour with an unforgiven one without feeling guilty if they haven't preached a sermon or manifested a "sober Christian spirit." They know nothing of balance. And they're miserable because of it. . . . They think the gospel

is 'good news' until you obey it and then it becomes an endless guilt-trip.[2]

The Westminster Catechism has it right: "Man's chief and highest end is to glorify God, and fully to *enjoy* him forever" (emphasis added).[3]

Don't Forget to Be Thankful for God's Gifts

And also that every man should eat and drink and enjoy the good of all his labor—it is the gift of God.
—ECCLESIASTES 3:13

Luke 17 is a healing story of Jesus. He restores ten lepers to perfect health, but only one has the good manners to come back and say thank you. Why was this leper different? We have no clue, but it's logical to believe that long before Jesus came to town, this one showed evidence of a different heart. And we can imagine the other nine grumbling, rumbling, dwelling in the considerable misery of their lives.

This one leper must have been different—thanking God for the sunshine and the blue sky, bowing before meals to offer thanks. Disease is a terrible thing, but its power to inflict misery over us is, to a great extent, within our control. Godly people cope with amazing adversities by simply refusing to bow to misfortune. The most powerful weapon in the attitudinal arsenal is gratitude: "In everything give thanks; for this is the will of God in Christ Jesus for you" (1 Thessalonians 5:18).

The best-known evangelist in the world during the early 1900s was Billy Sunday, a former professional baseball player who preached with acrobatic vigor and powerful results. His wife, Helen, was heavily involved in his ministry. On November 19, 1935, Billy died in her arms, and she felt she had lost both her husband and her life's work. But the following week at a memorial service in Buffalo, her subject was "Things I'm Thankful For." She had a long list, but she began like this:

> Folks, it's surprising how many things God can reveal to you to be thankful for, if you really want to know and ask Him to help you. I had no idea there were so many! But when I prayed and asked God to help me write them down, they came into my mind one after the other—the very first one was: If Billy had to go, oh, how thankful I was to God Almighty that He called him away in an instant. . . . He just cried out to me, "I'm getting dizzy, Ma!" and he was gone! How wonderful to be here one second, and up in heaven the next second! Never knowing any real pain or any real suffering of that type—I think God was so good to take Billy that way, and I thank Him for it.[4]

Life is like one of those Rorschach tests administered by psychiatrists. Some look at it and see the black inky stains. "It's a monster, preparing to attack me," they say. Others look at the same blot and define it by the whiteness that encloses the ink. "It's a heavenly cloud and a hovering angel," they say.

Optimistic people see blessings amid burdens. They realize the sun always breaks through sooner or later. It refuses to be defined by the presence of dark clouds. After all, the dark clouds are nothing but mist; the sun is built to last.

We have the opportunity to look at life through the powerful eyeglasses of God's promises, which magnify blessings and keep trials in perspective. The more we peer through those spectacles, the more we want to send thank-you notes, the more we want to commit random acts of kindness, the more we want to stop during the day and offer silent thanks for the subtle blessings that cover us all the time.

Don't Fear Life—Fear God

I know that whatever God does,
It shall be forever.
Nothing can be added to it,
And nothing taken from it.
God does it, that men should fear before Him.
That which is has already been,
And what is to be has already been;
And God requires an account of what is past.

—Ecclesiastes 3:14–15

God deals exclusively in *forever* and *flawless*. If God made it, you can't add to it, subtract from it, or put a stop to it. Though even a sunset over the Rockies is not forever, you have these feelings as you stand in its presence: "This is a work of perfection; a masterpiece. I can add nothing to it, nor can I detract from it one iota. Therefore I simply stand, humble and speechless."

God's design for your life is every bit as awe-inspiring as tomorrow's sunset. What? You have your doubts about that plan? It is perfect; it is a forever thing; it cannot be edited. We should rest in the knowledge of His perfection, but we should also respond in a healthy fear.

Did you read that correctly? Fear? Even though that word appears less frequently in today's sermons and Bible studies, it remains in God's perfect, uneditable Word. The phrases "fear God" or "fear the Lord" occur more than 114 times in the Bible. For example:

You shall fear the LORD your God and serve Him. (Deuteronomy 6:13)

Now therefore, fear the LORD, serve Him in sincerity and in truth, and put away the gods which your fathers served. (Joshua 24:14)

The fear of the LORD is clean, enduring forever. (Psalm 19:9)

You who fear the LORD, praise Him! (Psalm 22:23)

[Walk] in the fear of the Lord and in the comfort of the Holy Spirit. (Acts 9:31)

Therefore, having these promises, beloved, let us cleanse ourselves from all filthiness of the flesh and spirit, perfecting holiness in the fear of God. (2 Corinthians 7:1)

Does this imply that we should cower in fear of God—tremble as we enter the church or begin our morning prayer? Not in the way we fear any force of malevolence, such as a wild animal or a disaster or a misfortune for someone in our family. No, this kind of fear we feel in the presence of something too marvelous for words.

Have you ever visited Niagara Falls and ridden the Maid of the Mist right out into the basin of that thundering cataract? It is a bit terrifying to stand there, only a few yards from such power, deafened by the roar of six million cubic feet of water bursting over the cliff every minute and falling 170 feet into the basin before you. The spray hits you, and you can literally feel the sound waves beating against your face. You look at the awesome power of the pounding waters, and you feel small and fragile in your sense of wonder.

When you look at the sun setting over the Rockies, painting the sky in a spectrum of reds and oranges, you reflect on the size and heat of that solar star, and the fact that in a millionth of a second, you would cease to exist if you were in its near presence. You feel small, fearful, and awestruck.

The One powerful enough to set that sun in space and to create that waterfall is far more worthy of our fear and wonder. He holds all of space and time within His fist, and how small are we in that context?

This is a fear caught up in love—the way we may have once feared our earthly mothers and fathers, but to the trillionth power. It is a fear that inspires worship as the heat inspires warmth. Life? We have no reason to fear it. God? We have every reason. We fear His magnificence, His infinity, His wrath, and therefore we fear the prospect of ever wandering from His friendship, ever turning from His presence, ever losing His power, as Solomon did.

We fear the thunderous power of a love so relentless it could send One's own Son to die. We fear the utter blackness of God turning away, as endured by Christ on Calvary. We stand before the cross and realize we can add nothing. We can take nothing away. The act is perfect and forever, and our fear turns to abounding love and devotion.

8

When Justice Isn't Just

Ecclesiastes 3:16–22

The misty image of an ear sealed his fate.

In 1998, Mark Dallaher was convicted of killing a ninety-four-year-old woman in England. The key testimony was an expert witness who stated that the intruder had pressed his ear against the glass window of the woman's house, listening quietly before slipping into the room to murder her. The ear prints matched those of Mr. Dallaher, said Cornelius Van Der Lugt; in fact, he was "absolutely convinced" of the match.

The trial made headlines around the world because it was the first time ear prints had been used to convict a killer. Dallaher was sentenced to life behind bars in England's notorious "Old Bailey" prison.

It turned out the evidence against Dallaher was flawed. A DNA profile obtained from the ear print proved it did not belong to Dallaher at all. Instead, a new suspect was implicated. Dallaher was set free.

"I've waited seven years for this day," he told British newspapers as he left Old Bailey. "I've spent six of those years in prison, protesting my innocence to deaf ears. The last nine months has been a terrible ordeal—all as a result of the prosecution's reliance on now-discredited expert evidence."[1]

If there is a God of love, justice, and power, how do you explain the fact that life is not fair, and cruel injustices may stand? It is a story as old as humanity. The guilty walks free while the innocent suffers.

Injustice Under the Sun

Moreover I saw under the sun:

> In the place of judgment,
> Wickedness was there;
> And in the place of righteousness,
> Iniquity was there.
>
> —ECCLESIASTES 3:16

This deeply bothered Solomon—injustice under the sun. The wicked prosper in their sins while the righteous suffer in their integrity. People with money can oil the wheels of justice, making them turn in their direction and in their favor, while the poor often find themselves at the mercy of an overburdened court nearly bursting at the seams. According to one survey, one of every seventy-five men in the United States is in jail or prison.[2] The odds dictate that a few of these are surely innocent, but it is even more certain that the streets are filled with as many evildoers as ever.

Solomon uses a unique literary technique to make his point. With characteristic honesty, he tells it exactly as he sees it, using the phrase "I saw" no fewer than four times in this section (Ecclesiastes 3:16; 4:4, 7, 15). He takes a look around, records his observations, and draws his own conclusions. He thinks in his heart (3:17), he perceives (3:22), and he considers (4:1).

We do the same. We see the innocent suffer, and it cuts us deeply. There but for the grace of God go we. In time, we become angry, and we stand with Solomon to demand: Why must justice be so unjust?

Thousands of upright souls are suffering in filthy prisons under the tyranny of communism, militant Islam, and totalitarianism. The "crime" may well be that of bearing the name of Christ.

Few governments have been more brutal to Christians than that of North Korea. Soon Ok Lee was a prisoner in North Korea from 1987 to 1992. She did not become a Christian, however, until she escaped to South Korea. When she first received Christ, she was overwhelmed by her memories of what she had seen and heard in prison. It was the simple things, like the Christians who sang as they were being put to death. At that time, she did not understand and had thought they were crazy. She was not allowed to talk, so she never had the chance to speak with a Christian. She does remember hearing the word *amen*.

While she was there, she never saw Christians deny their faith. Not one. When those Christians were silent, the officers would become furious and kick them. At the time, she could not understand why they risked their lives when they could have said, "I do not believe," and done what the officers wanted. She even saw many who sang hymns as the kicking and hitting intensified. The officers would call them crazy and take them to the electric-treatment room. She did not see one come out alive. It was the singing that stuck with her. Perhaps it was the singing of those precious saints that planted a seed in her spirit and eventually led her to Christ.

As Solomon pondered the problem of faulty justice, he proposed a series of profound answers in verses 17–21.

And yes, there *are* answers.

Judgment Is Coming

I said in my heart,

"God shall judge the righteous and the wicked,
For there is a time there for every purpose and for every
work."

—Ecclesiastes 3:17

Times are just, Solomon said—but just wait, for here comes the Judge. And when He sits behind the bench, the rulings will be according to the secrets of men's hearts. Furthermore, there will be no partiality; no favoritism or influence peddling. The date has been set, and each of us will have his or her day in court.

As Ecclesiastes 8:6 puts it, "Because for every matter there is a time and judgment." Again, a time for every purpose under heaven.

We hate it when someone "gets away with it." Solomon tells us that in truth, nobody gets away with it. Paul Harvey illustrated this point when he told about a man named Gary Tindle who was charged with robbery. While standing in the California courtroom of Judge Armando Rodriguez, Tindle asked permission to go to the bathroom. He was escorted upstairs to the bathroom, and the door was guarded while he was inside. But Tindle, determined to escape, climbed up the plumbing, opened a panel in the ceiling, and started slithering through the crawl space, heading south.

He had traveled some thirty feet when the ceiling panels broke under him, and he dropped to the floor—right back in Judge Rodriguez's courtroom.[3]

When the guilty seem to have escaped judgment, it is only for a short moment and a short crawl. They will find themselves before the Judge once again in due time. Sooner or later the wheels of God's righteousness will right every wrong, balance every scale, and correct every injustice in the world. James Russell Lowell's famous poem, "The Present Crisis," describes this truth:

> Truth forever on the scaffold. Wrong forever on the throne—
> Yet the scaffold sways the future and behind the dim unknown
> Standeth God within the shadow, keeping watch above His own.[4]

William Wadsworth Longfellow elaborated on Lowell's original sentiment, saying:

> Though the mills of God grind slowly, yet they grind exceeding
> small;
> Though with patience he stands waiting, with exactness grinds he
> all.[5]

Small and all—good ways to characterize the extent of God's present and future judgment. As someone has said, "In the choir of life, it's easy to fake the words—but someday each of us will have to sing solo before God."

Death Is Certain

I said in my heart, "Concerning the condition of the sons of men, God tests them, that they may see that they themselves are like animals." For what happens to the sons of men also happens to animals; one thing befalls them: as one dies, so dies the other. Surely, they all have one breath; man has no advantage over animals, for all is vanity. All go to one place: all are from the dust, and all return to dust. Who knows the spirit of the sons of men, which goes upward, and the spirit of the animal, which goes down to the earth?

—Ecclesiastes 3:18–21

Here is Solomon's point: A man and his dog romp through the same field, breathe the same air, die on the same acre, and fade to dust together in the earth. They are more alike than different.

Some liberal interpreters of the Bible claim this passage argues against the eternal nature of the human soul. But Solomon is referring to issues of flesh and bone. These bodily temples are not built to last any more than was Solomon's temple of gold. Both topple someday; both become one with the dust.

But the issues of the soul are a separate discussion. Eternity is set in our hearts and engraved in our destiny—but it is not so for the animals. We are made in the image of God, and we are His children—but it is not so for the animals.

So death is certain. The criminal may run free today, but Death wears excellent running shoes and cannot be outrun.

Doctors and social scientists have been studying deathbed scenes for several years and interviewing people who have had near-death experiences. Dr. Maurice Rawlings, a Chattanooga cardiologist, has written about his research. He observes that death survivors tell us that the moment of death is absolutely painless, regardless of every instinct we have about it. "Feels like fainting," survivors say, or "like a missed heartbeat" or "a lost breath." Many have a sense of their souls leaving their bodies on a tranquil voyage down what seems to be a tunnel.

But not all the stories have happy endings. Dr. Rawlings was an agnostic and a cynic when something happened to him that changed his life. One day he was examining the heart of a forty-eight-year-old mail carrier named Charles McKaig, from LaFayette, Georgia.

McKaig was on the treadmill when his heart monitor became erratic, then flatlined.

Surprisingly, Charlie continued to talk for a moment, unaware that his heart had stopped. Four or five seconds later, he looked suddenly dumbfounded. Then his eyes rolled up in his head, and he fell, the treadmill sweeping his body away like so much trash, as Dr. Rawlings later put it.

Rawlings immediately began applying CPR. As Charlie's heart began beating, he screamed, "Don't stop! I'm in hell! I'm in hell!"

Rawlings thought the man was having hallucinations. But Charlie continued, "For God's sake, don't stop! Don't you understand? Every time you let go, I'm back in hell." Charlie begged Rawlings to pray for him, but Rawlings told him to shut up. "I'm a doctor," he said, "not a minister."

The nurses gave Dr. Rawlings such terrible looks that even while applying CPR he said, "All right. Say it! Jesus Christ is the Son of God. Go on and say it." Charlie said those words, and a strange thing happened. He was no longer a wide-eyed, screaming, combative lunatic. He was relaxed and calm and cooperative. He survived the experience, a changed man from that moment on. He went on to live a committed Christian life.

The experience shook Rawlings deeply. He began a long-term study into near-death experiences, and out of his research Rawlings himself became a Christian. What he discovered in his research is that near-death experiences are often horrifyingly negative and terror filled when the person has no relationship with God.

Dr. Rawlings summed up his findings, saying, "Most people are deathly afraid of dying. They say, 'Doctor, I'm afraid of dying.' But I have never heard one of them say, 'Doctor, I'm afraid of judgment.' And judgment is the main concern of patients who have been there and returned to tell about it."[6]

We need to be careful about building our theology on the ambiguity of near-death incidents. Even so, it is interesting that such information often harmonizes with what the Bible tells us. "And as it is appointed for men to die once, but after this the judgment," says Hebrews 9:27. And one chapter later we read this sobering verse: "It is a fearful thing to fall into the hands of the living God" (Hebrews 10:31).

Life Continues

So I perceived that nothing is better than that a man should rejoice in his own works, for that is his heritage. For who can bring him to see what will happen after him?

—ECCLESIASTES 3:22

Let's get personal here. Have you ever been the victim of injustice? Perhaps you received a speeding ticket when, in fact, you were well within the speed zone. Perhaps a coworker slandered you, preventing you from getting the promotion you deserved. Maybe an associate or family member accused you falsely.

What should you do about it? Grow bitter? Get even? Complain to everyone who will listen? Brood over the injustice until the bitterness springs forth like a weed? No. Just leave it in God's hands and get on with your life.

I heard of a pastor whose car was sideswiped by a speeding motorist. The stranger shot off down the road, never to be seen again. While he was not hurt physically, the young pastor was devastated financially. He was just getting started in ministry, and his little church could pay him only a small stipend. He did not have comprehensive car insurance, so he had to bear the cost of the repairs himself. He also knew he easily could have been killed.

The more this pastor thought about it, the angrier he became. For several days he drove around his neighborhood, searching for the offending car, primed to confront the driver with his fists if necessary.

Then he began to regain his perspective, saying to himself, *It was God who spared my life. It will be God who cares for me financially—and it will be God who sees that justice is done. I'll leave the matter in His hands.*

And so, for the pastor, as well as for you and me, there is wisdom and comfort in realizing that because life goes on, we can go on with life. Yes, injustices will go on as well on this side of eternity. Life is not fair—never was, never will be.

But justice *is* coming, whether today, tomorrow, or in a thousand lifetimes; it is as certain as death. Living in bitterness is not worth the trouble while joy is worth any price.

Therefore life goes on; we move on, and even with its entire catalog of inequities—life is good.

> God holds the key of all unknown,
>> And I am glad.
> If other hands should hold the key,
> Or if He trusted it to me,
>> I might be sad. . . .
> I cannot read His future plan,
>> But this I know:
> I have the smiling of his face,
> And all the refuge of His grace,
>> While here below.[7]

9

From Oppression to Obsession

Ecclesiastes 4:1–6

S imon Wiesenthal survived the Holocaust of World War II, but
his faith in God died somewhere in a Nazi concentration camp.
He told the story of watching a Nazi commander shackle
two Jews together, back to back. The commander pushed his revolver
into the mouth of one of the victims and pulled the trigger. One bul-
let killed both men.

The Nazi turned to his corporals and said, "See, I told you there's
no need to waste bullets. You can kill two with one."

Wiesenthal concluded, "When I saw the oppression and the wickedness and the injustice of that [act], I couldn't comprehend it, and I
turned from God."[1]

The Oppression of the Poor

Then I returned and considered all the oppression that is
done under the sun:

And look! The tears of the oppressed,
But they have no comforter—
On the side of their oppressors there is power,
But they have no comforter.
Therefore I praised the dead who were already dead,
More than the living who are still alive.
Yet, better than both is he who has never existed,
Who has not seen the evil work that is done under the sun.

—Ecclesiastes 4:1–3

The loss of faith is tragic, but in Wiesenthal's case, somewhat understandable. He simply lacked the perspective that Solomon offers you and me.

Yet the wise king must have seen a few atrocities too. Here he suggests that the oppressed—people like the two Jews in Nazi Germany—would be better off if they'd never been born. Job once thought the same thing about himself. After he lost his children, he said,

May the day perish on which I was born,
And the night in which it was said,
"A male child is conceived." . . .
Why did I not die at birth?
Why did I not perish when I came from the womb? (Job 3:3, 11)

Have you ever cursed the day you were born? Many of us have endured terrible times and unthinkable trials. There are more than a few of us who have, in rock-bottom moments, wished the Lord would go ahead and take us home. Others simply say, "I wish I were dead."

The suicidal impulse, of course, is a very serious emotional issue and requires professional care. But most of us have endured midnights of the soul. In such moments we can thank God that we know

He has a better place for us; we need only be patient. But what about those with no belief in heaven? What can we say to the temporally oppressed and eternally hopeless?

Through my years in ministry I have come to the conclusion that sometimes it is best to simply say, "I don't know. I wish I could give you a full and satisfying answer to your question." We would be foolish to claim an understanding of all the intricacies of God's ways when, in truth, we comprehend so little of them.

Psalm 73 offers a compelling take on this particular matter. I have returned to this passage again and again to draw on the fount of its wisdom and to lead others there. The psalmist tells us, "But as for me, my feet had almost stumbled; my steps had nearly slipped . . . when I saw the prosperity of the wicked" (verses 2–3).

The psalmist has had enough of the "haves" ravaging the "have-nots." The more wickedness he has seen, the bleaker his perspective has become. The psalm grows darker and more troubled until a tentative ray of sunshine breaks through in the middle portion. That is when something happens that shifts the psalmist's perspective:

> When I thought how to understand this,
> It was too painful for me—
> Until I went into the sanctuary of God;
> Then I understood their end. (Psalm 73:16–17)

Comprehension came to him through the act of worship.

We look at our jobs, our governments, and everything else through our own hazy viewpoints. Then, perhaps in church, perhaps in prayer, perhaps on some other holy ground, we gaze through the portal of "the sanctuary of God." The picture changes, like a kaleidoscope of dark colors shifting into a beautiful moonlight landscape. The colors all remain, but we begin to get the picture too. God's perspective is based on different parameters—His love, His grace, His eternal purposes—and the moment we begin to account for these, we make wiser judgments about what we see under the sun.

Charles Tindley was one of the greatest African American preachers of the twentieth century. He had been born into slavery in 1851. After the Civil War, he moved to Philadelphia, where he began attending church and found Christ as his Savior. He was called into the ministry and made the impressive vocational journey from church janitor to senior pastor.

His congregation grew just as radically. Thousands eventually came to hear him preach each Sunday. Most of them were poor and black, in a time when there was particular oppression for the poor and the black. Tindley himself died in poverty, despite his fame, and was buried in an unmarked grave.

He faced great oppression in life: racial injustice, false accusations, plain mistreatment. When he was a candidate for a bishop's position, a competing minister told him to his face, "You are an unlettered ignoramus. You know you are not educationally fit to be a bishop." An anonymous letter accused him of immorality, and he was denied the position. Tindley's wife died; his son was killed during World War I. His ministry was a midnight landscape.

Tindley channeled the burden of his suffering into wonderful music. His hymns endure. "I'll Overcome Some Day," for example, became "We Shall Overcome," the basis for the great theme of the civil rights era. He also wrote "Stand by Me," "Nothing Between My Soul and the Savior," and "Take Your Burden to the Lord and Leave It There." That was what Tindley himself had learned to do.[2]

But one of his hymns has a special place in our hearts. "We'll Understand It Better By and By" goes hand in hand with Solomon's insight:

We are often destitute of the things that life demands,
Want of food and want of shelter, thirsty hills and barren
    lands;
We are trusting in the Lord, and according to God's Word,
We will understand it better by and by.

Trials dark on every hand, and we cannot understand
All the ways that God could lead us to that blessed promised
    land;
But He guides us with His eye, and we'll follow till we die,
For we'll understand it better by and by.

Temptations, hidden snares often take us unawares,
And our hearts are made to bleed for a thoughtless word or
    deed;
And we wonder why the test when we try to do our best,
But we'll understand it better by and by.[3]

Solomon's message for you and me is, "As we look upon the oppressed, our hearts are broken. We'd rather not see; we'd rather fix our minds on pleasant subjects. But how can we turn our backs on God's beloved children? We must look hard and accept that we don't have all the answers. Our Lord does, and we'll understand it better by and by."

Suffering Solomon aches for the huddled masses of the poor and hungry because he knows that God aches for them. But the down-and-outers are not the only objects of his pity. We watch him shift his gaze, and we are shocked to see him looking toward the rest of us—those who covet.

The Obsessions of the Prosperous

Again, I saw that for all toil and every skillful work a man is envied by his neighbor. This also is vanity and grasping for the wind.

The fool folds his hands
And consumes his own flesh.
Better a handful with quietness
Than both hands full, together with toil and grasping for
the wind.

—ECCLESIASTES 4:4–6

Basketball coach Pat Riley, in his book *The Winner Within*, tells the story of the 1980 World Championship and the Los Angeles Lakers. After they became the NBA champions, they were thought to be unbeatable. As the 1980–81 season approached, sports pundits agreed that the Lakers were sure to repeat their league domination.

Then, within weeks of the opening game, Magic Johnson tore cartilage in his knee and faced three months of recuperation. He was the star. He was the playmaker. The team and its fans were crushed, but they rallied. The Lakers reached within themselves, found their courage and intensity, and brought their team's game to a new level. They played their hearts out.

Magic was on the bench, but there was fresh magic on the court. The Lakers were winning at an amazing 70 percent clip as Johnson's return drew near. The fan anticipation mounted. During time-outs, the public address announcer would say, "And don't forget to mark your calendars for February 27. Magic Johnson returns to the lineup of your World Champion Los Angeles Lakers!"

Johnson's teammates would hear the announcement and grumble,

"Hey, we're on top of our game right now. What's so special about February 27?"

But even as they continued to overachieve, all the attention shifted toward the one player who had not yet seen the court. On the twenty-seventh of February, 17,500 ticket holders pushed through the turnstiles and were handed buttons reading "The Magic Is Back!"

At least fifty press photographers crowded onto the floor while the name of each player was called. Normally only the starters were introduced, and Magic was going to be on the bench when the game began. But he was, nevertheless, included in the introductions. At the mention of his name, the arena rocked with a standing ovation. Flashbulbs burst like popcorn. Magic Johnson was hailed as a returning conqueror, as if the games without him really had not counted.

The other Lakers burned with resentment. That night their games were off, and they barely overcame the worst team in the league. As the season progressed, team morale plummeted. There was finger-pointing and recrimination among what had been a tight-knit family of players. The coach was fired. The Lakers' win-loss record collapsed, and they took a quick exit from the playoffs.

"Because of greed, pettiness, and resentment," Riley later said, "we executed one of the fastest falls from grace in NBA history. It was the Disease of Me."[4]

The website PersonnelToday.com, a resource for human resource managers in the workforce, reported its survey on this subject. The headline read "Professional Jealousy Grips the Nation." The article under the headline gave the evidence:

> Almost nine out of 10 office workers suffer from "professional envy" of colleagues they perceive to have more glamorous or better paid jobs, according to a survey by Office Angels.
>
> The survey of 1,500 office workers by the recruitment

consultancy found more than two-thirds of respondents felt professional jealousy toward friends who made their own working life appear bland in comparison.

Almost a third envy a partner or spouse's job, while a fifth feel jealous of a work colleague who is further up the career ladder.[5]

Solomon shifts his gaze to envy, jealousy, and the drive to outdo others. The ancient king could have been writing for the *Wall Street Journal* as he summarized the driving motivation in today's workplace.

Most of us work hard at our jobs. But our motivations are ambiguous. Many workers push themselves simply because they want others to envy and admire them. They want the corner office, not because it has a nice view, but because their coworkers will be jealous. And the main reason for buying the high-end car is the hungry look they long to see on the faces of the Joneses next door.

We like being one step ahead. It is normal to want approval, but we want more than that—we want admiration and envy. Competitive drive is a deeper motivator for many of us than we realize.

Erwin Lutzer says that envy is basically a rebellion against God's plan. We do not want others to be blessed more than we are, regardless of God's master plan. J. I. Packer notes that envy is dangerous because it is fed by pride, "the taproot of our fallen nature."[6] Billy Graham has pointed out that envy ruins reputations, splits churches, and even incites murder. It is the precise opposite of love, for love rejoices in the good fortune of others.

Some of us realize the truth of this and determine that we will be different. We do not want to be the kind of people who step on everyone else on our climb up the corporate ladder. But we must also avoid the opposite extreme, as Solomon points out in verse 5. "Foolish people refuse to work and almost starve" (NLT).

During the 1960s and on into the '70s, some young people

decided to abandon what they called "the establishment." We called them "flower children." They sold what they had, piled what was left into their old VW buses decorated with psychedelic paint schemes, and moved into communes.

Naturally, this is less a rejection of competition than an excuse for laziness. And because we are designed to be fruitful, laziness does not sit well with the human spirit. Lethargy sets in, self-respect plummets, and relationships weaken. And don't forget that for every lazy person, society pays a price. The unproductive become social burdens in various ways.

Neither overcompeting nor underperforming is the answer. Solomon suggests the true solution in 4:6: "Better a handful with quietness than both hands full, together with toil and grasping for the wind." Translation: Seek balance. One hand filled with prosperity, contentment, and quietness is far better than two hands filled with envy and rivalry. Compete but cooperate; rest but resume.

Most of us would agree that our society has erred on the side of overwork. That's why an Associated Press article detailed the growing numbers of young adults who are scaling back their lifestyles. They are moving into smaller homes, selling their expensive cars, and often quitting their high-pressure jobs. "It's true among people of all ages," said Bruce Tulgan, a Connecticut-based consultant who tracks generational relationships and trends in the workplace. "But it's much stronger, much more notable among the younger generations." Tulgan said these young adults want more time for "the *life* part of life."[7]

I have enjoyed using a daily devotional resource called *Daily Light*, an updated version of what was first compiled by Samuel Bagster in the nineteenth century. The plan is simple: exclusively Scripture, with one collection of verses for morning, another for evening, and a topical index. I call it the "Starbucks of devotional time" because it is pure spiritual caffeine—a powerful jolt of truth that comes from the all-Scripture program. I have developed a discipline of putting myself in the Scripture passages and offering them as my own prayers to God. Here is an example, recorded in my journal, for the topic of financial stewardship:

> Lord, I ask that You give me neither poverty nor riches—please feed me with the food allotted to me; lest I be full and deny You, and say, "Who are You, Lord," or lest I be poor and steal, and profane the name of my God. Give me this day my daily bread.
>
> Lord, help me not to worry about my life, what I will eat or what I will drink; nor about my body, what I will put on. Isn't my life more than food and my body more than clothing? . . . So Lord, let my conduct be without covetousness; help me to be content with such things as I have. . . . for You yourself have said, "I will never leave you nor forsake you."

If you are familiar with the Bible, you will recognize the verses I was reading on those days. The Scriptures were speaking to me about financial contentment, and this was my way of replying to God in the power of His Word. I realize the crucial nature of contentment in life. Every one of us involved in a race to accumulate the most toys will come out the loser in the end. Solomon, the world's richest man, knew this and knew it early on. As a younger man he wrote, "Better is a little with the fear of the LORD, than great treasure with trouble" (Proverbs 15:16), and along the same lines, "Better is a little with righteousness, than vast revenues without justice" (Proverbs 16:8).

Help us indeed to be content, Lord, in the pleasant valley between too much and too little; between slavery and sloth; between over-competing and underperforming. There, in that valley where heaven meets earth, we can walk with our hand in Yours rather than grasping at the wind.

10

When 1 + 1 > 2

Ecclesiastes 4:7–16

S ticks and stones may break my bones, but words will never hurt me." It has a nice memorable ring to it, but I'd guess whoever said it had very few close friends.

The fact is that the worst hurts of all come from people, their words, and the pains we suffer simply in trying to get along together in some semblance of a social life.

You twist an ankle—*ouch!* The immediate pain is considerable. You feel it for a few days, and you may even go to the doctor. But a year from now, maybe two years from now, will you even remember the incident? When someone mentions the day you twisted your ankle, will your face darken as you feel a jolt of fresh pain and sadness? I doubt it.

But consider a relationship wound—and we are not even considering divorces, lawsuits, or the truly serious issues. Just think about the last time someone you care about said something that *really hurt.*

As with the ankle, the immediate pain was considerable. You felt it with intensity for days. But there was no medical doctor who could help you, and few could even understand your pain. This was nothing as generic as a twisted ankle—this was personal. Someone hit a nerve of the emotional variety, and I would predict that in one year, two years, maybe even a decade, you'll remember exactly what was said and how you felt. Only time and God heal wounds like that.

Solomon knew this. Certainly he was king, and there were probably very few who chanced a biting remark in his direction. Still, he came from a family that had its share of discord. Absalom was his half-brother; David was his father. Solomon had plenty of opportunity to observe the profound suffering that can result from the fact that we always hurt the ones we love. Many of us struggle all of our lives to overcome the pain arising from early family life, even after we have committed the problem to God. The first cuts in life are the deepest.

T. S. Eliot provided a cynical definition for the typical family in one of his poems:

> Two people who know they do not understand each other,
> Breeding children whom they do not understand
> And who will never understand them.[1]

Yes, families are also beautiful, wonderful gifts from God. If they can be monstrous, they can also be marvelous through the bountiful blessings of God.

But you and I know the truth, don't we? Several times each year we are shocked at the hurtful things that happen to godly families we know. This teenager, so active in the youth group, ran away; that child, raised in Sunday school, got into some trouble; this couple, pillars of the church, is getting a divorce. We hurt with them. We whisper, though we should not. But the wiser ones among us throw no stones; we may be living in glass houses of our own. We know that life's most perilous task may well be that of maintaining an emotionally and spiritually successful family.

Solomon knew it, too, and within the fourth chapter of Ecclesiastes he begins to reflect on the terrible pain of relational discord.

Riches over Relationships

Then I returned, and I saw vanity under the sun:

There is one alone, without companion:
He has neither son nor brother.
Yet there is no end to all his labors,
Nor is his eye satisfied with riches.
But he never asks,
"For whom do I toil and deprive myself of good?"
This also is vanity and a grave misfortune.

—ECCLESIASTES 4:7–8

Solomon perceives that a problem arises when people choose riches over relationships. Perhaps he took a walk and studied the construction crew busily toiling over the temple. He looked off toward the valley and saw workers laboring in the fields even after sundown. He saw them arrive for worship and looked at their eyes, full of weariness within and dark circles beneath.

These people were working their fingers to the bone, putting in hundreds of extra hours. They were not having much fun—they simply refused to leave time for it. Many of them, from farmers to bricklayers, were amassing fortunes. Their labors were paying in the way labors pay: financially.

But there is a cost as well as a payout to our work. We all begin with the same number of minutes, and we invest them however we choose. If the bulk of our investment is in work, our relationship portfolio will be very weak. Solomon looked at a particular laborer, "alone, without companion," and said, "He has neither son nor brother."

What a lonely picture. We see images of the unforgettable character of Ebenezer Scrooge, created by Charles Dickens, sitting up by himself on Christmas Eve, eating his soup before a fire small enough for one. All the rich furnishings around him are slowly going to dust and mold, for who is there to share them with? Why polish the windows when no one looks in or out? He was a rich man, but money bought him no friends; in fact, it seemed to do the very opposite.

Do the math and you'll discover that $1 + 0 = 0$.

Relationships over Riches

Then Solomon turns to a happier image. It is one of the better-known passages in Ecclesiastes, but have you ever studied it in context? Solomon implores us to keep our relationships first. I am indebted to Warren Wiersbe, who came up with perfect titles for these truths about friendship, and I have appropriated them in the following four points.[2]

TWO ARE BETTER THAN ONE FOR WORKING

> Two are better than one,
> Because they have a good reward for their labor.
> —ECCLESIASTES 4:9

So simple—so painfully simple. Two are better than one because they are more effective that way, because God made it that way, and because it's simply more fun that way.

Have you ever noticed the strong friendships that blossom over shared labor? A small group from church goes overseas for a mission project, or they build a house for Habitat for Humanity. There is something about the environment of the hammers and the heavy lifting, the mortar and the muscle, that forces us to drop our usual inhibitions and let people really know us. You can know someone for twenty years in an office or a church environment and hardly know him at all. But spend an afternoon of yard work together and you may become inseparable friends for life.

Work is a sacrament of sweat by which God reconciles us one to another. It works for both sexes, married and single, family and strangers, and across the races. When it comes to labor, "two are better than one."

Two human souls combine their strength, creativity, talent, and ambition. Synergy (the intangible chemistry of working together) takes over. You share the work but you also share a greater reward.

The whole can be greater than the sum of its parts. When you do the math, you find that 1 + 1 adds up to some value greater than two.

TWO ARE BETTER THAN ONE FOR WALKING

> For if they fall, one will lift up his companion.
> But woe to him who is alone when he falls,
> For he has no one to help him up.
> —ECCLESIASTES 4:10

Life is a marathon, an epic journey. They who walk together, walk farther. The path can get steep and rough, and walking with another brings help should we stumble and fall. I pity the person who has no friends to lean on when life gets hard. Not only does he face the difficulties of life, but he faces the discouragement and loneliness of confronting those challenges alone.

Have you ever noticed that even the Lone Ranger had Tonto? He would have been more honest to call himself the Almost-Lone Ranger. He must have known that a campfire with one can be lonely and depressing, but a campfire with two is lively and fun. That's just the way God made things for us. The modern emphasis on being "independent" and "going one's own way" is not a biblical one. We were made to work, walk, and live together, for God understood that it wasn't good for us to be alone (Genesis 2:18).

Loneliness is a warning light on an inner gauge that confirms we are running short on a primary fuel we require to run efficiently. We were made for relationships. Otherwise, who would want to be married? Who would want to have an evening out with the guys or the girls? Who would enjoy family reunions or Bible study groups, as opposed to individual study? We crave all these groups because we need each other, and we need each other daily in the same way we need food, water, air, and shelter.

In truth, Solomon shouldn't even have to remind us of such obvious facts of life. But there are many who try to go it alone as much as possible, and it is for these true lone rangers that Solomon makes his point. "Woe to him who is alone when he falls."

Two Are Better Than One for Warmth

> Again, if two lie down together, they will keep warm;
> But how can one be warm alone?
>
> —Ecclesiastes 4:11

Does your spouse have cold feet?

When we lie down for the night, warmth becomes much more

important because our bodies go into cold storage. We are almost completely sedentary for eight hours. Few calories are being burned; therefore, even in the summertime we need to be covered by some kind of sheet when we sleep. No one likes those cold feet or the chilly floor tile when we walk into the bathroom early in the morning; everyone likes warmth.

And as we all know, two bodies create more heat than one as we sleep. There is something pleasant and secure about having someone sleep beside you.

In Solomon's time cold was a much more serious issue. When forced to sleep in the open, or even in a tent, the more bodies that huddled together, the warmer all would be. It reminds me of the Australian aboriginal phrase, "a three-dog night," that refers to a freezing cold night in the outback. One requires at least three dogs sleeping around him to ward off the chill.

So Solomon says that two are better than one in staying warm. Love is a warm blanket of affection and affirmation that keeps us safe from life's bitter chills.

Two Are Better Than One for Watchcare

> Though one may be overpowered by another, two can
> withstand him.
> And a threefold cord is not quickly broken.
> —Ecclesiastes 4:12

Notice the pattern? Solomon begins his discourse by speaking of one, then two; he ends with three, a number that signifies perfection and holiness. A friend is a treasure; two friends is a treasure-house.

The emphasis here is safety in numbers. One is not only the loneliest number, but the riskiest. Surely that's partially why Jesus sent His disciples out "two by two" to preach the gospel (Luke 10:1). Imagine those groups of two young men each, spiritually unconfident, walking into strange towns with such a message. The good news was really good but really *new;* they were certain to encounter hostility, and the "buddy system" made sense not only for working and walking together, but for watching out for each other.

And if our own world is so much more civilized, why do we have pepper spray, alert whistles, and personal defense classes? Through the nighttime cityscapes of today, you'll never walk alone—if you have good sense. As Solomon says, however, "a threefold cord is not quickly broken."

We can be attacked physically but also spiritually, emotionally, or financially. The world is filled with snares, and there is wonderful security in the feeling of community we have. It is heartbreaking to read of people who grow old without the comfort of friends and family. One day the police or a neighbor force open the door to find the lonely old soul passed away several days ago, and there were no loved ones to notice the silence. How any normal person can get by today without a church family, I'll never understand.

The great hymnist Charles Wesley is not as famous as his brother John, the founder of Methodism, but Charles's hymns are far better known than John's sermons. All over the world Christians still sing "O, for a Thousand Tongues," "Christ the Lord Is Risen Today," "Hark! the Herald Angels Sing," and "Jesus, Lover of My Soul."

Charles wrote hymns day and night, sometimes jumping off his horse to run into nearby houses, shouting, "Pen and ink! Pen and ink!" He reportedly composed 8,989 hymns during his lifetime, an average of ten poetic lines every day for fifty years. He was still writing hymns on his deathbed.

When Charles fell in love, he wrote his love letters in the form of hymns. As he pondered his love for Sally, and as he studied Ecclesiastes 4, he brought the two together in this hymn that began:

> Two are better far than one
> For counsel or for fight;
> How can one be warm alone,
> Or serve his God aright?
> Join we then our hearts and hands,
> Each to love provoke his friend;
> Run the way of his commands
> And keep it to the end.
> Woe to him whose spirits droop,
> To him who falls alone!
> He has none to lift him up,
> To help his weakness on:
> Happier we each other keep,
> We each other's burdens bear;
> Never need our footsteps slip,
> Upheld by mutual prayer.[3]

Are you struggling to make and keep friends? Are some of your relationships going sour? Don't worry so much about *making* friends; work at *being* a friend. Solomon writes elsewhere: "A man who has friends must himself be friendly" (Proverbs 18:24).

Dale Carnegie observed that we can make more friends in two months of showing interest in others than in two years of trying to get them interested in us. And Andy Rooney said good old friends are worth keeping, whether we like them or not!

All that we see around us will pass away, but every person you ever meet is an eternal creature. Treat people with profound love and respect as the fellow citizens of heaven they are or could become. Guard your friendships as you would guard the world's largest diamond, because you can be certain the least of your friends is infinitely more valuable in the eyes of God than any jewel.

Relationships over Popularity

Better a poor and wise youth
Than an old and foolish king who will be admonished no more.
For he comes out of prison to be king,
Although he was born poor in his kingdom.
I saw all the living who walk under the sun;
They were with the second youth who stands in his place.
There was no end of all the people over whom he was made
    king;
Yet those who come afterward will not rejoice in him.
Surely this also is vanity and grasping for the wind.

—ECCLESIASTES 4:13–16

Solomon takes one more look at the industrious workers hauling great stones into place as they build the temple. He sees them helping each other instinctively, hardly thinking about it; protecting each other; bolstering each other through the heat and perspiration of the day. He looks at the great edifice being built, then at the little people doing the building. And Solomon suddenly realizes that as great as this temple will be—surely the world's finest and holiest building—it is worth less than the people for whom and by whom it is built, because the God of this temple loves every one of those souls with an everlasting love. And He made it possible for us to love, support, encourage, and protect in the same way.

It's all about people, the older and wearier Solomon reflects in his later years, as he composes Ecclesiastes. People needing people. And what is needed from those people is true, sincere love and friendship, not the power that comes through fame or envy. That's the point Solomon drives home in these verses.

Fame is like a lover to avoid: beautiful to the eye, seductive to the spirit, and fickle to the end. Fame is expensive, requiring obsessive pursuit. Once apprehended, its attractions are not only fleeting but profoundly disappointing.

Winning the Super Bowl is the professional dream of every NFL player. It is not the money they make; the winner's earnings from a Super Bowl appearance amount to less than a full game's check for the average NFL player. It is not the Vince Lombardi trophy, which they do not get to take home. It is the fame, the respect, that moment of supreme glory.

The players do receive a ring, and the Super Bowl ring is perhaps the most coveted prize in the world of sports—on par with an Olympic gold medal.

But even such a ring may not last. Charlie Waters of the Dallas Cowboys found that out when his *five* Super Bowl rings were stolen from the closet in his home.

Joe Gilliam won two Super Bowl rings as a member of the 1974 and 1975 Pittsburgh Steelers, but he later pawned them for a few dollars after being caught in a vicious cycle of drug addiction and homelessness. Another former Steeler, Rocky Bleier, sold his four rings to cover divorce and bankruptcy proceedings.

The Cowboys' Thomas Henderson had his Super Bowl XII ring seized to pay back taxes. Former Raiders All-Pro cornerback Lester Hayes sold his to pay for dental work. Mercury Morris of the Miami Dolphins sold his to raise money to clear his name during a drug-trafficking case.

That ring, symbolic of months and years of hard work crowned by a season at the top, is as fleeting as the glory for which it supposedly stands. The hype may be spectacular, the TV ratings may be the biggest of the year, the commercial time may cost millions . . . but the glory is fool's gold. Its ephemeral luster is quickly tarnished. As Houston sportswriter Steve Campbell puts it, "One of the dirty secrets about the Super Bowl is that the winner's high often has less of a shelf life than a container of cottage cheese."[4]

With those insights in mind we take another look at Ecclesiastes 4. We find mysterious references to certain individuals:

> *A poor but wise youth;* which one?
> *An old and foolish king;* hmm, who might that be?
> *The second youth;* dare we venture a guess?

Most authors, as we all know, write what they know (the first law of literature). Naturally, they use their own family experiences, perhaps changing the names or using some other literary subterfuge. I think the shady characters in this passage are members of Solomon's family circle.

For example, he points out that a poor and wise youth is better than an old and foolish king. We quickly think of Saul, the first and ill-fated king of Israel. When Saul was crowned, he had palatial fame and acclaim. His approval ratings soared. For Saul, it was good to be king. He ascended in glory but eventually went down in flames.

That would identify the poor and wise youth for us as David, born a peasant shepherd from a small town, destined to bestride the Old Testament like a Colossus, to build a kingdom, to ensure military supremacy, to write psalms and become a man after God's own heart.

But verse 15 speaks of "a second youth who stands in his place." I believe that young man is David's son, Solomon himself, who replaced his father on the throne. Solomon got off to a fast and promising start as a leader, relying on God's wisdom and his own considerable gifts. He extended the empire for which his father had laid the foundation. People all over the world knew about Solomon and the ascendancy of the children of Israel—once slaves in Egypt, now rulers of the Mediterranean world.

But what does Solomon say about this second youth? "But then everyone rushes to the side of yet another youth who replaces him. Endless crowds stand around him, but then another generation grows up and rejects him, too" (NLT).

Fickle, fleeting fame. Solomon knew that his footprints in the sand of time may be deep at the present, but the tide of history would quickly wash them away. His father had reminisced over the days when he rode through the streets to hear people singing, "Saul has slain his thousands, and David his ten thousands" (1 Samuel 18:7). It was a lovely hit tune if you were David, but if you were Saul it was a funeral dirge.

Saul died and was quickly and happily forgotten in the glory of David's prowess as a military king over Israel. But like his predecessor, David's approval rating could not soar forever. The young Solomon had to realize that his newfound glory had bittersweet taste for his aging father.

Now Solomon himself was growing old. He could already hear the people preparing their hearts for a new hero.

Super Bowl rings, Oscars, and chart-topping songs are like the flavor of the month at your local ice-cream parlor. They are smooth, delicious, and they go down easy. But they will be replaced shortly enough. The apostle Paul would refer to a much better crown than any the world could offer. This was a crown worth striving for, one that can only be applied by nail-scarred hands.

I believe Solomon would have appreciated the wisdom offered

in 1 Corinthians 9:25: "And everyone who competes for the prize is temperate in all things. Now they do it to obtain a perishable crown, but we for an imperishable crown." We seek the crown not of supreme fame but supreme faith.

11

A God Who Can't Be Used

Ecclesiastes 5:1–7

There I sat, immersed in thoughts of the ancient king and his quest for meaning. As I worked on this chapter, our community was swept by one of California's largest and most destructive fires ever. Several of our church members lost their homes, and many of the rest—including my own family—were evacuated for safety.

We were beneficiaries of God's severe mercy, as our home was spared. But to this day I take little comfort in that. Again and again, God has allowed my preaching itinerary to overlap with events in the wider world.

After great natural disasters, people walk among the rubble and ask the big questions: Why did this have to happen? What was the meaning of our years building this home, only to see it literally go up in smoke? What could possibly be God's purpose for all this? Pastor, are you listening? We'd like some answers!

I turn to my Bible and find that it happens to be opened to Ecclesiastes this week. That's the way I planned it—at least I *thought* it was me. But here is Solomon, walking among the rubble of his own devastated life, asking all the same questions from a distance of three thousand years. Again the point comes home to us: This is a book for all seasons.

Still, we are left with questions that demand good answers.

Solomon has already spent two chapters discussing the emptiness of a life apart from God. Then, in the third chapter, he has admitted that even so, the stubborn questions remain. But Solomon stands boldly on the declaration that God has a plan, and that even when it is cloaked in several layers of mystery, it is a good plan—a trustworthy plan.

Now we come to Ecclesiastes 5 and the rubble around our ankles. This is the site where all that we built once stood: our hopes right here, our dreams in that pile over there. You can still reach your finger down and find wet traces of our blood, our sweat, and our tears. But now all of that has been leveled. It lies in ruins around us, and nothing is left standing but these towering questions—questions too tall for us to see past, even when we stand on tiptoe.

In times like these, life is hard, spirits are low, and faith is hanging by the adhesive on its bandages. God? A no-show. And maybe that's for the best, because what would we say to Him right now, anyway?

Don't Blame God

Author John Killinger tells about the manager of a minor league baseball team who got so frustrated with his center fielder's performance that he jerked him out of the game and played the position himself. The first hard-hit ball that came to the manager took a bad hop and smashed into his mouth. His next play was a high fly ball that he lost in the sun—until it smacked him in the forehead. The third ball that came his way was a hard line drive that flew between his hands and popped him in the eye.

Furious, he ran off the field to the dugout, grabbed the center fielder by the shirt and shouted, "You've got center field so messed up, even I can't play it!"[1]

God is the subject of more than His share of finger-pointing. As a matter of fact, a seventeen-year-old was accused of burning down a church in Nashville, Indiana. At his trial, he explained that he took a cigarette lighter to the nearly century-old building because "I was angry with God."

One woman, having lost both her husband and son in separate accidents, posted a notice on the Internet: "I am ANGRY at God. I am VERY ANGRY!" She dared to say out loud what you and I really feel sometimes.

God understands our anger, and when we pray, it's a good thing to tell Him what we honestly feel. But sustained bitterness toward the Lord who loves us is irrational and unwise.

The *Journal of Health Psychology* reported an interesting study. Social psychologist Julie Juola-Exline and her team of researchers found a link between anger toward God, and anxiety and depression. Those who couldn't get beyond their resentment toward God were more likely to experience problems with negative emotions. The good news, according to Juola-Exline, was that "those who were able to forgive God for a specific powerful incident, reported lower levels of anxiety and depression."[2]

"Forgiving God" is a term I would rather avoid. It implies that God has done something wrong that requires our pardon. We should underline the statement that by the perfection of His nature, He will not and cannot do wrong. What seems like misdeed is mystery. The important thing to remember is that His love and compassion are perfect, unbroken, and forever.

Just the same, it's all too easy to blame God for our losses and sorrows. Here in Ecclesiastes 5:1–2, Solomon gives us some pointed instruction.

Walk Carefully Before Him

> Walk prudently when you go to the house of God; and draw
> near to hear rather than to give the sacrifice of fools, for they
> do not know that they do evil.
>
> —ECCLESIASTES 5:1

Imagine stumbling into the house of God loaded down with a heavy burden. It is the dead weight of all your sorrows. You are certainly bringing them to the right place, but you need to bring them in the right way. When you are overloaded, it is important to watch your step.

We want to lay them carefully at the altar rather than violently at His feet. That is, we need to give Him the burden but not the blame. There is a difference. That is why we need to tread carefully in the house of the Lord.

Remember that Solomon was the builder of the temple, the most beautiful building on earth in its day. There had never been such a place to bring God and His children together. It was, in a sense, the one place for heaven on earth. The architect understood that such a place should not be entered carelessly or thoughtlessly—particularly not resentfully.

We must decide which side we are on: Do we honor God as the Lord of life or not? Do we trust Him in the rough times or only when it's convenient? Our modern expression, "Watch your step!" comes from Solomon's warning: "Walk prudently." Literally, the Hebrew says, "Keep your foot."

You may remember a time when you heard that phrase from your parents. You were angry, and your words were approaching the territory known as *disrespect* when Mom or Dad said, "Watch your step, young man" or "young lady."

Due respect for parents and for God is a sufficiently urgent issue to be enshrined in the Ten Commandments. Life without boundaries is chaos; and when we treat God as if He is not in control and not loving, when we cut Him down to our size through a petty approach, when we wander outside of the boundaries between us, we invite chaos into our lives.

When we come into the house of God, we are to draw near to hear, to understand, to learn, and to worship. We are to cultivate an attitude of reverence, expectation, and a holy sense of resignation to His will.

Talk Cautiously to Him

Do not be rash with your mouth,
And let not your heart utter anything hastily before God.
For God is in heaven, and you on earth;
Therefore let your words be few.
For a dream comes through much activity,
And a fool's voice is known by his many words.

—Ecclesiastes 5:2–3

Now that we have walked the walk, we have to talk the talk. We must talk cautiously to Him as well as walk cautiously before Him—always keeping in mind that we are speaking from a basis of ignorance.

I think about the terrible fire that burned a path through our community. We often do not know how such a blaze begins. An electric storm could send a bolt of lightning. Some disturbed individual could engage in a conscious act of arson. A careless person could innocently start a great fire without realizing it.

What about God? Could He start a fire? Of course.

Could He also prevent or suppress one? Yes. Could it be that He has done so many times in many places without any human being realizing it? Yes! That is something we seldom consider. We see every fire God allows but none that He prevents.

So when we philosophize about His character based upon our limited observations, we speak from ignorance. On a given day His intervening hand may have prevented some horrendous act of global terrorism—then five minutes later, a single automobile with a drunk driver crashes, and all who knew the victim are giving God a tongue-lashing.

Nothing illustrates this insight more vividly than a widely watched episode of television's *The West Wing* in which the fictional president, Josiah Bartlet (played by Martin Sheen) lashes out at God. Bartlet, battling multiple sclerosis, is anguished over the death of his longtime secretary in a drunk-driving accident. After attending her funeral in the National Cathedral, he waits until everyone leaves, then orders the doors sealed so that he is alone. Standing before the altar, Bartlet, a Roman Catholic in the television series, lashes out at God. "She bought her first car, and You hit her with a drunk driver," shouts Bartlet into the cavernous cathedral. "That's supposed to be funny? Have I displeased You, You feckless thug?"

The angry president then launches into a tirade in Latin. Translated, his words are: "Am I really to believe that these are the acts of a loving God? A just God? A wise God? To hell with your punishments!" Then, in a gesture of contempt, the fictional president lights a cigarette and crushes it on the cathedral floor.[3]

The reaction of viewers was predictable. While some were shocked at Bartlet's anger and blasphemous words, others commended him for his expression of brutal honesty and for representing thousands of people in his anger toward God.

Solomon would feel differently. He reminds us that God knows the time and appointed season of every life. He counts the very hairs on your head, and a sparrow does not plummet to earth without His awareness. And as Jesus tells us, "You are of more value than many sparrows" (Matthew 10:31). Moreover, God knows every implication of every event: positive, negative, or neutral. We live in the goldfish bowl of time and space, with all the limitations imposed by that habitation. God is outside that bowl entirely, and He sees past, present, future, and all across every inch of His creation simultaneously. We cannot wrap our minds around that one any more than a goldfish can understand a map of your county.

Seeing, hearing, knowing, and planning all things, and based upon His own mysterious purposes, God governs the affairs of this planet. There will be a time for intervening and a time to refrain from intervening. To feel angry and frustrated is human; but to chastise God is to make a cosmic spectacle of our own folly in the presence of the Alpha and the Omega, the King of kings who loves us so much that He bears the nail marks in His hands, in the presence of the seraphim and cherubim and all the heavenly realm.

Solomon counsels us to be men and women of few words, for the mark of a fool is his airy gust of reckless speech. Verse 3 is difficult to translate, but Solomon seems to say that a fool babbles on relentlessly, like a man who has had a busy day and experiences dream after dream all night long. And we do sleep better when we don't dwell on our short-sighted grievances against a loving Father.

Don't Bribe God

When you make a vow to God, do not delay to pay it;
For He has no pleasure in fools.
Pay what you have vowed—
Better not to vow than to vow and not pay.

Do not let your mouth cause your flesh to sin, nor say before the messenger of God that it was an error. Why should God be angry at your excuse and destroy the work of your hands? For in the multitude of dreams and many words there is also vanity. But fear God.

—ECCLESIASTES 5:4–7

As a troubled young man walked through a field in Germany, a terrible electrical storm filled the sky. A lightning bolt struck a nearby tree, and he instantly took it as a sign from God. "Help me!" cried the young man, "and I will become a monk." That sudden vow changed the life of Martin Luther.

Another young man, a disreputable character named John Newton, made a similar promise to God in the middle of a deadly storm at sea. "Help me," he prayed, "and I will change my life." Out of that prayer came a gradual transformation that led Newton into the ministry and made him a world-class hymnist, the author of "Amazing Grace."

There are times when God uses a storm or crisis to awaken us, and we make life-changing vows and commitments to Him. The problem is that most of us are quicker to make a commitment than we are to keep it. We live in an age of halfhearted vows and ill-kept promises. If every single person kept the promises he made to God in a pinch, then Africa and Asia would be swarming with millions of missionaries.

We sometimes call this "foxhole Christianity." It is the ultimate expression of using God. Bargaining with God is an extremely questionable activity, generally one to be avoided. But if you do put yourself on the line, don't even think about not making good, for God is not mocked. What is vowed before Him is *binding*, just as He is bound by His many promises in the Scriptures.

Solomon is teaching us that vows are serious. They are lasting and, in the eyes of God, not subject to "on second thought" revocations.

I love what David says in the Psalms as he thinks about a vow he had made to God. "I will go into Your house with burnt offerings; I will pay You my vows, which my lips have uttered and my mouth has spoken when I was in trouble" (Psalm 66:13–14).

We do not know exactly what kind of trouble David was in, but whatever it was, God apparently got him out of it. And in the process David made a vow to God. Making vows were not uncommon in the Old Testament, nor was breaking them. Otherwise, Solomon would not have warned against it, nor would Jesus have commented on it when bringing a spiritual perspective to what had become pharisaical traditions surrounding the Mosaic Law (Matthew 5:33–37). But David kept the vow he made to God.

Eva J. Alexander was born to believing parents in Chennai, India, and was born again at age twelve during a Billy Graham meeting. In 1963, she married R. D. Alexander, and the two took positions with the government of India. Eva's job exposed her to the plight of women in her country, and she began speaking out about their status and suffering. For a while she became so socially active that her spiritual life suffered. Politics became more important than her faith.

But the Lord sent a serious illness that brought her to her knees, where she made a solemn vow before the Lord. As she hovered near death in the hospital, she prayed, "God, if You're real, do not allow me to die. I will serve You."

Eva ultimately recovered from her illness. When she returned home, she began reading her Bible again. Two words in Matthew 21:31 tore through her mind like torpedoes, the words *and harlots*. Jesus said, "Tax collectors and harlots enter the kingdom of God before you." Our Lord wants to bring harlots into His kingdom.

A week later, a nearby pastor told her of a prostitute who had run away from the brothels, and he asked Eva to provide a room for her. "I can't," Eva said. "You keep her." Eva had a husband and four children at home, including two teenage sons. But once again the Lord brought Matthew 21:31 to mind, and Eva relented.

Her family was aghast: "What is this? You're turning our house into a brothel!" But their attitudes soon changed, and they accepted this ministry as coming from God. Other girls began showing up, and the Alexander home became a rehabilitation center. Police officers and prisons referred troubled women to Eva, and today up to fifteen women live in the Alexander home at any one time. The Alexanders provide medical treatment, job training, and a strong gospel witness.

As a result of her vow made to God when she was near death, Eva has started a home for the children of prostitutes. In this home sixty children—ages twelve months to thirteen years—find refuge. Her husband and children joined her work and, spurred on by that passage in Matthew, they are bringing many harlots into God's kingdom.[4]

We have seen it throughout church history. A promise to God, honored by the one who made it, can lead to a touch of heaven on earth. But a vow in danger of being broken is an idea that should make us shudder with fear. At this moment, when the flames are at the door, a vow comes easily to the lips; but tomorrow, when a cool rain drives calamity from memory, it is too easy to double-cross God. The soul implications could be far worse than the original danger that brought about the vow.

My recommendation? Keep your mouth shut when your back is to the wall, and keep the faith with God. Then keep on keeping on. That is the only vow He is really looking for.

12

Governments Never Change

Ecclesiastes 5:8–9

Nikita Khrushchev stood in a high Kremlin window and glared in the direction of the West, home of democracy and freedom. He shook his fist in defiance and shouted, "We will bury you!" Another translation of his Russian phrase reads, "We will be present at your funeral."[1] He spoke of a time when Soviets would rule the world, and they would see the last Christian of the last free nation taken to his execution.

Translation aside, his meaning was clear and unambiguous. The Union of Soviet Socialist Republics had reached its zenith. It measured one-sixth of the world's land mass—two and one-half times the size of the United States of America. Its mastery of science and military technology forged ahead of American progress. And on a clear evening in 1957, North Americans stood on their roofs and watched Sputnik, the first satellite, take a victory lap around the very planet that some felt would be overrun by Soviet Communism.

Within thirty-five years—little more than a generation—that

same proud Communist government lay in ruins, one more casualty of political hubris. What had happened? The demise of the USSR is a complex matter and not to be oversimplified. There were many factors, including a changing world-economic climate. But historians agree that one of the largest contributors to the toppling of Soviet Communism was the incredible personal corruption of government officials. They used their positions not to serve the nation's starving farmers and factory workers but to line their own pockets. They exploited the system, nibbling at its foundations until the whole edifice teetered and collapsed from the inside.

Remember, this empire was the shining fruit of an idealistic revolution. It was to be a socialist organism that would prefigure a new world order, according to Lenin and its champions. Production and prosperity would be in, of, and for the working classes. So went the pledges of the insurgents.

But in December of 1991, when Gorbachev signed the papers that dissolved Lenin's dream, all of that was long gone. The ideals-driven government of the worker classes had quickly given way to the most totalitarian of regimes. As we have long observed, today's revolutionaries become tomorrow's bureaucrats—or, as rock philosopher Pete Townshend put it, "Meet the new boss—same as the old boss."[2]

To which Solomon, presiding over his own idealistic regime, would nod vigorously in agreement.

Imperfect Institutions

If you see the oppression of the poor, and the violent perversion of justice and righteousness in a province, do not marvel at the matter; for high official watches over high official, and higher officials are over them.

Moreover the profit of the land is for all; even the king is
served from the field.

—ECCLESIASTES 5:8–9

A timelier passage cannot be imagined—and as we have seen, it
is timely for any era. If you poke your nose too far into government,
Solomon says, do not be shocked at what you find: graft, injustice,
exploitation. The great palace of state always has a termite problem.
As the *New Living Translation* words verse 8, "For every official is
under orders from higher up, and matters of justice get lost in red tape
and bureaucracy."

How is that for a bleak summary of the wheels of state that make
the world go 'round?

The church is imperfect because it is made of flesh and blood, not
bricks; it is the same with government. Human institutions always
fall prey to corruption, and—because of the presence of wealth and
power—governments most of all.

So we must retain a certain realistic level of pessimism. We expect
the system to fail occasionally, and we have to wash out the stains
every now and then, keeping the laundry of state as pure and clean as
possible. Therefore, we cheer on the honest representatives and leaders, and we use the system to uproot those who break the trust. But
we cherish no illusions of keeping the machine in perfect repair. This
is Solomon's point: creeping corruption cannot be prevented.

In England the established church persecuted those who identified with Martin Luther's Reformation movement throughout the
sixteenth and seventeenth centuries. The "divine right of kings" was
the unbiblical doctrine used by monarchs to establish their will as the
will of God.

Against such tyrannical rule in the British Isles rose the thunderous voice of John Knox. And from this Scot's inspiration came the

writings of Samuel Rutherford. His book, *Lex Rex: or The Law and the Prince* (1644), resulted in his own sentence of death, though he died of natural causes before the sentence was carried out.

Lex Rex stated the biblical view of kings: they and their laws are subject to God and His laws. Everything God is, earthly kings should be: just, righteous, good, merciful, generous . . . everything the established kings of the period were not. Rutherford's treatise was consistent with the New Testament teachings about civil rulers: that they are an extension of the hand of God on earth to carry out His will (Romans 13:1–7; 1 Peter 2:13–17).

With that kind of philosophy, it's easy to see why Rutherford gained the disfavor of kings who asserted their "divine right" to rule.

Unfortunately the kings of the post-Reformation period in England are not the only government rulers who failed to rule with God's priorities. Even the United States, the most successful government in the history of the world, has had to constantly remind itself of its obligations and responsibilities to the governed.

And long before American, English, or any other governments lost sight of their priorities, rulers in Solomon's day had lost the vision for good government. Solomon says the poor were oppressed, and justice and righteousness were perverted. Corruption followed the trickle-down rule as it flowed through one layer after another of back-scratching rulers.

In the 1980s, there was a succession of benefit concerts held by the "glitterati"—rock stars and film idols concerned about issues such as hunger, disease, famine, or the plight of the farmer. They raised huge sums of money, only to discover that the money too often had to be funneled to the third world through corrupt governments. Instead of serving as humble stewards to the people, officials siphoned off large amounts for personal gain.

We spend a great deal of energy railing about these things, and well we should. Righteous anger is natural, but Solomon tells us it is simply naive to be surprised.

In good times, people look at government as their protector, and in bad times as their savior. The failings of governments are nothing more than the failings of men. Why should we expect government to be any different from other segments of society since all are populated and overseen by sinners? Anyone who puts his hope in the government is surely bound to be disappointed. That does not mean we do not appreciate the righteous things government does. It just means that our ultimate hope for protection and salvation is in a God who never disappoints.

Russian author Aleksandr Solzhenitsyn says, "The line separating good and evil passes not through states, nor between classes, nor between political parties either—but right through every human heart."[3]

The government is nothing but human beings gathered together for a particular purpose. Sometimes they make good decisions, sometimes they do not. In that regard, looking at the government is like looking in a mirror. If you feel the government should be doing a much better job of governing the people, what about the job you are doing governing your life? Are there integrity issues? Health issues? Effective use of time and resources?

The problem is the same with principalities as it is with princes: sin. We are foolish to expect the work of government to be any more effective than the lives of its people.

God, Grace, and Governing

We sometimes forget the wonderful idea of the providence of God. Someone has defined this as "God's hands behind the headlines." A preacher named T. DeWitt Talmage once said, "Despots may plan and armies may march, and the congresses of the nations may seem to think they are adjusting all the affairs of the world, but the mighty men of the earth are only the dust of the chariot wheels of God's providence."[4]

Providence is the belief that God will have His way in the end. He rules over land and sea, and He guides the course of history toward His appointed ends. Benjamin Franklin admitted this when he said, "The longer I live, the more convincing proofs I see of this truth— that God governs in the affairs of men."[5]

King David referred to providence when he wrote, "The kingdom is the LORD's, and He rules over the nations" (Psalm 22:28). Proverbs 8:15–16 says, "By me kings reign, and rulers decree justice. By me princes rule, and nobles, all the judges of the earth."

These are particularly difficult promises for us to claim in these days. We know more about the governments of the world. Secrets are harder to keep. Just the same, the Bible assures us that God is in control. We cannot and should not expect the government to be the highest court of appeal or trust. Every ruler in this world serves at God's pleasure—and so do you in your own position, for that matter. Our God is in control of everything; why should we think His divine authority ends on the Capitol steps?

So our first response to the political and governmental sphere should be to trust in the sovereignty of Almighty God. In doing so, we will sleep much better.

Second, we are to pray for our officials. Paul commands, "Therefore I exhort first of all that supplications, prayers, intercessions, and giving of thanks be made for all men, for kings and all who are in authority, that we may lead a quiet and peaceable life in all godliness and reverence" (1 Timothy 2:1–2). How often do you actually pray for your president, your elected representatives, your governors, mayors, and council members? Pray for them, and then take one extra step: write them to encourage them, and let them know you are girding their work with prayer every day. Perhaps if we all did these things, we would begin to see a positive effect on the people who toil to serve us.

Involvement and Insurrection

Third, Peter tells us to be good citizens—actually *excellent* citizens: "Therefore submit yourselves to every ordinance of man for the Lord's sake, whether to the king as supreme, or to governors, as to those who are sent by him for the punishment of evildoers and for the praise of those who do good" (1 Peter 2:13–14). We obey our leaders loyally, knowing that in serving them we serve God. An ordinance is a law. Many of us have grown cynical about our laws and our duties toward them. Be an upholder of the law and a proactive servant of the public good in your community. Get to know your policemen and other public servants. Ask them how you can help.

It is troubling to see Christians withdraw from public discourse. Our influence needs to be present in every event that occurs in this world. Will Durant said:

> Civilization is a stream with banks. The stream sometimes is filled with blood from people killing, stealing, shooting, and doing things historians usually record, while on the banks, unnoticed, people build homes, make love, raise children, sing songs, write poetry, and even whittle statues. The story of civilization is the story of what happened on the banks. Historians and journalists are pessimists because they ignore the banks for the river.[6]

Some of that activity on the riverbanks regrettably reminds us of church activity: singing songs, having covered-dish dinners, enjoying our evangelical culture as we build steeples high enough to block our view of the stream. We need to dive in and make our presence known.

Fourth, take a stand for God when the government clearly defies Him. Peter and John were faced with such a choice. The gauntlet was thrown down when the authorities commanded them not to preach the name of Jesus. They replied, "Whether it is right in the sight of God to listen to you more than to God, you judge. For we cannot but speak the things which we have seen and heard" (Acts 4:19–20).

There was a time when Christians looked into the depths of that stream and saw the evils of slavery. In eighteenth-century England, for example, Christian voices were among the few that spoke out against it. Of course, some Christians defended it with passages from the Bible, such as when Paul tells slaves to submit to their masters. But the conviction of the Holy Spirit was giving a different interpretation. Slavery was a disgraceful plight that needed to be addressed. Many believers devoted their lives to combating the outdated institution. They collected data on the mistreatment of the human cattle who were being exploited for the sake of economic growth. These concerned believers began to build a following that raised an outcry. Still, they needed someone in power to take up their cause. They needed a voice within the seat of government.

William Wilberforce became a believer in 1785, five years after his election to Parliament. Interestingly the work of former slave trader John Newton was a factor in Wilberforce's conversion. Newton was a man with a burden of guilt; he had piloted vessels filled with groaning, bleeding, dying souls. "Amazing Grace" was the first legacy of Newton's wretchedness; Wilberforce was the second. Under Newton's influence Wilberforce began to fight in Parliament for the abolition of slavery.

This was no election-year stunt; it was a twenty-year pursuit of a godly vision. The proslavery lobby had terrible clout in the government. At every turn Wilberforce spoke of God's heart against such inhuman exploitation, until Lord Melbourne sniffed, "Things have come to a pretty pass when religion is allowed to invade public life."

The army of Christ won the victory when the slave trade was abolished in 1807.

We are inspired by Wilberforce, who persevered against the Goliath of slavery. We are inspired by Martin Luther King Jr., a martyr to the Goliath of racism. And we realize that Christians must walk the tightrope of respecting government (as both these men clearly did) while working within it to the glory of God. Following their example, we can make a difference. We can weed out the corruption Solomon warned us about and strike a blow for the kingdom of God.

But never, never expect utopia to come to a Capitol near you. Heaven on earth cannot be established at the ballot box but only through the hearts of men. One day we will see the descent of the New Jerusalem, and there will be at last, one Governor before whom we will bow, with no more use for intermediaries; one Party to serve, with no more use for debate or dissension; one Lord, one faith, one baptism into the world that has always been our destiny as His divine constituency.

13

Dollars and Sense

Ecclesiastes 5:10–20

You might as well admit it: you have had those fantasies. You cannot grow up in this country—or perhaps any country— without having them.

I'm talking about those dreams of unbounded riches. You have visualized winning the lottery or, perhaps, having the Prize Patrol walk up to your door with the cash prize for the Publisher's Clearinghouse. You have watched those TV shows about the lifestyles of the rich and famous, and you have wondered what it would be like to have just a little of that for yourself.

You have daydreamed about April 15 being just another day, when that tax deadline no longer looms like a predator over your home, of having an army of servants who fix the meals and do the laundry, of cruising up to your mansion in a brand-new luxury car.

We all build castles in the air, but Solomon warns us not to get too carried away. It is all an illusion, he says, no matter how it appears—and today's magazines and TV cameras can make it appear pretty lovely.

Solomon wants us to understand that the deepest desires within us are for heaven, and that they will never materialize on earth through the paper paradise of wealth.

Wealth underachieves when it comes to bringing happiness, but it overachieves when it comes to bringing misery. It is true now, it was true in old Jerusalem, and it will always be true under the sun.

An Associated Press article covered the story of a man with stomach pain. The report said,

> French doctors were taken aback when they discovered the reason for the patient's sore and swollen belly: He had swallowed around 350 coins—$650 worth . . .
>
> The 62-year-old man came to the emergency room of Cholet General Hospital in western France . . . [having] a history of major psychiatric illness. . . .
>
> His family warned doctors that he sometimes swallowed coins, and a few had been removed from his stomach in past hospital visits.
>
> Still, doctors were awed [by what they saw on the X-ray. There was] an enormous opaque mass in his stomach that turned out to weigh 12 pounds. . . . It was so heavy it had forced his stomach down between his hips.
>
> Five days after his arrival, doctors cut him open and removed his badly damaged stomach with its contents. He died [a few days] later from complications.[1]

Doctors said the man was suffering from a rare illness that makes people want to eat things other than food.

But that is simply insanity. You and I are nothing like this mentally unhealthy fellow, are we? We would never become consumers of wealth—well, at least not literally. But what about spiritually?

In the realm of faith, we require a certain kind of nourishment. As the body thirsts for water and the lungs yearn for air, so the soul is hungry for heaven. We feed ourselves through His Word, His presence, His service, and His vision for us—so many good and healthy nutrients. He has set a full table before us, and we need only share the banquet.

Instead, the world seduces us away from His table. It draws our hungry gaze toward its shiny trinkets until we become ravenous consumers of the American Dream. We feed the hunger of the soul with the empty calories of the world, and we end up as bloated and unhealthy as the man in the news story. Perhaps the only difference is that this man's price was $650. What is ours?

We are spirits in the material world, "ghosts in the machine" as someone has said. We live on earth, but our true home is heaven, and that creates a dissonance in the soul. We will never be at peace until we find the bridge between the two worlds. So we continue to search for the things that really matter in life.

So thoroughly have we been hypnotized that no matter how many times we tell ourselves that wealth is not contentment, no matter how many times we witness the utter bankruptcy of that myth in real life, no matter how many miserable millionaires walk the earth, and no matter how powerfully our own experience points to the truth—we keep returning to the empty dream, mesmerized by the mirage.

And when life goes wrong, we look first to the financial remedy. Her marriage fails, and she wonders if a bigger house would have made the difference. He faces depression, so he goes out and buys an expensive sports car. They are losing their kids, so they shower them with gifts.

Very simply, *wealth is not the answer.* Don't you think it's significant that this idea permeates the whole Word of God, from Moses to Paul? Isn't God urgently trying to tell us something?

The illusion is powerful, persistent, and deadly. It promises heaven but delivers heartbreak. In this chapter of Ecclesiastes, Solomon offers us five points on finance, then two profound truths about God.

Five Things We Should Know About Money

1. THE MORE WE HAVE, THE MORE WE WANT

> He who loves silver will not be satisfied with silver;
> Nor he who loves abundance, with increase.
> This also is vanity.
>
> —ECCLESIASTES 5:10

Look up the richest tycoons in town. Meet them at the country club for a game of golf or tennis; discuss their dreams. I predict you will discover that they are focused on getting *more*.

You can be the poorest peasant or the richest land baron, yet it seems you will always want *more*. The more we get, the more we want. The fire is fed but never quenched.

Jesus said, "Take heed and beware of covetousness, for one's life does not consist in the abundance of the things he possesses" (Luke 12:15).

There are not many "Uncle Bud" Robinsons among us. Robinson, a well-known holiness preacher of an earlier generation, was taken by friends to New York and shown all the sights of the city. That night in his prayers, he said, "Lord, I thank You for letting me see all the sights of New York. And I thank You most of all that I didn't see a thing that I wanted."[2]

Wouldn't it be wonderful to be truly content? To be eased of the burden for more accumulation, and to be at peace with where we are in life? Why do we make ourselves miserable over what has no track record of satisfying?

Part of Paul's incredible power in his ministry comes from this trait: "I have learned in whatever state I am, to be content: I know how to be abased, and I know how to abound. Everywhere and in all things I have learned both to be full and to be hungry, both to abound and to suffer need" (Philippians 4:11–12).

There is wisdom and power in knowing how to be content with much or little.

2. THE MORE WE HAVE, THE MORE WE SPEND

> When goods increase,
> They increase who eat them;
> So what profit have the owners
> Except to see them with their eyes?
>
> —ECCLESIASTES 5:11

The big promotion comes through with its expected raise. We could simply keep the same lifestyle and use the extra money wisely, but in a microsecond we are salivating over the prospect of new cars, new furniture, perhaps a second home. Solomon says that when possessions get thick, so do we. He wants to know, what is the point of having more money? We will just go out and spend whatever we get.

Author William MacDonald says, "When a man's possessions increase, it seems there's a corresponding increase in the number of parasites who live off him: management consultants, tax advisers, accountants, lawyers, household employees, and sponging relatives."[3]

The more you have, the more you want. The more you want, the more you spend. The more you spend, the more you need. The more you need, the more you have to have. Stop the world—I want to get off!

3. The More We Have, the More We Worry

The sleep of a laboring man is sweet,
Whether he eats little or much;
But the abundance of the rich will not permit him to sleep.

—Ecclesiastes 5:12

When the San Diego County fires began approaching our neighborhood, the order came to collect our valuables and evacuate our homes. Driving down the hill from our home, I turned to my wife, Donna, and said, "Do you realize it only took us ten minutes to collect our valuables? Everything else is just 'stuff.'"

When you can fit all your life's valuables in the backseat of your car, you can sleep well at night because you have cut down your "worry field." By God's grace I can say I have never lost a night's sleep over the status of my investments. Many people think that the more money they have, the more soundly they will sleep at night, but the opposite is true. The more they get, the more they worry about preserving it.

When money is your shield and bulwark, you will spend all your time worrying about what will happen if you lose your shield. Thankfully, my Shield and Protector is One who has already said, "I will never leave you nor forsake you" (Hebrews 13:5).

When he was fifty-three years old, John D. Rockefeller was the world's only billionaire. His income was one million dollars per week. But he was a sick man who lived on crackers and milk and could not sleep because he worried so much about his money. Eventually, he learned how to give money away, and his health improved radically. As a philanthropist, he lived to celebrate his ninety-eighth birthday.

Elderly couples reminisce about the box of macaroni days in the tiny apartment. They conclude that those may have been the best times in their marriage. The Great Depression was a severe time for people, yet many folks have remembered those same years fondly.

Lack of money flushes us out of self-satisfied isolation. It forces us to go out and meet people and to need some of them. As we grow richer, we draw away from community. We miss a lot of the little graces and relational encounters that make life real and satisfying—and we replace them with trinkets that never live up to their shiny allure.

4. The More We Have, the More We Lose

> There is a severe evil which I have seen under the sun:
> Riches kept for their owner to his hurt.
> But those riches perish through misfortune.
> —Ecclesiastes 5:13–14

Let me be clear on this point because it is easy to misunderstand what Solomon is saying. The essence of his message is this: you cannot lose what you do not have.

We should not avoid seeking things just because we could lose them. But we realize from the very beginning that we are adding one more element to our lives, one more dependency, one more responsibility. Anyone who has ever bought a home for the first time understands that concept. We become attached to our possessions at our own risk because we now have so much more to lose.

5. The More We Have, the More We Leave Behind

> When he begets a son, there is nothing in his hand.
> As he came from his mother's womb, naked shall he return,
> To go as he came;

And he shall take nothing from his labor
Which he may carry away in his hand.

And this also is a severe evil—
Just exactly as he came, so shall he go.
And what profit has he who has labored for the wind?
All his days he also eats in darkness,
And he has much sorrow and sickness and anger.

—ECCLESIASTES 5:14–17

We all know the modern translation of this one: you can't take it with you.

It's just common sense. You pay sweat and toil for the things you accumulate. But you never own anything permanently; you only rent it for a season until you pass from this earth. Your precious possessions, even if they outlast you, will belong to someone else.

The flip side of that coin is positive: much good has been done by sizeable bequests to charities, Christian ministries, or individuals. Accumulation can work hand in hand with goals for God's kingdom. For now, we only need to remember that in eternal terms, there is no *own*—only *loan*. Jesus reminds us to act wisely, therefore, and invest in the treasures that are indeed permanent, for they are fixed in heaven. "But lay up for yourselves treasures in heaven, where neither moth nor rust destroys and where thieves do not break in and steal. For where your treasure is, there your heart will be also" (Matthew 6:20–21).

One way we find heaven on earth is to make investments in it from earth. And that bank is accessed through what we set our hearts upon.

Two Things You Need to Know About God

Now Solomon turns to insights about God.

1. Our Ability to Earn Money Is a Gift from God

> Here is what I have seen: It is good and fitting for one to eat
> and drink, and to enjoy the good of all his labor in which he
> toils under the sun all the days of his life which God gives
> him; for it is his heritage.
>
> —Ecclesiastes 5:18

It is the American tradition to be a self-made man or woman. The Horatio Alger stories of the late nineteenth century, about impoverished boys who achieved wealth and respect through hard work and virtue, instilled a work ethic in the burgeoning industrial culture of America that has never faded.

We cannot say anything negative about hard work or virtue; Scripture promotes personal industry (Proverbs 6:6–11; 2 Thessalonians 3:10). But motives tell the tale, and the American tale lacks a spiritual premise, for there is no such thing as a self-made man or woman. Every person who ever earned a dime did so with a heart, mind, soul, strength, talents, and opportunities supplied by God. And what God gives, God can take away (Job 1:21).

Solomon says you have worked for what you have, so go ahead and enjoy it. "Knock yourself out," he would say in modern terms. "You've got it coming to you." But remember that every gift is from God, and those gifts are not ends in themselves but reminders of His goodness. He gives us things for the same reason you buy birthday presents for your children. It makes them smile. God, too, enjoys our pleasure—which increases exponentially when we see His gifts for what they are; maintain hearts of humility, contentment, and gratitude; and thank and praise Him daily as the source of all that is good in life.

2. Our Ability to Enjoy Money Is a Gift from God

> As for every man to whom God has given riches and wealth, and given him power to eat of it, to receive his heritage and rejoice in his labor—this is the gift of God. For he will not dwell unduly on the days of his life, because God keeps him busy with the joy of his heart.
>
> —Ecclesiastes 5:19–20

God gives us not only the gift but also the ability to enjoy it, the food and the mouth to eat it, the art and the mind to appreciate it, the beautiful earth and the feet to run upon it. Every component of life, down to the smallest molecule, is part of His gift. But we cannot enjoy any gift properly without reference to the Giver.

As I prepared to preach this particular chapter of Ecclesiastes, God offered me a living illustration in the fires that our community endured. Material things that people had spent a lifetime accumulating were consumed in mere moments. People came through it well if their hearts were set on the Giver rather than the gifts. Those people knew that what went up in smoke was little more than smoke to begin with. Life itself is a vapor that lingers a moment before evaporating (James 4:14). But for those whose hearts were set on their material possessions, the devastation of the loss was terrible indeed.

We have mentioned John D. Rockefeller, who learned the life-giving therapy of generosity before it was too late. In a 1905 interview he said,

God gave me money. I believe the power to make money is a gift from God . . . to be developed and used to the best of our ability for the good of mankind. Having been endowed with the gift I possess, I believe it is my duty to make money and still more money and to use the money I make for the good of my fellow man according to the dictates of my conscience.[4]

God is a loving and generous Father, but He does not want our things to possess us. What a joy to learn the lesson Rockefeller learned: money and possessions are not evil as long as they do not enslave us. Instead of destroying lives, wealth can serve the kingdom of God. Every good and perfect gift comes from God and has a good and perfect use. As long as we can find it and honor it, we honor Him. And we are one step closer to happiness, rather than one foot deeper into the golden mirage of a fool's paradise.

14

Money Without Meaning

Ecclesiastes 6:1–6

W hat happens after "happily ever after"? Where do you go after your dream comes true? Three lottery winners had the chance to find out.

Carl D. Atwood of Elwood, Indiana, appeared on an Indianapolis TV show called *The Hoosier Millionaire*. When he received the good news of his winnings, he was ecstatic. "I'm very thankful," the seventy-three-year-old told viewers. "I must admit that I never expected to be leaving the show with this amount of money. Now I can purchase a very nice car."

Hours later Atwood took a walk to the same grocery store where he had bought the lottery ticket. He was struck by a truck and killed.[1]

A winning lottery ticket brought Rosa Grayson of Washington four hundred dollars a week for life. But she hid in her apartment and suffered nervous disorders. "People are so mean," she said. "I hope you win the lottery and see what happens to you."[2]

Then there was Jack Whittaker, winner of the richest undivided lottery jackpot in US history at the time: $314.9 million. The West Virginia construction contractor, already owner of a multimillion-dollar business, took the lump-sum, after-tax payout of $113 million in December 2002.

Whittaker's fondest wish was to help the people of his home state. He, his wife, and his daughter held a press conference on national television, announcing he would give a tithe of his winnings to his church and start a foundation to help the poor of West Virginia.

That's when reality came crashing in. Floods of letters and visitors to the door of his office and home and thousands of pleas for help, enough to fill file cabinets lining three walls in the conference room of Whittaker's new office.

Security guards watched his house and office around the clock, and visitors from all over the country brought their hard-luck stories.

There were some positive results of his win. Jack expanded his business, spent about $14 million on charity work, and established the Jack Whittaker Foundation to help West Virginians find jobs, buy food, and get educations. He also donated more than $7 million to three of his denomination's pastors.

The one goal he hoped the lottery would allow him to reach has not happened: spending more time with his family. Whittaker, who worked fourteen-hour days before winning the lottery, became busier than ever: "I was hoping I could start taking naps in the afternoon. But that hasn't happened yet," he said. "One study claimed that instant millionaires have about the same level of happiness as accident victims."[3]

Story after story can be cited of people whose newfound fame and fortune have made them more miserable than when they were just average citizens. Some people manage to keep heart and home together, but their stories are few and far between. Yet people still line up at convenience stores and gas stations across the nation to put down their money for a chance at unhappiness.

If we were to hold a convention of lottery winners, I have a hunch they would agree with Solomon's five truths from the last chapter:

1. The more we have, the more we want (Ecclesiastes 5:10).
2. The more we have, the more we spend (5:11).
3. The more we have, the more we worry (5:12).
4. The more we have, the more we lose (5:13–14).
5. The more we have, the more we leave behind (5:14–17).

I would hope those lottery winners would agree that it is God who gives us our ability to earn money (5:18) and to enjoy money (5:19–20). We think we are talking about something very material, but actually it is all about God. Without reference to Him, money cannot be enjoyed.

Ecclesiastes 6 shows the results of violating that principle. Without Him there can be no meaning, joy, or answers. Wealth in itself is not evil; wealth apart from God is another thing entirely.

Solomon's Insights

There is an evil which I have seen under the sun, and it is common among men: A man to whom God has given riches and wealth and honor, so that he lacks nothing for himself of all he desires; yet God does not give him power to eat of it, but a foreigner consumes it. This is vanity, and it is an evil affliction.

—ECCLESIASTES 6:1–2

Ecclesiastes, we are again reminded, is a kind of veiled memoir. Solomon's conclusions about the world are colored by his own fortunes and misfortunes. It is not surprising that wealth becomes an important subject in this book.

Running the numbers on Solomon's net worth is a chore of some complexity, but we know he was the wealthiest man alive. And we know how he acquired his fortune. When he was twenty, the Lord appeared to him as he worshiped and invited him to ask anything he desired. Solomon asked for wisdom, and God was pleased.

> Then God said to Solomon: "Because this was in your heart, and you have not asked riches or wealth or honor or the life of your enemies, nor have you asked long life—but have asked wisdom and knowledge for yourself, that you may judge My people over whom I have made you king—wisdom and knowledge are granted to you; and I will give you riches and wealth and honor, such as none of the kings have had who were before you, nor shall any after you have the like." (2 Chronicles 1:11–12)

It is characteristic of God to give us more than we ask. He knows we possess neither the wisdom nor the boldness to ask what we should of Him. Our little minds cannot fathom all that He longs to bestow upon us, so He always gives us more than we request. He blesses us "exceedingly abundantly above all that we ask or think, according to the power that works in us" (Ephesians 3:20). Our cups overflow, and goodness and mercy follow us all the days of our lives.

Solomon asked God for wisdom and got it—but so much more came along with the blessing: wealth, success, power, fame. With God in His rightful place at the center, the young king and his empire flourished as never before. He built the temple in Jerusalem, a place for God to dwell in the midst of His people. He developed trade and commerce initiatives that had an economic trickle-down effect throughout the land as money flowed into and out of Israel.

Solomon was a kind of King Midas for Israel; everything he touched turned to gold.

But even blessings from God come wrapped in the trials and temptations by which He develops our characters. Like the rest of us, Solomon had to conquer his own appetites to attain the godliness his Lord wanted for him. But he began to fail these tests.

He established relationships with neighboring pagan countries. As part of that diplomatic process, he took wives from these countries— something he had been specifically warned by God not to do (1 Kings 11:1–8). These foreign women brought their idolatrous worship into Solomon's life. Tragically, the king's spiritual center, God Himself, gradually was moved more and more to the sideline of his life. "For it was so, when Solomon was old, that his wives turned his heart after other gods; and his heart was not loyal to the LORD his God" (1 Kings 11:4).

Solomon began to compromise his commitment. He went so far as to build centers of worship for his wives' idols on a hill overlooking Jerusalem.

As Solomon later looked back over his life, he wrote about his own frustration of trying to find meaning in life through money and godless marriages. It reminds me of a poignant sentence by Jerry White in his little book *The Power of Commitment*: "Christians have never worn the clothes of affluence well."[4]

The same Solomon who wrote, "As for every man to whom God has given riches and wealth, and given him power to eat of it, to receive his heritage and rejoice in his labor—this is the gift of God" (Ecclesiastes 5:19), later rejected God's banquet table of provision and decided instead to go out for fast food.

As Solomon began to lean on his financial wealth to the exclusion of his spiritual wealth, his life and his national empire quaked. He permitted and abetted idolatry, introducing a deadly virus into the kingdom of which God had made him shepherd. It would take four centuries for that virus to run its course.

David began as a shepherd and had to learn to be a king; Solomon began as a king and had to learn to be a shepherd. Allowing other gods was tantamount to letting in wolves among his sheep.

Author Warren Wiersbe summarizes the lesson we should learn from this failure:

> To enjoy the gifts without the Giver is idolatry, and this can never satisfy the human heart. Enjoyment without God is merely entertainment, and it doesn't satisfy. But enjoyment with God is enrichment and it brings true joy and satisfaction.[5]

Solomon's Illustrations

> If a man begets a hundred children and lives many years,
> so that the days of his years are many, but his soul is not
> satisfied with goodness, or indeed he has no burial, I say that
> a stillborn child is better than he—for it comes in vanity and
> departs in darkness, and its name is covered with darkness.
> Though it has not seen the sun or known anything, this has
> more rest than that man, even if he lives a thousand years
> twice—but has not seen goodness. Do not all go to one
> place?
>
> —ECCLESIASTES 6:3–6

Solomon uses two illustrations to drive home his point about the vanity of money and pleasure apart from God.

First, he offers us the eye-opening comparison of a stillborn child and a two-thousand-year-old man who fathers one hundred children. One enjoys the full rich feast of life and comes back for about twenty-five second helpings; the other doesn't quite make it to the table.

Solomon exaggerates to make his point. The longest life span recorded in Scripture is Methuselah's, and he lived to be "only" 969 years old (Genesis 5:27). Imagine the man who lives more than twice that long, to be two thousand years old, and has a hundred children in the process? I know of no one who has fathered one hundred children, though Solomon's own son Rehoboam came close. According to 2 Chronicles 11:21, Rehoboam had eighteen wives and sixty concubines, and he fathered twenty-eight sons and sixty daughters!

In the Old Testament an Israelite family was considered blessed by God if the patriarch lived long and had lots of children (Psalm 92:14; 127:3–5). Solomon's point here is obvious: you could live twice as long as anyone else and have more children than anyone else—but if God is not involved, it's all worthless.

Notice that Solomon afforded his fictional geriatric no burial. For an Israelite to have no burial was a sign of disrespect and dishonor. Jeremiah 22 tells about a king named Jehoiakim who was not given a burial, which illustrated how disrespected he was by the people. Solomon's fictional character lived a long time and had lots of children. But in the end, his family did not want anything to do with him; and when he died, they did not even give him a funeral.

King Solomon now travels to the other end of the spectrum, using a stillborn baby as his illustration. According to Solomon, such a child never sees the light of day, never experiences the disappointment the rich man has known. The stillborn baby knows only the bright shadow of time while the other greets twenty centuries.

We all want long lives. But imagine for a moment twenty centuries of loneliness, twenty centuries of never finding what really counts in life. We want heaven on earth, but that would come close to the equivalent of hell. It is like the story of a man who is granted the gift of immortality only to be apprehended for some crime and locked up for life in prison. What value would eternal life be in a tiny cell?

As I wrestled with this text, I told Donna that this might be the hardest passage in the book of Ecclesiastes. But with Scripture the strongest boxes bear the richest treasures. This one yields a profound point: life without God and without meaning is worse than never having been born at all.

On the other hand, life *with* God is deeply satisfying, whether one has little or much. It is not the years in life but the life in the years. Only God can give us the wisdom to know what to do with what we have. As Jesus says:

> Don't store up treasures here on earth, where moths eat them and rust destroys them, and where thieves break in and steal. . . . Wherever your treasure is, there the desires of your heart will also be. . . . No one can serve two masters. For you will hate one and love the other; you will be devoted to one and despise the other. You cannot serve God and be enslaved to money. (Matthew 6:19, 21, 24 NLT)

I have talked with more than a few individuals who have a lot more money than I will ever see in this life. Many of them discuss wealth as a great burden. Jesus once talked about those who hear the Word of God but become distracted by wealth, as Solomon did. "Now he who received seed among the thorns," said Jesus, "is he who hears the word, and the cares of this world and the deceitfulness of riches choke the word, and he becomes unfruitful" (Matthew 13:22).

My friend Adrian Rogers told of a man who loved gold. When he inherited a fortune, he decided to redecorate his bedroom to reflect his first love. He hung gold parchment wallpaper, highlighted by yellow curtains, a golden rug, and a yellow bedspread. He even bought some yellow pajamas. But then he got sick and came down with yellow jaundice. He died because when the doctor came to treat him, no one could find him!

A lighthearted illustration, but the sad truth is that many great people have disappeared into their wealth. They have built railroads and restaurant chains, mills and malls, empires of every variety. But instead of ruling over those empires, they woke up one day to find themselves in shackles. J. C. Penney, having built a flourishing business, became filled with despair, checked himself into a hospital, and waited to die. No doctor could do a thing for him.

One evening, the certainty of impending death flooded across Penney's troubled soul. He was writing farewell notes to his wife and his loved ones when he heard the singing of nurses in a chapel down the hall. "No matter what may be the test," they sang, "God will take care of you."

To Penney these were the voices of white-clad angels. Something was suddenly born within his soul: an absolute assurance that the old faith was true—that he was completely in the loving hands of Jesus, and need fear no more.

J. C. Penney climbed out of his bed immediately—fully cured physically, emotionally, and spiritually. He was a brand-new creation. He left the hospital immediately, rebuilt his sagging business empire to unprecedented heights, and served God magnificently all his days. We need not disappear into the golden quicksand of our wealth, as Solomon did and as countless other lost souls have done.[6]

That quicksand is a valley of lost souls. It is among the most treacherous tests we face on the trail to finding what counts in life. But we can get through it as long as we cling to the knowledge that whatever the test, God will take care of us. Then when we get beyond that golden trap, we will see the true cities of gold on the horizon—the heaven on earth for which we have longed. We will see the eternal wealth of a life ruled over by the God who gives us the ability to earn, to enjoy, and to finally, quite happily, lay it all at His feet for His use.

That is a life of richness beyond imagining.

15

Employment Without Enjoyment

Ecclesiastes 6:7–9

Stan Collymore's dream came true. Not only did he want to make it as a world-class soccer player, but he signed the most lucrative contract in British soccer history. His fans called him "Stan the Man," and he was powering forward to peak career performance.

Then something unexpected happened. England was rocked with reports of strange, public sexual antics on the part of "Stan the Man," who abruptly checked into a clinic to be treated for depression. He told reporters:

> I remember one day sitting in the bath feeling empty inside. It was as if my energy levels had gone from 100 percent to flat battery overnight. I lost all interest in my appearance, and my self-esteem was low. There was this terrible void and emptiness inside. I couldn't even cry.[1]

"Stan the Man" had a clear field before him, but he instead encountered a pit of quicksand, not far from the deathtrap of wealth without God. He discovered the hazard of work as the meaning of life.

Work is not, in fact, our greatest adventure, and most of us are okay with that proposition—particularly when we are burned out on the job or lazy or simply not up to giving our very best to the task. It seems like a good time to say, "Solomon tells us that work is vanity, and that's good enough for me. My boss is not God, so why give Him my all?"

Not so fast, my friend. Solomon is not critical of work in itself. The world would not be much of a place to live in if everyone started calling in sick a couple of times a week because they just did not care. Would you like to use the services of a surgeon who felt that way? Would you trust your financial investments to a stockbroker whose mind is on his next ski trip?

I find genuine joy in my job, and I hope you do, too—whether you are a governor or a garbage collector. We stand with Solomon to assert that work is one more gracious gift from God. Work makes life compelling. It teaches us about ourselves. It gives us the pleasure of fruitfulness. But if you approach your job as the reason for being here, you will come to one more dead end.

Jobs are earthly, and joy is heavenly. A job is not what really matters in life, but it offers a number of clues to what does. It is not the whole picture but one more jigsaw-puzzle piece that fits into the vast panorama we are developing.

According to Solomon, here are three reasons your job cannot supply ultimate joy in this life.

Your Job Can't Satisfy Your Soul

All the labor of man is for his mouth,
And yet the soul is not satisfied.

—Ecclesiastes 6:7

Solomon tells us that work is about food for the stomach rather than the soul. Who could say it any better? Your work is based in the tangible world—the world of material things—and it pays in that same coin. You receive money, which translates to food, shelter, clothing, and other material needs. In itself, your work does not pay in the currency of heart fulfillment, nor is there any exchange rate between the two worlds.

I have many friends who work hard, grueling weeks. They put in sixty hours, barreling right on through evenings and weekends. Occasionally I talk to a friend about church, and he tells me, "I'm really in over my ears with the job right now. This is a crucial time in my career, and I can't really stop for worship or Bible study."

Five years later I talk to him again and discover it is still a crucial time in his career. He is five years older, five years wearier, not noticeably happier, but he has given his all to that company. And is the company grateful? Actually, I often find that my friend is not even working for the same company; that one chewed him up and spit him out a few months back, and now it is a crucial time with this new one.

On and on goes the cycle until my friend might look and sound like Solomon: tired, cynical, and possibly deeply angry about a life that somewhere took the wrong turn.

We can and should work hard, and all of us do at times. But do not miss the caution flag Solomon is waving here. Trade those minutes and hours of your life carefully, for they repay you in the coin of the realm, which does not satisfy the hunger of the soul.

God is the ultimate worker. "We are His workmanship, created in Christ Jesus for good works, which God prepared beforehand that we should walk in them" (Ephesians 2:10). That means we are wired to work in the manner He previously arranged.

Our grandson, David Todd, was at our house several years ago. My wife had purchased a computer toy for David to play with when he came to visit us. It worked through our television, and it was a pretty cool little game. As I was about to leave for my office, Donna stopped me. "I can't get this thing to work," she said. "Can you help me with it?"

After a few moments' inspection, I said, "Honey, I don't think this thing has any batteries in it. It's not heavy enough." I got the Phillips screwdriver, removed the top, and sure enough, it needed four batteries. It was in perfect working order, and it looked like it would be a lot of fun, but it would not work without the batteries.

As I came to my office to finish my study on this passage in Ecclesiastes, I could not help thinking that this is the way life is for us. We are complicated, impressive, and made for a specific purpose. But we do not work because there is no power source deep inside. We are empty shells without the battery of the Holy Spirit's power.

Men in particular must take heed. We are made to find our meaning in work, but we had better have the right kind of voltage powering us.

Your Mind Can't Replace Your Heart

> For what more has the wise man than the fool?
> What does the poor man have,
> Who knows how to walk before the living?
> —ECCLESIASTES 6:8

A wise man with the greatest education in the world has no ultimate advantage over a fool when God is absent from his life. On the day when we all stand before God, He is not going to ask to see anyone's diploma. He is not going to inquire about the number and source of academic degrees. He is not going to ask about IQ, SAT or GRE scores, or bank balances. All He is going to ask about is our hearts.

The problem is that our work begins by requiring our strength. We do it during the best hours of our day, and we find that we need to be rested and at our physical best. Then we find that our work requires our minds if we are going to do better at it. We are soon mulling over challenges and problems even when we are away from work. We begin to come up with some solutions, and we become emotionally involved in the work before us. It has taken a piece of the heart. And finally, when we are completely sold out to the world of nine to five, we discover that our work has required our very souls.

But Jesus says the number one commandment includes loving God with all your heart, soul, mind, and strength (Luke 10:27). Work, in short, becomes another idol that displaces (and displeases) God.

Forty miles south of downtown London is a tiny village named Piltdown. One day in 1908, a lawyer named Charles Dawson, a member of the prestigious British Geological Society, claimed to have discovered an ancient skull. More bones were soon discovered, and suddenly the world had "proof" of Darwin's theory of evolution: Piltdown Man. The scientific literature that came out about Piltdown Man was enormous, with more than five hundred doctoral dissertations written about the discovery. School children were shown pictures of what Piltdown Man looked like and where he fit into the evolutionary chain.

Sir Arthur Keith, one of the world's greatest anatomists, wrote more about Piltdown Man than anyone else. His works include the widely acclaimed book *The Antiquity of Man*, based on the Piltdown discoveries. He had based a lifetime of work on his faith, and he was fascinated by the Piltdown development.

Sir Keith was a frail eighty-six years old when Kenneth Oakley and Joseph Weiner paid a sad visit to his home. They were breaking the news that after a half-century of study, Piltdown Man was a hoax, nothing more than an old human skull, the jawbone of an orangutan, and a dog's tooth.

For forty years, the brilliant scientist had trusted in a fraud.

Keith was a rationalist and a profound opponent of the Christian faith. Yet in his *Autobiography* he tells of attending evangelistic meetings in Edinburgh and Aberdeen, seeing students make a public profession of faith in Jesus Christ, and often feeling "on the verge of conversion." He rejected the gospel because he felt that the Genesis account of Creation was just a myth and that the Bible was merely a human book. It causes profound sadness to know that this great man rejected Jesus Christ, whose resurrection validated everything he said and did, only to put his faith in what proved to be a phony fossil.[2]

The Bible warns about those who think they are wise but are really fools (Romans 1:22). While a good education is desirable, it's not as important as a heart that knows God through Jesus Christ our Lord. The Bible says, "The fear of the LORD is the beginning of knowledge" (Proverbs 1:7). Your mind cannot replace your heart.

Your Dreams Can't Replace Reality

Better is the sight of the eyes than the wandering of desire.
This also is vanity and grasping for the wind.
—ECCLESIASTES 6:9

Solomon is comparing the vanity of living in a fantasy world with the wisdom of living in the real world. Proverbs 28:19 says, "He who works his land will have abundant food, but the one who chases fantasies will have his fill of poverty" (NIV). There is nothing wrong with dreaming and vision-casting. But if we live in a fantasy world, we live in a world that will likely never come to pass. Too many people say, "We'll take the children there when . . ." or "We'll start saving for retirement when . . ." and the "when" is always tied to something big that is "just around the corner." People who are continually talking about the future never seem to get around to enjoying the present.

If your career is the determining factor in your life—you are constantly waiting for the next raise, the next promotion, the next assignment, the next transfer—then you are living with the "wandering of desire." Keep your dreams and goals, but stop and smell the roses. Today is the day the Lord has made, and you ought to stop and rejoice in it (Psalm 118:24).

Solomon is saying something over and over again in Ecclesiastes: between now and the time you go to heaven, enjoy what God has given you. Do not be so caught up in earning money and building a career that you do not have time to enjoy your life. What happens if you take a surprise day off for your family? You will be one more day behind on the job, but think of the memories you will make with your wife, kids, or grandkids. Twenty years from now, which will matter more? One touches godly relationships with heavenly companions; the other is simply another acre plowed, another clock punched, another day, another dollar.

Perhaps Solomon gained some insight on these issues by thinking about his father, David, the king of Israel before Solomon. David's Psalm 16 so captures the spirit of what Solomon is advising that I am going to reproduce it in its entirety here:

> Keep me safe, O God,
>> for I have come to you for refuge.
>
> I said to the LORD, "You are my Master!
>> Every good thing I have comes from you."

The godly people in the land
    are my true heroes!
    I take pleasure in them!
Troubles multiply for those who chase after other gods.
    I will not take part in their sacrifices of blood
    or even speak the names of their gods.

LORD, you alone are my inheritance, my cup of blessing.
    You guard all that is mine.
The land you have given me is a pleasant land.
    What a wonderful inheritance!

I will bless the LORD who guides me;
    even at night my heart instructs me.
I know the LORD is always with me.
    I will not be shaken, for he is right beside me.

No wonder my heart is glad, and I rejoice.
    My body rests in safety.
For you will not leave my soul among the dead
    or allow your holy one to rot in the grave.
You will show me the way of life,
    granting me the joy of your presence
    and the pleasures of living with you forever.

People talk about "mission statements" these days. I cannot think of a better one than Psalm 16. Try adopting it as your personal creed for your lifework.

George Young was a carpenter. He and his wife were dedicated to following the Lord wherever He led. "He does the leading," they often said, "and we do the following." God led the Youngs to the rural

Midwest, and they traveled from church to church in revival efforts. Their finances were always tight, but "through the many years we never went hungry!" as Mrs. Young said years later. "Oh, sometimes we didn't have too much of this world's goods, but . . . we always had so much of Jesus."

Finally they saved enough to buy a small piece of land on which George built a cottage. Though humble, it was the fulfillment of a life's dream, and when they moved in they dedicated the house to God and sang the Doxology. But some time later, when the Youngs were away on a ministry trip, a thug who had been offended by George's preaching set the house afire. Returning home, the Youngs found a heap of ashes. All their worldly goods and cherished possessions were gone.

As George gazed at the ruins, he recounted the precious possessions fire could never destroy—his family, his relationship with Christ, his ministry, his eternal home. There and then, the words of a hymn began forming in his mind. Within a few days, he had written all three stanzas of the great hymn "God Leads His Dear Children Along." The chorus says:

> Some thro' the waters, some thro' the flood,
> Some thro' the fire, but all thro' the blood.
> Some thro' great sorrow, but God gives a song
> In the night season and all the day long.[3]

Years later music publisher Dr. Harold Lillenas decided to track down George's widow. Driving to the small Kansas town where she resided, he stopped for directions and was alarmed to hear that Mrs. Young was living in the run-down county poorhouse. Lillenas was deeply troubled that the widow of the author of such a hymn about God's guidance should spend her final days in the poorhouse.

Mrs. Young only smiled and said,

One day God took my sweet husband home. Oh, how I missed him, for we had always served the Lord together. In my heart I wondered, where will God lead me now? Dr. Lillenas, God led me here! I'm so glad He did, for you know, about every month someone comes into this place to spend the rest of their days, and Dr. Lillenas, so many of them don't know my Jesus. I'm having the time of my life introducing them to Jesus! Dr. Lillenas, isn't it wonderful how God leads?[4]

Some people are so caught up with their jobs, careers, and acquisitions that their song is, "God, leave me alone!" But others keep Christ in the center of their lives, and they sing, "God leads me along."

Which song are you singing?

16

Solomon Answers Your Questions

Ecclesiastes 6:10–12

Time out! You and I have handled some big ideas in the last couple of chapters, haven't we? Heavyweight contenders for the battle of the soul—a great load of issues in a small number of pages. We have plunged deep into our study, and it's time to come up for air.

We talked about the place of money in your life. I do not know anyone who would not consider that a central matter to be confronted on a daily basis.

Then we discussed the place of your work. Whoever you are, CEO or CPA, student or homemaker, your work is at the very core of your life experience.

And above all, we have taken on one towering monolith of an issue: the matter of God's role in your life. That is the biggest one of all, the great sea into which all the little rivers of your life expressions flow.

This book is a thirty-one-day study, but at times it is like touring

Europe in a week—"If it's Tuesday, this must be Belgium." We have a wonderful and thought-provoking book by Solomon, but I want to be certain we are making the most of it. Are you still there? Have you absorbed all that Solomon is saying? How is all this coming across to you? What changes are being forged in the way you see the purpose of your life?

Readers will come to these pages from many different points on the spiritual compass. Some of you have grown wise in the seasons of life. You nod in recognition of these truths and could probably add a few insights of your own to every chapter in the book.

Others come from a direction of ongoing struggle. You, too, recognize the frustration and the disappointment of dead-end pathways. But at this juncture of life, you are stuck. You have come to one of the many walls that define the geography of living.

Or perhaps you are just one of those many who are found somewhere in-between. For you it is fairly smooth sailing through the voyage of life right now. You have a few instruments on the boat that need adjustments. But for the most part, your ship is moving full speed ahead, on course for a destination you feel good about.

Where do you fit? What particular life issues do you bring to this book? I believe that there are many key moments in life: whenever the sermon begins, whenever you read the first page of a book, whenever you find yourself in a thoughtful conversation about life with a trusted friend. I do not believe these moments are random and coincidental, but that in some important way they are divine appointments, potential crossroad moments.

God is speaking to us all the time, and He will use whatever megaphone catches our attention. His wisest children have figured that out, and they are always discerning what He is trying to tell them in those instances of inspiration.

That is why I firmly believe that your reading of this book, like many of your other experiences, represents a "message moment" for you. What you come away with will depend upon what you are willing to take seriously about this moment.

For example, what does God want you to see about this journey to happiness? What key life decisions can you make because of the insights the Holy Spirit is even now implanting in your heart? Are you countering the enemy's distractions, knowing he would rather you look the other way than think seriously? Do you feel him trying to "fiddle with the remote control" of your attention span, put other thoughts in your mind, convince you this is, after all, just another book, no different than a good novel?

Okay, those are a lot of questions. I'll stop right there. But I hope you will stop right here, too, and reflect a bit on what is happening in your life between God, His Word, this book, and your future. I would predict that if you are facing some of the serious issues about your life and your values, you will find yourself encountering some personal turmoil. You could be saying, "My approach to God needs to change" or, "I've been making wealth the center of my life."

The still, small voice will be guiding you toward the life that God has always wanted for you: the embracing of what really matters in your life. But another part of you will argue, will come up with objections, will question whether this is just another wild-goose chase, will roll its eyes and say, "What does Solomon know about anything?"

Solomon has anticipated the kind of arguments we might have. And as we come to the middle of our book, he offers us four reasons that competing arguments about the purpose of life will fail. These are not four separate arguments, but four ways to approach one bedrock truth. If you hold up a spectrum to the sunlight, you'll see that all the colors come together to make what we call light. Solomon is going to offer us four colors that form one core argument: your life without God is meaningless.

This is your time to take stock of your own life as Solomon nails down the great theme of his book, and what should be the theme of life on earth for you and me.

God Has Ordained Life as He Desires It to Be

Whatever one is, he has been named already,
For it is known that he is man.
—ECCLESIASTES 6:10

The New English Translation is right on target: "Whatever has happened was foreordained, and what happens to a person was also foreknown" (Ecclesiastes 6:10).

In the last chapter we talked about the soccer player "Stan the Man." He went wrong when he began to think he was the Man; what he discovered was that he was only "Stan, *a* man"—just another man created by God to do greater things than simply play good soccer. "For it is known that *he is man*," said Solomon (emphasis added). And God planned how life will be for a man—and for a woman.

Success and riches won't satisfy us because God did not design us to be satisfied that way. He made horses for galloping gracefully, He made eagles for soaring spectacularly, and He made us purely for himself, as His special companions. When we try to live some other way, we are like horses trying to fly or eagles trying to gallop.

He made us creatures who enjoy work because He enjoys it. He made us as creatures who enjoy gathering wealth because He owns the cattle on a thousand hills. But He did not make us to *exist* for these things—only to recognize Him more clearly through them.

Solomon says this is simply the way God planned it, from the foundation of eternity. It's useless to try living outside of the parameters He created for us.

Arguing with God Is an Exercise in Futility

> And he cannot contend with Him who is mightier
> than he.
>
> —ECCLESIASTES 6:10

So you have come to the middle of this book, and you find yourself facing a far greater commitment to God than you are prepared to offer. You begin to argue with Solomon, but he cuts you off in midsentence. "I don't make the rules," he says. "I just work here."

You scratch your head. "I thought you were king."

"Yeah, well, not *the* King," says Solomon. "*A* king—same deal as Stan the Man." Solomon points upstairs. "Your argument is with *God*."

And that quiets you down because you realize the obvious: arguing with God is an exercise in futility.

> But indeed, O man, who are you to reply against God? Will the
> thing formed say to him who formed it, "Why have you made
> me like this?" Does not the potter have power over the clay, from
> the same lump to make one vessel for honor and another for dis-
> honor? (Romans 9:20–21)

Job had the same conversation with God one day. Even when facing the devastation of his entire life, as Job did, he was in no position to argue with God. There are no circumstances in which the clay gets the last word over the sculptor. Many characters in the Bible argued with God, from Abraham to Jonah. God was always willing to talk it over, but He made the decisions. He is the Lord, and His vision and justice and providence are perfect. The right approach is to discover the plan of God and live it out; it is arrogance of a cosmic intensity to try to change the plan.

God Is Willing to Bring Meaning to Life

Since there are many things that increase vanity,
How is man the better?

For who knows what is good for man in life, all the days of
his vain life which he passes like a shadow?

—ECCLESIASTES 6:11–12

Solomon asks a simple question. Any child could answer it. He says, "There are so many ways to completely foul up my life. Who has the best idea about what will actually work?"

Any child could answer it, but only the wisest will follow it. The fact is that deep down, we each think we have better ideas. We wait for the really big decisions in life to ask God's opinion and then only after we have weighed all the options ourselves.

Parents know what it is like to watch a child struggle to make life a success. We, the veteran life-livers, know a lot of the answers. When they are tested, we can't help but try to pass them the answers. "Honey, popularity is not the highest priority in junior high school," we say. Or "Son, don't make your college decision based on where your girlfriend goes. Down the road you may wish you had looked at the bigger issues."

To which our kids may well roll their eyes and say, "Sure, Pop," or "Whatever you say, Mom." And we wish they would trust us just a little more, the way they did when they were younger. Hey, we are not on a power trip, trying to run anyone's life. We love our children. We want them to be happy, and when they stumble, we often hurt more than they do.

That is just the way God looks at us. We think we are pretty sharp and that we already have the answers. And God patiently keeps speaking to us through His Word, through His Spirit, through our believing friends, wishing we would trust Him just a little bit more than we do.

The secret of life is not some exotic puzzle to work out. It is right there in front of our noses, just as the promised land was for the Israelites—only a couple of weeks' walk in their case. Heaven on earth is near, but the problem is not the lack of a treasure map. It is our disobedience.

God Alone Is in Charge of the Future

Who can tell a man what will happen after him under the sun?
—Ecclesiastes 6:12

Who knows the future?

Americans went through a time of fascination with horoscopes—the ones printed in the daily newspaper on the comic page. People generally took them no more seriously than the comic strips themselves, but these columns paved the way for astrology and other New Age philosophies for divining the future.

Now it seems the pendulum has swung back the other way toward a more cynical view of the future—a fatalism that says, "Whatever will be, will be." For people who embrace the postmodern view that life has no controlling theme or story, the future is a game of chance. The idea that today is all that matters is a repackaging of the existentialism of the 1950s.

The Bible has a great deal to say about the future. First and foremost, it says that God is in control of the future and has already determined what it will be. The best way to be ready for the future is to stick close to God. He's the One in charge of it. Solomon says that trying to figure out the future for oneself is an exercise in vanity: "Nor can anyone tell [a man] what the future will hold for him on earth" (Ecclesiastes 6:12 NET). For that reason, arguing with Him will change nothing.

Solomon's points in these verses are logical and clear:

- God created all of us to find meaning a certain way.
- Ultimate meaning is not found in money or in vocation.
- Ultimate meaning is found only in God.
- To argue with God about this arrangement is an exercise in futility.

I have already described the impact of the San Diego County fires on my neighborhood, including some who are members of our church. My friend Lee and his family were in our church when I first came. They have given themselves in service to the Lord for years. They are known and loved throughout our congregation, and they lived near the church.

While our church and college campuses survived, Lee's home was totally consumed. I talked to Lee shortly after the fire, and he told me he only had time to dash into his home and grab three books related to his job, his Bible, and a daily devotional book he was reading. Everything else was lost. Lee was alone when the house went up in flames because his wife was in Virginia visiting their daughter, a cancer patient. When he told me about placing the phone call to his wife, it took my breath away.

This couple, fighting to save their daughter from cancer, lost their house and all their worldly goods to a wildfire. He said, "Pastor, you know, my wife and I have talked about what's happened to us in these last days. God has been wonderful to us. We've experienced very few difficult times in life. For some reason that we don't understand, He has trusted us with some trouble right now. We know He's going to be with us in the midst of it and help us through it. So we're just honoring Him through this time and trusting Him for everything that we need."

As I listened to the voice of this humble, godly man, I knew his family was going to come through the furnace of life. They were like Daniel's three friends who were in conversation with an angel as the flames should have broiled them. Lee and his wife, because they stick closely to God, were ready when the future came.

We do not know what the future holds, but we do know who holds the future—and that is enough. It ends every argument or objection we can pose. And coming to the end of all the questions, we can only bow before the One with all the answers.

Praise God, for knowing Him is better than knowing the answers.

17

The Joy of Misery

Ecclesiastes 7:1–4

While we are here at the middle of the book, halfway through our journey to happiness, it seems like a good time for a midterm exam.

Don't worry. No grades will be sent out, and it's a short test. No trick questions. No essays or multiple choices. No pressure. Just six simple true/false statements for you to consider:

True or False—I like laughter better than crying.

True or False—I like weddings better than funerals.

True or False—I like thinking of my birthday better than my dying day.

True or False—I like compliments better than criticisms.

True or False—I like shortcuts better than the long way around.

True or False—I like the "good old days" better than the way things are now.

If you marked true on any or all of those statements, Solomon would flunk you. If he were giving the test, all these questions would be answered with *false*. That is, he prefers crying, funerals, death reflections, criticism, the harder way, and the bad old days.

You may be asking yourself, what kind of man is this Solomon? Is he a glutton for punishment? But as we read Ecclesiastes 7:1–10, we begin to catch on. Solomon teaches us the lessons most teachers would avoid. This is the TV infomercial you are not likely to come across late at night: "The Joy of Misery."

The key word in Ecclesiastes 7:1–10 is *better*. It was also the key word in your test. The Lord shows us that some of the medicine that tastes the worst has the best cure. In these verses, Solomon is going to goad us into thinking outside the box.

The first thing he tells us is that sorrow is better than laughter. No kidding—literally.

Funerals Are Better Than Festivals

A good name is better than precious ointment,

And the day of death than the day of one's birth.
—ECCLESIASTES 7:1

Okay, you had decided this is an odd chapter. But now you feel like throwing the book against the wall. *Death, better than birth? Come on.*

Just humor me for a moment (even if sorrow is better).

It is not that Solomon is buying into the philosophy of despair. If that were true, he would not tell us eight times in this book to enjoy life. I have underlined those passages in my Bible; it is clear that Solomon—and the Lord—are in favor of joyful and abundant living.

In his book of Proverbs, I counted at least thirty verses emphasizing the goodness of enjoying life. A few examples:

> A merry heart makes a cheerful countenance,
> But by sorrow of the heart the spirit is broken. (Proverbs 15:13)

> All the days of the afflicted are evil,
> But he who is of a merry heart has a continual feast. (Proverbs 15:15)

> A merry heart does good, like medicine,
> But a broken spirit dries the bones. (Proverbs 17:22)

Solomon liked to have a good laugh, just like you and I do. So what's all this about preferring funerals? Warren Wiersbe has said that laughter is medicine for a broken heart, but sorrow is a hearty meal for the soul.[1]

There are two phrases in verse 1, and the first explains the second: "A good name is better than precious ointment, and the day of death than the day of one's birth."

This was originally written in the Hebrew language, and Hebrew scholars tell us something interesting about this verse. The word "name" in Hebrew is *shem,* and the word "ointment" in Hebrew is *shemen.* So Solomon is saying a *shem* is better than a *shemen.* He gets a Hebrew reader's attention with a play on words.

There are two days in our lives when our name is prominent: the day we receive our name at birth, and the day our name appears in the obituary column. What happens between those two determines whether our name is a lovely ointment (a *shemen*) or a foul stench.

The late Bill Bright, founder and president of Campus Crusade for Christ, International, told about growing up in Oklahoma in the

1920s and '30s watching his father and grandfather conduct business affairs with other men. It was all done on a handshake (which is almost unheard of today) because of his grandfather's reputation in the area. He did not realize exactly how respected his grandfather's name and word really were until years later.

In 1948, Bill was driving from California to Oklahoma to marry his sweetheart, Vonette Zachary. As he passed through Okmulgee, Oklahoma, where his grandfather had lived for many years, he remembered that he had forgotten to purchase gifts for several members of the wedding party. Stopping at a jewelry store, he asked if he could make a purchase with an out-of-state check and was told no, that it was against store policy.

As he turned to leave, the owner asked him, "Do you know anyone in Okmulgee?" thinking someone might be able to vouch for his honesty.

"No, I don't," Bill replied. "My grandfather used to live here, but he died a few years ago."

"Who was your grandfather?" the store owner asked.

"Sam Bright."

"Are you Sam Bright's grandson?" the store owner asked, his face lighting up as he approached Bill. "Why, Sam Bright was the most honorable man I have ever known! If you're anything like your grandfather, I'll sell you anything in the store—and I'll gladly take your check."[2]

As a result of looking back to his grandfather's honorable life and standing on the name he had established in his community, Bill Bright was able to accomplish what he needed to do. That is an example of what Solomon means when he says, "A good name is better than precious ointment, and the day of death than the day of one's birth."

Notice the way we mark a person's life span. We write a person's name, and below it we put something like this: 1934–2003. We list the year of birth and the year of death. Between the two is what? *A dash.*

Solomon might agree that this life is a quick dash between birth and death—just a vapor. All we will ever do on earth, all the influence we will ever garner, all the reputation we will ever build is summarized in a simple line between one year and another. It is not much time to serve God but plenty of time for making a huge mess of things.

Solomon was suggesting that if you die with a good name, you can no longer do anything to tarnish it. But on the day of your birth, you have an entire life before you yet unwritten. In that respect, if you have a good reputation, the day of your death is better than the day of your birth. Looking back on a life well lived is better than looking forward to a life unlived. Ending a good life is better than beginning an unknown life.

Mourning Is a Better Teacher than Feasting

> Better to go to the house of mourning
> Than to go to the house of feasting,
> For that is the end of all men;
> And the living will take it to heart.
> Sorrow is better than laughter,
> For by a sad countenance the heart is made better.
> The heart of the wise is in the house of mourning,
> But the heart of fools is in the house of mirth.
> —ECCLESIASTES 7:2–4

Solomon does not want you to spend daily time thinking about your death. What he wants you to see is that wisdom is forged in the fires of mourning, trouble, and disappointment. Fools with frivolous, carefree attitudes do not learn from the experiences of life. When wise men and women face adversity, such as death, disease, and destruction, they learn fresh lessons from God, they take the lessons to heart, and they become better instead of bitter. It is a choice.

This has been one of the deepest secrets of the greatest saints. Listen to this passage from the founder of the China Inland Mission, Hudson Taylor:

> The great enemy is always ready with his oft-repeated suggestion, "All things are against me." But, oh, how false the word! The cold, and even the hunger, the watchings and sleeplessness of nights of danger, and the feelings at times of utter isolation and helplessness, were well and wisely chosen, and tenderly and lovingly meted out. What circumstances could have rendered the Word of God sweeter, and the presence of God so real, and the help of God so precious.[3]

Have you ever had a day where you missed every green traffic light, spilled your coffee on your best jacket, saw your baseball team lose in the ninth inning, and generally seemed to be living out an audition for poster child for Murphy's Law? You grumble, "Everything is against me! It's all set up to make my life miserable!" Taylor is saying it's precisely the opposite. God desires to lovingly use every inconvenience, every bad day, every trial, to make us stronger and wiser and closer to Him.

There is an old clipping from the devotional magazine *Our Daily Bread* that illustrates this in a practical way. During World War II, a man in Sussex, England, sent some money to the Scripture Gift Mission. He enclosed a letter saying that he longed to give more, but the harvest on his farm had been very disappointing because of a lack of water. He was also fearful because German bombs were being dropped in the area, and his family and farm were at risk. He asked the workers of Scripture Gift Mission to pray that no bombs would fall on his land.

Mr. Ashley Baker wrote back from the mission and said that while he did not feel led to pray that exact prayer, he had prayed that God's will for their lives would prevail. Shortly after, a huge German missile crashed down on the farm. None of the man's family or livestock was harmed, but the bombshell went so far into the ground that it liberated a submerged stream. The stream yielded enough water to irrigate the man's farm as well as neighboring farms. The next year, due to a bountiful harvest, the man was able to send a large offering to the mission.[4]

Sometimes even bombs are blessings. They fall from heaven, make a lot of noise, and liberate something wonderful within us—streams of living water that refresh us and draw us closer to Christ.

Of course, we never seek the bombs or the burdens. We like festivals—parties. The truth is that no one grows wiser who lives the party life. The year in your life when everything goes well is the year you will gain the least maturity. As someone says, if we learned from our mistakes, we ought to be PhDs by now. We should also be all the wiser in our faith.

I can speak by experience. The richest and most probing time in my life as an adult began when cancer became a part of my vocabulary. I never sought it, I never welcomed it, but I have never doubted the blessings that God has indeed showered upon me through it. There are things I simply never could have learned with an unmitigated, unbridled, uninterrupted success pattern in my life.

That is why God is not as concerned about our being momentarily happy as He is about our being mature. We wonder why He does not seem to answer the prayer by the side of the road when the tire is flat or why He is silent during this or that crisis. God seems cruel and unfeeling at those moments, but the truth is that even though He hurts for us, He knows that if He protected us from every inconvenience, we would never cease being infants. There must be rain, and there must even be a few tornados and wildfires. Such is the university of life.

We are beginning to see the light. The highest purpose of life is not happiness. But as we take the blows that life brings us on the way home from the festival, as we suffer the unpitying rain that falls on the just as well as the unjust, as we keep right on moving down the road toward heaven on earth, often not happy at all—miserable is more like it—we begin to see the light in the distance. We begin to realize that, when we reach that final destination, then we will be paid richly in the coin of happiness. We will realize that, until now, we never knew what happiness was—and never could have enjoyed it so richly now without the sorrow that was preparing our hearts all along the path.

18

The Pleasure of Rebuke

Ecclesiastes 7:5–6

Mark Twain said, "I can live for two months on a good compliment."[1] And it's probably true. But he could have gotten more out of those two months on a good criticism.

Do you agree?

I am just like you. I get a lot more pleasure from people telling me the things I want to hear. After a church service I appreciate people who tell me the sermon was absolutely perfect—the jokes funny, the quotes compelling, the Scripture selection powerful, and the stories inspiring. Music to my ears. Just once I'd like to preach such a good one that the deacons carry me out of the sanctuary on their shoulders, cheering!

But then there is that one fellow who says, "You may have slam-dunked your first outline point, Pastor, but you had to rush the next three. And I noticed how you slipped your final outline point into the closing prayer."

Ouch. Now I'm *still* thinking they will carry me out of the sanctuary—but *without* the cheering.

Nobody loves a critic. But let's get beyond the feel-good factor. Life is not always about feeling good. That second fellow has given me food for thought. It may not taste like ice cream, but it is probably good for me. And later on, after my bruised ego recovers, I'll find that advice not only humbling but helpful.

I am starting to realize that rebukes are really compliments turned inside out, designed to mold and mature us in wonderful ways. Conrad Hilton established one of the greatest hotel chains on earth. In his autobiography he tells of a time early in his career when he was practicing his public speaking, preparing to address an issue before the New Mexico state legislature. His mother walked in and listened politely, and when he finished he asked for her opinion.

"Very good for poetry. But you'll have to unlearn all this," she said bluntly, referring to his oratorical flourishes and dramatic gestures. "Connie," she continued, seeing his deflated expression, "all those trimmings are sinful. You are hiding yourself behind a lot of gestures. If you're afraid to be you, Son, you're throwing dust in God's face. He made you. If you have confidence in Him, you'll relax and be just what you are. You'd do better to pray about it than practice this."

It was a little disheartening to him at first, but by accepting her rebuke he became an influential man and a polished speaker who delighted audiences around the world.[2]

Yes, the critics can be cruel. Some advisors make the medicine taste as sour as possible, and it's true that any fool can give advice. We think of Lucy, Charlie Brown's crabby friend who has advice for everyone—often dispensed for five cents at a neighborhood psychiatric booth. But she also plays left field on the baseball team. In one of the late cartoonist Charles Schulz's strips, Lucy makes a visit to the pitcher's mound and rakes Charlie Brown over the coals, telling him his fastball is slow, his curveball is straight, and his change-up is a letdown. In conclusion, she yells, "Why don't you win one for a change?" and returns to her position. The batter hits the next pitch in the air, right to Lucy—who makes no attempt to catch it. When Charlie Brown asks her why she let it drop, she replies, "I work strictly in an advisory capacity."

But we are not here to talk about the Lucys of the world. You and I both know that caring people also work in an advisory capacity: spouses, associates, good friends. Most of us are sharp enough to sort out the malicious jabs from the wise guidance.

The Rebuke of the Wise

It is better to hear the rebuke of the wise
Than for a man to hear the song of fools.
For like the crackling of thorns under a pot,
So is the laughter of the fool.
This also is vanity.

—ECCLESIASTES 7:5–6

Gordon MacDonald, in his book *Ordering Your Private World*, tells how he was corrected by one of his seminary professors—a mild rebuke that changed his life. He had prepared a paper on a controversial moral issue and was to read it to a special gathering of students and faculty. In order to finish the paper, he cut two of his regular classes during the day prior to the meeting that night. After the meeting, the professor in charge of one of the classes he had cut approached him and said, "Gordon, the paper you read tonight was a good one, but it wasn't a great one. Would you like to know why?"

Suspecting that "yes" would be painful, he nevertheless said he would.

Poking his finger into Gordon's chest, the professor said, "The paper wasn't a great one because you sacrificed the routine to write it."

Here is what Gordon MacDonald said about the rebuke:

> In pain I learned one of the most important lessons I ever needed to learn. Because my time as a Christian leader is generally my own to use as I please, it would be very easy to avoid routine, unspectacular duties, and give myself only to the exciting things that come along. But most of life is lived in the routine, and [my professor] was right: The man or woman who learns to make peace with routine responsibilities and obligations will make the greatest contributions in the long run.[3]

The specific lesson was a good one, but what counts here is his first sentence: "In pain I learned one of the most important lessons I ever needed to learn." Do you think MacDonald would agree with Solomon that it is better to hear the rebuke of the wise than the song of fools? Based on his own testimony, I think he would.

Solomon likens the meaningless praise and laughter of fools to "the crackling of thorns under a pot." This was a culturally relevant comparison that we do not readily understand. Branches of a thorn bush thrown on a fire will flame up with rapid intensity, providing a short, hot burn. If you needed to heat up something quickly, instead of preparing a fire for slow cooking, you would throw thorn branches on the fire. Solomon uses this illustration to say that the praise of fools is quick, hot, showy—but gone quickly. It flames up and dies out, and you need something else to stoke the fire. The rebuke of a wise man, however, can change your life forever.

Receiving rebuke and correction is a major theme in the writings of Solomon, especially in Proverbs, no doubt because it goes against human nature. Left to our own devices, we are not very teachable. It often takes us the awkward struggle of the teenage years to learn how to handle criticism—and some of us never do, even then.

We would rather hear from the fan club. We like the schmoozing, stroking, and back-patting of those who have some motive to keep us propped. (At some point we need to ask what that motive is.) But take a look at Solomon's advice about the value of receiving correction and the folly of rejecting it:

> He who keeps instruction is in the way of life,
> But he who refuses correction goes astray. (Proverbs 10:17)

> Whoever loves instruction loves knowledge,
> But he who hates correction is stupid. (Proverbs 12:1)

> A fool despises his father's instruction,
> But he who receives correction is prudent. (Proverbs 15:5)

> Rebuke is more effective for a wise man
> Than a hundred blows on a fool. (Proverbs 17:10)

> Like an earring of gold and an ornament of fine gold
> Is a wise rebuker to an obedient ear. (Proverbs 25:12)

> Open rebuke is better
> Than love carefully concealed. (Proverbs 27:5)

> He who is often rebuked, and hardens his neck,
> Will suddenly be destroyed, and that without remedy. (Proverbs 29:1)

> The rod and rebuke give wisdom,
> But a child left to himself brings shame to his mother. (Proverbs 29:15)

Famous New York Yankee Mickey Mantle tells how as a teenager playing in the minor leagues, he began playing poorly. Growing discouraged, he gave in to homesickness and self-pity, and tearfully called his father to come and take him home. But when Charles Mantle arrived, he did not give the expected sympathy and reassurance. Instead, he looked at his son and said, "Okay, if that's all the guts you've got, you might as well come home with me right now and work in the mines."

It was a stinging slap in the face, but the young man got the message, stuck it out, and went on to make baseball history.[4]

Have you made it known to people who care about you that they are free to share a word of advice, correction, or even rebuke with you when necessary? You don't need to paint a big target on the front of your shirt, with "Hit me with your best shot" printed in the center. You also don't need to put on the false humility act when you know you've done a good job—people see right through it.

Instead, just be humble. Be open. And at the right time, tell your spouse, coworker, or friend that his or her feedback is valuable to you. Make it known that you are always interested in getting better at what you do, whether it is marriage, parenting, vocation, or hobby. The moment you open that particular door, a number of wonderful things will come through. For example:

- You'll receive invaluable advice that God gives us through others.
- You'll improve your relationship with the person whose advice you've invited.
- You'll combat pride and enhance humility.

Don't be enamored with the praise of people who don't really care about you. Be more interested in the rebuke of a wise person who really loves you. Listen carefully to that person's instruction.

Test Yourself for Pride

The late J. Oswald Sanders wrote biblical books packed with remarkable insight and common sense. In one of them he said, "Pride is a sin of whose presence its victim is least conscious. There are, however, three tests by means of which it can soon be discovered." He went on to suggest these three tests:

> THE TEST OF PROCEDURE: How do we react when another is selected for an assignment we expected, or the office we coveted? When another is promoted and we are overlooked? When another outshines us in gifts and accomplishments?
>
> THE TEST OF SINCERITY: In our moments of honest self-criticism, we will say many things about ourselves and really mean them. But how do we feel when others, especially our rivals, say exactly the same things about us?
>
> THE TEST OF CRITICISM: Does criticism arouse hostility and resentment in our hearts, and cause us to fly into immediate self-justification?[5]

Find a friend and trust him enough to tell you when you are doing something wrong. Be humble enough to listen to the advice of your husband, wife, or parents. The next time your boss makes a suggestion, do not react defensively. Listen with a quiet prayer for wisdom and pass the "test of criticism," for the Bible tells us that rebuke is better than praise.

When he was a young pastor, Gordon MacDonald was walking down the street with a missionary friend one day when Gordon made a derogatory comment about a mutual acquaintance. The missionary immediately rebuked him with these words: "Gordon, a man of God would not say such a thing about another person."

Writing about the experience in his book *Restoring Your Spiritual Passion*, MacDonald said,

> The rebuke stung, and I lived with its pain for many days afterward. But I will always be thankful for that rebuke, painful as it was, because I hear those words every time I am about to embarrass myself with a needless comment about another person. That was a rebuke that forced me to grow. . . .
>
> Looking back, I realize that rebukes were and still are among my greatest learning moments. They set me free from things that otherwise would have destroyed my spiritual passion. They spotlighted things that were hurting me badly but that I did not understand. So I am thankful to my wife and other special friends who play the position of rebuker. I understand the proverb that says, "In the end, people appreciate frankness more than flattery." (Proverbs 28:23 TLB)[6]

Finally, if defensiveness is a problem for you, that is an issue you need to hash out with God. Some people are overly sensitive. This could come from basic insecurity or an amplified need to be admired and accepted. Some of us fly off the handle when someone criticizes us.

What happens then? Once you have snapped at someone, he or she will conclude that it does not pay to share certain things with you. We need to remember that for people like friends and spouses, it is more wretched to give than to receive. They know they are risking your displeasure and possibly the relationship by giving you unwelcomed words.

Think of the husband who will not tolerate his wife's guidance. She takes a verbal lashing every time she tries until she stops trying. One little crack opens in the foundation of that marriage, and for every occasion when the wife grits her teeth rather than make a needed observation, the crack widens.

Or what about the account representative who has an anxiety attack whenever the boss calls her in for a performance rating? It is very unlikely she will receive any promotions.

Not only can we afford to listen to advice—we must. Surround yourself with good people who will help you, advise you, guide you, and hold you accountable. Your life will be like a river fed by many streams. Such a river grows broader and stronger, pounding its way through rugged territory, rushing along joyfully on its way to the vast sea.

But the person who shuts off criticism is like a river fed by no streams. That one moves along neither broadening nor picking up momentum. As it hits the higher, more rugged territories, it slows to a trickle, until it finds its journey's end in some stagnant lake.

One of the glories of life is the sharing of gifts, talents, insight, love, and burdens through the community of faith. To shut ourselves off from that is a great tragedy. But as we join together with that loving assembly, the Bible tells us that something supernatural occurs. We become the very body of Christ, head to toe. We care for the things He cares about. We share in His mind, His wisdom, even His power. Then and only then, with hands joined in mutual support across the spectrum of other seekers, do we begin to see heaven on the horizon.

19

The Hard Way Made Easy

Ecclesiastes 7:7–9

I had set out to drive to our college's basketball game at a nearby school when I happened to remember a shortcut someone had told me about, a route around the California freeways. Being in no mood for traffic, I turned down side streets and back roads. Before long I realized it was a shortcut to nowhere. After wandering around for a couple of hours in a maze of detours, bypaths, culs-de-sac, and bridle paths, I finally arrived back home with every nerve on edge.

Have you ever taken a "shortcut" and discovered it took twice as long to get somewhere? The message of Ecclesiastes 7:7–9 is that the hard way is better than the easy way. We get what we pay for, and we reap what we sow.

Isn't that what we tell our kids? Study hard. Practice, practice, practice. Work, work, work. Keep at it. Don't give up. Don't take the easy way out. There aren't any shortcuts to success. That is the constant refrain of parents, coaches, and teachers.

The Hard Way Is an Investment

Surely oppression destroys a wise man's reason,
And a bribe debases the heart.

The end of a thing is better than its beginning;
The patient in spirit is better than the proud in spirit.
Do not hasten in your spirit to be angry,
For anger rests in the bosom of fools.

—ECCLESIASTES 7:7–9

Notice how Solomon makes his point. Verse 7 says, "Surely oppression destroys a wise man's reason, and a bribe debases the heart." A bribe is nothing but a shortcut dressed in green. It's using money or some other asset to get your way without earning it. It will corrupt your integrity and destroy the purity of your heart.

One man climbs a mountain. He struggles up the path, taking frequent stops to catch his breath before continuing the slow trek to the top. He reaches the crest just as his friend steps off a helicopter. Which man enjoys the view most? The one from the helicopter says, "It's a nice view, but probably not worth the price of a 'copter ride."

His friend looks at him for a moment and says, "It's the most beautiful view I've ever seen. Every aching muscle in my body makes it look that much better."

And it is true. The hard way is an investment. If you personally work to upgrade your home, rather than hiring workers, you invest what real-estate agents call "sweat equity" in that house. The financial value increases but not nearly as much as your sense of pride in the home. You have earned it. You have owned the betterment process. And in some cases, you may have done a better job than hired workers, because this was your own home and you cared that much more.

186

Yes, the hard way is better. As Robert Frost said, "The best way out is always through."[1]

Imagine Jesus in the wilderness, on the very periphery of His ministry and mission to the world. There, in the most vulnerable possible zone of His life, the devil made his approach. He gave Jesus his three best pitches, and what were they? Shortcuts all.

"If you want food, just turn these stones into bread."

"If you want fame, just leap from this temple, into the arms of angels."

"If you want followers, just bow down to me."

The devil knew exactly where Jesus was going, but he suggested the wrong ways to get there.

Yes, Jesus wanted food, but He needed fasting, not fast food.

Yes, Jesus wanted fame but through the way of the cross, not ways that were crass.

Yes, Jesus wanted followers but through victory over sin, not by giving sin the victory.

The testing of Jesus was all about convenience versus commitment. He refused "wonder bread" for himself but offered it to a crowd of five thousand. He refused to make an impressive spectacle at the temple but made a shocking spectacle at the temple. He refused to accept the kingdoms of the world by bowing down to Satan but bowed down to death so that the kingdoms of heaven and earth would bow at His name (Philippians 2:9–10).

Perhaps it came easier for someone who was the Son of God. Never think that. There was a night when Jesus prayed and wept in the Garden of Gethsemane, asking God if there might be some other way. He actually perspired in blood, which modern doctors have recognized as a legitimate symptom of profound anxiety. In the end Jesus acknowledged that God's will was the only way, even when it was the hard way—the way of the cross. And because Jesus took the hard way, He opened heaven to those on earth.

God's Way Is the High Road

There is a saying: "Let the devil take the high road." But in fact, the devil takes the shortcut and wants us to do the same. He knows that if we can be persuaded to take the easy way, we have shortchanged ourselves. We have sold ourselves out in the name of convenience and opened the door to selling out everything else that is meaningful.

When you are in school, the easy way is to cheat on the big test. It's all about the grade and graduation and getting on with life, and who is going to know?

When you are in business, the easy way is to cut some corners, turn in the phony expense report, give the customer a little less than he contracted for. It's a jungle out there, and who is going to know?

When you are married, the easy way is to give in to that extramarital flirtation and have a little fling. It's all about animal drives, and who can help it? Besides, who is going to know?

And when you are a parent, the easy way is to buy your kids televisions and computers and toys rather than to spend a lot of time with them. They have never turned down the gifts, right? And what difference could it make?

Then you come to a time in life when you realize you have no moral compass. There is no inner strength, no marital closeness or family solidarity. You made the journey, took the shortcuts, and this is where they led. Who knew? *You*—and your Lord.

Solomon says the hard way is, in the end, the happy way. He says that it is better to make the right decision now and to be patient in spirit than to be proud. God's way may be the hard way, but it is always the high road, and if we will simply wait on Him it will lead us to higher places in life.

This thought is continued in the next verse: "The end of a thing is better than its beginning." It's true over and over in life. When you learned to ride a bicycle, the beginning was nothing but hard spills on the road and skinned knees and hurt pride. But once you got the hang of it, the end was worlds better than the beginning.

Your first year in high school—what was that like? Low man or woman on the totem pole, new standards, tougher teachers. But by the time you were a senior, you felt like you owned the place. The best way out is always through.

Joseph in Egypt found that out. The end was the Egyptian throne, but by way of slavery and the darkest prison in the country.

Job found it out. He ended up with twice as much as he had ever had. But he got there the hard way, including the collapse of his wealth and the loss of his family. God provided two blessings for every bruise.

Jesus knew it too. His road led through a trial, beatings, and the most violent and painful death we can imagine. But the destination was an empty tomb, a glorious ascension, a seat at the right hand of the Father.

The hard way will always be tough; there are no shortcuts. But it's made just a bit easier when we stop to remember that God never fails, that all His endings are happy ones, and that every bruise leads to deeper blessings.

Begin with the End in Mind

The second habit in Stephen Covey's popular book *The 7 Habits of Highly Effective People* says we should begin with the end in mind. Covey suggests that we isolate where we want to end up, then keep that as an image that frames the way we think and act on a daily basis.[2] He's right, but Solomon knew that all along. He made the point here in Ecclesiastes, nearly three thousand years ago.

Many people today have lost the art of thinking things through.

We have so much noise around us, so many urgent demands upon us, and so little time for reflection that we make snap decisions without taking the time to mull over our choices and prayerfully work them out.

Wise people don't let that happen. In his biography of Napoleon, André Castelot wrote that sometimes the great emperor would stretch out on a settee near his fireplace, close his eyes, and appear to be asleep. But he wasn't; he was meditating, thinking through his actions:

> "If I always seem to be ready for everything, to face up to anything," he told his advisors, "it is because I never undertake anything at all without first having meditated for a long time and foreseen what might happen. It is not a genie, but meditation, that suddenly reveals to me, in secret, what I must say and do under circumstances not anticipated by others."[3]

When you have to make an important decision, take a quiet walk or shut yourself in your room and pray over some questions: Where will this lead me? What will be the result of this action? What are the possible outcomes of this particular deed? Try to determine the end from the beginning.

In the process, remember that God saves His best for last, whereas Satan points out the shortcut. As C. S. Lewis put it, "The safest road to hell is the gradual one—the gentle slope, soft underfoot, without sudden turnings, without milestones, without signposts."[4] It all begins with the little compromises, the "so what, no big deal" moments. It's just one pornographic image, just one snort of cocaine, just one night in a hotel room somewhere. Those little access roads always take us off the King's highway—the "narrow way," as Jesus called it. We can see that highway from the access road, and we can get back on it anytime we want (or so we say). But the roads get farther apart, and the slope gets steeper, and soon it becomes very difficult to apply the brakes.

Life on the King's highway is different. As His plan for us unfolds, it becomes richer and better; we grow happier and holier as time goes by. "The path of the just," wrote Solomon in Proverbs 4:18, "is like the shining sun, that shines ever brighter unto the perfect day."

Because I have participated in many weddings as a pastor, one myth I have heard over and over again is among the greatest of misconceptions. People believe that the beginning of a marriage is better than the end. Maybe our awareness of the divorce plague makes us think that. Maybe it's the abuse marriage takes on television and in the movies.

But marriage is not that way by nature. When we persevere at it, work on it, grow in it, and do it the hard way, the institution of marriage gets better and deeper and sweeter in time. When we weather the storms together like two strong oaks growing by the stream, the end is profoundly richer.

As a matter of fact, I have found through counseling that the early days of marriage are often the most tumultuous and challenging. Two distinct personalities bring their worlds together, and frequently they collide with great force. But the best part of marriage is the part that endures and mellows as the years pass and couples have smoothed off the rough edges and molded themselves together as one.

Donna and I have been married for fifty years, and I can honestly say it gets better every year. When she happens to be away for a few days traveling or visiting our children and their families, I miss her terribly. She is the one person in the world who is committed to loving me in spite of my many imperfections. Marriage done right gets better over time, because the end of a thing is better than the beginning.

We remember Fanny Crosby as the blind hymnist who wrote such amazing gospel songs as "Blessed Assurance" and "To God Be the Glory." But there is a lesser-known Crosby hymn that underscores the truth that the end is better than the beginning. Fanny wrote this particular song during the summer of 1886, when she was staying in the home of her friend Ira Sankey in Northfield, Massachusetts. Ira, himself a noted hymnist, composed a tune. After playing it for Fanny, he suggested, "Why not write a poem for this tune tonight?" She deferred, saying she could not do it at present. But the next day, while her friends were out for a drive, Fanny wrote the following words:

> O child of God, wait patiently when dark thy path may be,
> And let thy faith lean trusting on Him Who cares for thee;
> And though the clouds hang drearily upon the brow of night,
> Yet in morning, joy will come, and fill thy soul with light.[5]

Our destination is true happiness, but to get there we will have to walk through some difficult terrain. The clouds will often cover us. The darkness will often cause us to stumble and despair of ever rising. But when the clouds break through, there is joy in the morning. The hard way is the only way, for it makes that joy even sweeter.

20

Time to Move On

Ecclesiastes 7:10

E veryone loves the "good old days"—even young people who never lived in them. The pop music charts are filled with more song remakes from the 1960s and '70s than ever. Kids call it "retro" and consider it cool in the way that "futuristic" used to be. There is a fascination with the cultural remnants of certain decades, as embodied by TV shows such as *That '70s Show* and any number of movies. Even in professional sports it has become fashionable for teams to have "throwback days" when they play their games in the caps, jerseys, helmets, and uniforms of bygone eras.

Something within us smiles and sighs when we think about yester-year. Something within us insists that things were better then—music more melodious, movies more entertaining, the news more encourag-ing, and life in general more manageable. If asked for proof, we would quickly and passionately spit out examples to prove the point. At any given time, the best time to be alive was twenty or thirty years ago—often known as "when I was your age."

Is it really true? Consider a few facts about the good old days in America:

- From 1970 to 1992, a typical new home increased by an average of six hundred square feet of living area.
- Today at least 45 percent of homes now have dishwashers, up from 26 percent four decades ago.
- In 1990, 75 percent of homes had clothes washers, up from 66 percent in 1970. The percentage of homes with clothes dryers jumped from 45 to 70 during the same period.
- The average home had 1.4 televisions in 1970, but 2.1 in 1990, and gained 4.5 times as much audio and video equipment, 50 percent more kitchen appliances, 30 percent more furniture, and 100 percent more equipment for sports and hobbies.
- Median real wealth rose by 2 percent per year from 1970 to 1990.
- The Dow Jones Industrial Average increased sixfold from the early 1970s to the 1990s.
- Microwave ovens, food processors, camcorders, home computers, home exercise equipment, cable TV, Rollerblades, fax machines, and soft contact lenses became staples of the American life in the 1990s. Multitudes of other products are better in quality and lower in price than ever before.
- Three decades ago motorists had to stop and look for a pay phone to make a call. Now most Americans enjoy the safety and convenience of cell phones.
- Today's drivers go farther on a gallon of gas than ever before and drive safer cars equipped with antilock brakes, airbags, fuel injectors, turbochargers, cruise control, and sound systems better than many home systems.
- Since 1973, workers have added the equivalent of nearly five years of waking leisure hours to their lives . . . and the list goes on.[1]

Hold it! Wait for the disclaimer. Allow me to acknowledge what's wrong with that list: most of it is about stuff—material things for which Solomon would have three words: *vanity, vanity, vanity*. The list does not mention our increasing national debt, relatively low rates of personal savings, and declining moral standards, to be sure.

But the list also neglects to drive home the truth that Americans are living longer, retiring sooner, and traveling more widely than ever before. They are reaping the benefit of radical advances in medicine, giving them more years of life and more life for their years.

Can we agree that life is better in some ways and not nearly as good in others? I hope you will concede the point that even the most nostalgic of our elders, given the choice, would not climb into a time machine to go live fifty years in the past without the daily medication that helps them enjoy life. We enjoy the highest standard of living in America of any country in history.

Yesterday's Glory . . . Tomorrow's Promise

Do not say,
"Why were the former days better than these?"
For you do not inquire wisely concerning this.

—ECCLESIASTES 7:10

The good old days is a state of mind that has no coordinates in the real world. It is just a few blocks south of the pot of gold at rainbow's end, and it's another few blocks east of that other entrancing fantasyland, "what might have been."

Your kids will someday sit back in their easy chairs, sighing over this very moment, crowning it as the new *good old days*. It's hard to imagine, because today never seems like anything special to the people inhabiting it. Today is always just short of yesterday's glory, just shy of tomorrow's promise. But today is all we have. It holds all the stakes. Today is the only day we can directly affect, and all our hopes of a better life lie right there in the calendar box where you stand—the day marked today.

If you come up short on courage and decide not to live totally in the present, you begin to take that detour into the land of nostalgia. But Solomon says, "You do not inquire wisely concerning this." When you talk about the past, you are not speaking from a position of careful rationality, comparing and contrasting all the micro-differences between eras (that would be impossible). You are speaking purely from emotions: feelings of fear, a sense of loss from yesterday, an insecurity about the future.

Solomon would agree that there were elements of his father's regime that were superior to his own. But his point is the same one he has made in other parts of this book: the stillborn child and the two-thousand-year-old super-senior citizen face side-by-side cemetery plots. Even a two-thousand-year life span is a vapor, here today and gone tomorrow, from the perspective of eternity—not to mention that a few feet away, in the same cemetery, we find people from the good old days buried right beside those from our "brave new world."

The issue in life is not your times, your trade, or your take-home pay. It is all about the question, what are you doing with today? Are you electrically charged with the prospect of all that God can do with your life in this window called *Today*? After all, we can do all things through Christ, and He promised we would do miracles greater than His (John 14:12). Those are not verses about the good old days or the world of the future—those are Today words.

The idea of heaven on earth is a Today idea. Remember how the Israelites took three steps toward the promised land, then two steps backward into nostalgia? Slavery never seemed so enticing. Why, those

Egyptian masters actually *fed* their slaves occasionally, and there were some days when there were no whippings at all, and fifteen-minute rests between hauling those great bricks. The Israelites were anxious about the wilderness of Today, and it kept them from the promise of Tomorrow. We do much the same, forgetting that all of the great pictures our lives can paint will be painted on the canvas of Today.

The superiority of your yesterday is no more real than the good old days of slavery for the Israelites. As Paul Simon pointed out in a song, everything looks nice in Kodachrome.[2] The only problem is that when you stare too long into your rearview mirror, you collide with the life that is coming at you.

Meanwhile, the ultimate reality in life is God, who wants to fill your life with His presence and power right here and right now. Happiness has nothing of the past mixed in it or of what lies ahead. The heaven awaiting us, when we come face to face with our Savior, will be an eternal Now, and it stands to reason that the way to bring that heaven to earth is to live in this Now completely and consistently.

Upside Down, Inside Out

The kingdom of God always appears upside down to the human perspective. We think it is strange to die in order to live, to give in order to receive, or to serve in order to lead. Solomon captures the perpetual enigma of our looking-glass values just as Jesus describes them in the Sermon on the Mount. He insists we should embrace sorrow over laughter, rebukes over praise, the long way instead of the short, and today instead of yesterday.

The truth is that it is not the kingdom of God that is upside down—it is the world. It is not the Word of God that turns life inside out—it is the world that has reversed all the equations that God designed for our lives. After all, we can all verify the common sense of these upside-down propositions—it really is better to give than to receive, it really does help more to embrace criticism than praise, and so on. Everyday life is a proving ground for kingdom proposition.

Arthur Bennett wrote a prayer called "The Valley of Vision" that wonderfully summarizes some of the things in this section of Ecclesiastes. He uses the language of paradox, which is really the language of the kingdom about which Solomon wrote and Jesus Christ taught—the language of truth:

> Lord, high and holy, meek and lowly,
> Thou hast brought me to the valley of vision,
> Where I live in the depths but see thee in the heights;
> Hemmed in by mountains of sin I behold thy glory.
>
> Let me learn by paradox
> That the way down is the way up
> That to be low is to be high
> That the broken heart is the healed heart,
> That the contrite spirit is the rejoicing spirit,
> That the repenting soul is the victorious soul,
> That to have nothing is to possess all,
> That to bear the cross is to wear the crown,
> That to give is to receive,
> That the valley is the place of vision.
> Lord, in the daytime, stars can be seen from the deepest wells,
> And the deeper the wells the brighter thy stars shine;
> Let me find thy light in my darkness,
> Thy life in my death,
> Thy joy in my sorrow,
> Thy grace in my sin,

Thy riches in my poverty,
Thy glory in my valley.[3]

Three Things We Know

In our journey to happiness the first essential is vision—to see where we are headed; in this case, to step out of all these upside-down worldly assumptions and see from God's perspective. But even then it is a challenge to keep our "valley vision" of the invisible world of heaven from the visible context of earth. When I am tempted to lose focus in the midst of this life's events, to wonder if the seeming paradoxes of God are really true, I cling to three "knows" in Romans 8 that are the perfect complement to what Solomon teaches in Ecclesiastes 7.

First, I *know* that "the whole creation groans and labors with birth pangs together until now" (Romans 8:22). That is, I know that the way things are now is not the way they were supposed to be, nor the way they will be. Troubling things happen in this world for a multitude of reasons, all of which are rooted in sin. When bad things happen, the frailty of my flesh is tempted to yield to the pressure of those events because I am fallen. But this is all unnatural, not the way God designed it. So I do not become discouraged or deceived by something that I know is temporary. I cling to the image of heaven on earth, that which I know is eternal.

Second, I *do not know* what I should pray for as I ought, but "the Spirit Himself makes intercession for [me] with groanings which cannot be uttered" (Romans 8:26). This means that I am not alone in the battle. When I become tempted to do things the world's way—the way of laughter and flattery and the good old days—I fall to my knees and depend on the Holy Spirit to pray through me when I cannot find the words. When I am tempted to take the short and easy way instead of the long and difficult way, I cry out to God for strength with the Spirit's help. He is there for me at every turn, for every challenge. He is my Comforter and Counselor and Guide, the deposit of God that ensures what He has begun in me will be completed in the day of Christ Jesus. Even when I do not know what to pray, I know the Spirit does.

And third, I *know* that "all things work together for good to those who love God, to those who are the called according to His purpose" (Romans 8:28). As one of those who love Him, I can latch onto the prospect that every single event is part of an equation with a positive solution. There is power, incredible power, in grasping that paradigm.

This world seems out of control, and I have to depend on the Spirit to help me through. But ultimately I know that God is in control of everything. Nothing that happens in my life falls outside the bounds of His reach. He corrals every seemingly random and stray event and brings them together for good in my life because I love Him and have been called according to His purpose. That means that I am free to live paradoxically in this world, free to embrace the truths of God's kingdom in the face of every contrary teaching of the majority. Free to be a contrarian for Christ and His kingdom.

Ecclesiastes helps us see that God's plan is good and clear but sometimes mysterious. When we know what we know, it does not matter because to God it is not a mystery. He is the Author of the Book of Life, and He knew the ending before He set the beginning in place. Therefore, it is okay for Him to know and for us *not* to know, because He is God and we are not. And we choose to let Him be God in our lives.

I encourage you to embrace sorrow when it comes, a rebuke when you feel its sting, the hard way when it is the right way, and especially the power of Today—*carpe diem!* Seize the day He has given you. This is the day He made, so rejoice and be glad in it. Heaven is at hand, not in the rearview mirror nor in the unknown future. It is within your grasp. Take hold, take counsel, and take advantage!

21

The Perspective of Wisdom

Ecclesiastes 7:11–18

A wise old Chinese woodcutter lived on the troubled Mongolian border. One day his favorite horse, a beautiful white mare, jumped the fence and was seized on the other side by the enemy. His friends came to comfort him. "We're so sorry about your horse," they said. "That's bad news."

"How do you know it's bad news?" he asked. "It might be good news."

A week later the man looked out his window to see his mare returning at breakneck speed—beside a beautiful stallion. He put both horses into the enclosure, and his friends came to admire the new addition. "What a beautiful horse," they said. "That's good news."

"How do you know it's good news?" replied the man. "It might be bad news."

The next day, the man's only son decided to try the stallion. It threw him, and he landed painfully, breaking his leg. The friends made another visit, all of them sympathetic, saying, "We're so sorry about this. It's such bad news."

"How do you know it's bad news?" replied the man. "It might be good news."

Within a month, war erupted between China and Mongolia. Chinese recruiters came through the area, pressing all the young men into the army. All of them perished, except for the woodcutter's son, who could not go off to war because of his broken leg.

"You see," said the gentleman. "The things you considered good were actually bad, and the things that seemed bad were actually good."[1]

This wise woodcutter expresses the heart of Solomon's words in Ecclesiastes 7. We have already learned that mourning is better than laughing, funerals are better than weddings, a dying day is more important than a birthday, rebuke is better than praise, the long way is better than the shortcut, and the good old days are highly overrated.

Life is a paradox, and we are not always sure which end is up. The movie character Forrest Gump says life is like a box of chocolates because you never know what you will get; Solomon would add that even after you take a bite, you can't be certain how it is going to digest.

We have to rely on our Lord, who knows the end from the beginning. His values are often different, and that's the underlying theme of Ecclesiastes 7.

Solomon teaches us that wisdom is knowing we cannot know; it is realizing how small is the single puzzle piece we hold—that only God controls the final picture. We see through hazy glass, but His vision is perfect and all-encompassing; we know little, but His wisdom is perfect and all-knowing. Our perseverance is weak, but God plays every issue for the long haul.

Our response to all this should be Thanksgiving with a capital *T*.

Thank God for the Perspective of Wisdom

American Olympic speed skater Dan Jansen suffered a series of devastating defeats and setbacks in his career until 1994, when he finally took the gold in a thrilling 1,000-meter race in Lillehammer, Norway. As a young skater he learned to keep defeat in perspective. Competing in the youth national skating championships in Minnesota at the age of nine, he was positioned to capture the title when he tripped on a lane marker coming around a turn.

That mistake cost him the victory. He was so distraught that he cried through the awards ceremony and the entire six-hour drive home. His father did not say anything about the loss until they pulled into their driveway, but what he said then has stuck with Jansen ever since: "You know, Dan, there's more to life than skating around in a circle."[2]

That might strike you as an insensitive remark from a father to a heartbroken son, but it is true. It arises from the father's enhanced perspective, which indeed renders the pain smaller and less significant. Dan Jansen, being a veteran competitor even at age nine, needed that greater perspective. It helped him pursue his Olympic dream while remembering the true place of victory and defeat.

Wisdom may not solve all our problems or smooth out all the bumps in the road, but it gives the mind the right information for controlling the emotions.

Several years ago there was a popular style of picture featuring an optical illusion. At first glance the picture only seemed to be a pattern of swirling blue or green lines. Then as you placed your focus on the dot in the middle and slowly stepped backward from the picture, an image would emerge. The effect was startling. The work of God's perspective is similar. We look at the scene and see only random swirls of events until we fix our gaze on Christ, who is at the center of creation and holds all things together (Ephesians 1:10). As we step slowly back, we see the picture through new eyes.

Perspective is seeing things in their true size and significance, in their proper relationship to each other. Children's art is notable for a lack of perspective. Everything is on one flat plane. There is no distance, no horizon. A good artist can suggest a distance of several miles on a single canvas—such as a country road narrowing until it vanishes into the sunrise. God's wisdom allows us to take the long view and to see how all roads lead back to Him in the end.

Wisdom gives us depth, relationship, meaning—the long view of things. There are three ways wisdom increases our perspective on the events of life.

Wisdom to Deal with Prosperity

Wisdom is good with an inheritance,
And profitable to those who see the sun.
For wisdom is a defense as money is a defense,
But the excellence of knowledge is that wisdom gives life to
    those who have it.
—ECCLESIASTES 7:11–12

The world's brand of wisdom fluctuates like a roller-coaster week on Wall Street. The former *Newsweek* featured a weekly column called "Conventional Wisdom Watch," to chart the "up and down arrows" of fleeting popularity. One week a president or a pop singer might receive an "up arrow" for some positive publicity event; the next week the arrow may be pointing dead south. But the wisdom of God holds consistent and unchanging, now and forever.

Solomon tells us that wisdom and wealth make good companions.

The Living Bible says, "To be wise is as good as being rich; in fact, it is better. You can get anything by either wisdom or money, but being wise has many advantages" (Ecclesiastes 7:11–12).

Solomon wrote something similar in Proverbs: "For whoever finds [wisdom] finds life, and obtains favor from the LORD" (8:35). Rich people who lack wisdom end up miserable; their wealth becomes a curse instead of a blessing. Wisdom gives perspective to prosperity. Wisdom keeps wealth in perspective.

Worldwatch Institute, an environmental/economic think tank in Washington, DC, issued a surprising report showing increasing numbers of people in the world are "fat, rich, and unhappy." Private consumption expenditures (the amount spent on goods and services at the household level) increased fourfold in the world since 1960, topping more than $20 trillion in 2002. In America, where consumption has skyrocketed, there are more private vehicles on the road than people licensed to drive them. The average size of refrigerators in US homes increased by 10 percent between 1972 and 2002, and new homes in America were 38 percent larger than those built in 1975, despite having fewer people in each household. Yet increased consumption has not brought Americans happiness, said the report. "Only about a third of Americans report being very happy, the same as in 1957 when Americans were only half as wealthy."[3]

Wealth we have; wisdom we need. We can only thank God that while wealth is hard to come by, wisdom is actually freely available through God. A lifetime supply is available in this book of Ecclesiastes.

Wisdom to Deal with Providence

Consider the work of God;
For who can make straight what He has made crooked?

In the day of prosperity be joyful,
But in the day of adversity consider:
Surely God has appointed the one as well as the other,
So that man can find out nothing that will come after him.
—Ecclesiastes 7:13–14

As we have seen, providence is God's supervision of all creation, ensuring that all His plans work out. It means that things will come to pass in our lives that only He understands. You may be trying to fill in a certain picture with your life, such as the picture of you as an entrepreneur who owns your own business; or of you as courting and marrying a certain candidate. God may be (and usually is) filling in a completely different picture, a vaster and more comprehensive one involving any number of people and having implications that might be played out in coming centuries.

So you might not understand why God didn't allow you to start your own business or marry that specific person, but He has His reasons. And they are always reasons we would heartily approve if we were only wise enough.

"See the way God does things and fall into line," reads *The Living Bible*. "Enjoy prosperity whenever you can, and when hard times strike, realize that God gives one as well as the other" (Eccleslastes 7:13–14).

Affliction, that crooked thing we cannot fix, is the appointment of God. I wrote a book called *A Bend in the Road*, in which I affirmed God's presence with His children in the difficulties of life. But if you are like me, you would rather not have a bend in the road to begin with, or at least you would like a bend you could straighten on your own. But wisdom says there is something deeper to be learned in the bends than in the straight lanes of life.

As I studied Solomon's words, I thought of Job, a man blessed by God with incredible wealth before suddenly losing it all. The only thing left was his wife, and she gave him the most offensive advice we can imagine: "Curse God and die!" (Job 2:9).

Job replied, "You speak as one of the foolish women speaks. Shall we indeed accept good from God, and shall we not accept adversity?" (v. 10).

When good things happen, we never ask why God allowed them. Apparently we figure we have them coming. But when bad things happen, that is when we talk theology. Wise people know that God is in all of it, that He is never closer than in our affliction. Pity those who have never known the comforting presence of God in the eye of the storm.

Bible teacher and author Warren Wiersbe puts it this way:

> God balances our lives by giving us enough blessings to keep us happy and enough burdens to keep us humble. If all we had were blessings in our hands, we would fall right over, so the Lord balances the blessings in our hands with burdens on our backs. That helps keep us steady, and as we yield to Him, we can even turn burdens into blessings.[4]

Blessings in the hand plus burdens on the back equals balance in the spiritual life—a formula for contentment and maturity.

Wisdom to Deal with the Puzzles of Life

A long-standing holiday tradition in the Jeremiah household is the annual jigsaw puzzle. We get a new one each year, one with a gazillion pieces, and work on it during the Christmas holiday season. All the pieces are spread out on a table that is reserved solely for the holiday puzzle. Various Jeremiahs will stop and try a few more pieces until the picture is finally completed. (I won't reveal what percentage of these puzzles have been completed over the years.)

It is a great diversion when friends and family are gathered and a good opportunity to exercise our puzzle-solving skills. We always get the sides completed so that we have a nice frame that needs a picture inside. Corners and straight edges are simple. It's what is inside that gives us trouble.

In the puzzles of life we are often able to work out the borders of things—the places where life is straight, where its corners meet neatly. But to solve the big picture, we need wisdom, persistence, and perhaps the help of loved ones. There are two puzzles in particular.

The Puzzle of Reversed Rewards

I have seen everything in my days of vanity:

There is a just man who perishes in his righteousness,
And there is a wicked man who prolongs life in his wicked-
ness.
—ECCLESIASTES 7:15

Once again we come to the question everyone asks (you and I included). Why do good people suffer and bad people prosper?

I once worried over the hazy areas of my faith, like those spots on a sparkling car window that simply will not come clean. Now the hazy areas tell me that our God is real, dynamic, and too great for our conception. His ways are higher than mine. If there were no hazy areas, the whole thing would be too neat, too trite. If I could fully understand His thoughts, He would be no more God than I am.

We hear those who approach this puzzle with an ultimatum: solve it or God is not real. This is like approaching a ten-thousand-piece jig-saw puzzle and saying, "If I can't assemble this in five minutes, I will deny that it's a picture."

That's unfair, isn't it? It is also irrational. Our inability to work out an answer reflects only on our limitation, not God's.

God is both loving and powerful, but He allows the rewards to be reversed—success for the evil, suffering for the good—for reasons relating to His eternal plan, and because it is the consequence of a fallen world in which we ourselves have invited such chaos. And remember the wisdom of the woodcutter. We see only a fragment of life at a time, but God sees the whole.

The Puzzle of Righteous Rhetoric

Do not be overly righteous,
Nor be overly wise:
Why should you destroy yourself?
Do not be overly wicked,
Nor be foolish:
Why should you die before your time?
It is good that you grasp this,
And also not remove your hand from the other;
For he who fears God will escape them all.

—ECCLESIASTES 7:16–18

Some liberal-leaning Bible scholars love this passage because it seems to suggest that a middle-of-the-road approach to the spiritual life is acceptable: "Do not be overly righteous, nor be overly wise. . . . Do not be overly wicked, nor be foolish."

In other words, be "sorta righteous," but don't let this thing get out of hand by trying to make the world a better place. This is the basic posture of those who say, when asked if they know where they will spend eternity, "Well, I'm not as good as some, but not as bad as most. I'm hoping that's good enough to get me there!"

Let me state emphatically that there is no "sorta holy" any more than there is a "kinda pregnant." Sorta holy is the way to "sorta hell." Partial obedience to God is total disobedience.

Let's clarify what Solomon does mean. He is not telling us to be moderately godly; he is telling us not to exalt our godliness before others. You have seen people with Christian bumper stickers who get more than their share of honks when they do inconsiderate things in traffic.

The fact is that self-righteousness is not good for the self, and it is not righteous. It arises from sin, and it is the central reigning sin. Solomon counsels staying in the middle of the road, which is described in verse 18: "It is good that you grasp this, and also not remove your hand from the other; for he who fears God will escape them all."

A man was caught in adultery, but he confessed and repented. He began to spend all his time in church activities until he became very self-righteous. Pretty soon he was giving the pastor preaching advice. The pastor told him, "I liked you better as an adulterer. At least you were humble."

Better to avoid both adultery *and* self-righteousness. Those who live by the world's wisdom will never be content in their quest for happiness. But the perspective of God's wisdom helps us see a better road and a more blessed destination.

22

The Power of Wisdom

Ecclesiastes 7:19–29

One word for wisdom in Hebrew is *hokmah.* It occurs more than three hundred times in the Old Testament. While *hokmah* (and its derivatives) are usually translated "to be wise," "wise," or "wisdom," the root meaning of the word is "skill"—skill of all sorts.

For example, *hokmah* describes the high priest's tailors (Exodus 28:3) and the tabernacle's engravers (Exodus 35:35). Jonadab, a skillful man, has *hokmah* (2 Samuel 13:3), as does a good snake charmer (Psalm 58:5). Ants, badgers, locusts, and spiders have their own *hokmah* skill (Proverbs 30:24–28), as do idol makers (Isaiah 40:20) and navigators (Ezekiel 27:8).

The skillful are those who bring order out of chaos, who take raw materials and turn them into something useful or beautiful, and who have the ability to navigate chaotic situations such as storms at sea or to turn a chaotic situation to one's advantage. The ultimate image of *hokmah,* of course, is God creating an awesomely beautiful and complex earth from the chaos described in Genesis 1:2. The earth was without form and void before God applied His skill.

When we apply *hokmah* to the everyday course of human events, we could be said to possess the skill of living. We would be those who know how to bring order out of a sometimes chaotic life, who can gather up life's random bits and pieces and shape them into something that bears fruit, and who can keep from crashing on the shallows and shoals of life and make it safely to port.

Solomon cherishes that wisdom manifest in a godly perspective and godly power, wisdom to deal with whatever life brings his way.

Perspective on life is good. But power makes life a lot more exciting. Wisdom can help in understanding prosperity, providence, and puzzles in life, but it does not promise to provide perspective on everything. Nor does perspective exist alone. Perspective and power are like the two wings on a bird, the two blades of a pair of scissors, or the two sides of a coin. The whole of wisdom does not exist without both perspective and power.

Solomon notes four different areas of life in which wisdom can provide power.

Wisdom to Deal with the Problems We Encounter

Wisdom strengthens the wise
More than ten rulers of the city.

For there is not a just man on earth who does good
And does not sin.

—Ecclesiastes 7:19–20

"Wisdom," wrote Solomon, "strengthens the wise." Wisdom leads to strength and mastery. When we have aligned ourselves with the right Lord, we become more courageous. Ten city rulers hold no terror for us.

I think of Shadrach, Meshach, and Abednego in the book of Daniel. When they were told they would be thrown into a fiery furnace if they did not worship the king's statue, they shrugged and said,

> O Nebuchadnezzar, we have no need to answer you in this matter. If that is the case, our God whom we serve is able to deliver us from the burning fiery furnace, and He will deliver us from your hand, O king. But if not, let it be known to you, O king, that we do not serve your gods, nor will we worship the gold image which you have set up. (Daniel 3:16–18)

These three young men were not afraid of the problem they faced. Wisdom told them that God's plan, not Nebuchadnezzar's, would ultimately prevail.

Wisdom to Deal with the People We Employ

> Also do not take to heart everything people say,
> Lest you hear your servant cursing you.
> For many times, also, your own heart has known
> That even you have cursed others.
> —ECCLESIASTES 7:21–22

People who study the corporate workplace say that interpersonal problems are far more time-consuming than technical problems.

Psychologists tell us that one's "emotional quotient" (EQ) is more critical to life success than one's "intelligence quotient" (IQ). It is only by wisdom that employers can effectively manage those who work for them.

Solomon's advice to the wise is not to listen to the gossip people say about you, because you know in your heart you have said unkind things about others as well.

I stopped reading negative, critical notes from people a long time ago. My secretary reads them first, and if they are constructive and written in a spirit of love rather than antagonism, then she passes the notes to me. When they are carnal or unhelpful, she throws them away.

Listening to mean-spirited input isn't wise since it only serves to cause internal agitation when we hear it. So avoid it. One man said, "I never worry about people who say evil things about me because I know a lot more stuff about me than they do, and it's worse than what they are saying."

What Solomon means by his counsel is this: "Let's be honest. If we get upset when people talk about us, we are holding them to a higher standard than we hold ourselves to, because we are prone to do the same thing."

Wisdom to Deal with the Perplexities We Experience

All this I have proved by wisdom.
I said, "I will be wise";
But it was far from me.
As for that which is far off and exceedingly deep,
Who can find it out?
I applied my heart to know,

To search and seek out wisdom and the reason of things,
To know the wickedness of folly,
Even of foolishness and madness.

—ECCLESIASTES 7:23–25

Wisdom gives you power to live with what you do not understand. Solomon's experience is typical—we exercise our minds to try to find "the reason of things," but we can't. Those things that are "far off" and "exceedingly deep" may remain that way for the duration of our time on earth. The power that wisdom provides is to release such things into the hands of God lest our obsession with finding out ruin us.

When I was growing up, I would often hear this statement: "I don't know about the future, but I know who holds the future." That is more than a euphemism to quiet the quest of a curious mind. It is biblical truth. You have learned already in these pages that God's plan is good and His purpose is clear, but His program is mysterious. Wisdom gives us the power to live our lives in the realm of the first two and leave the third to God. There is power in not being a slave to knowing why everything in life happens as it does, a power that comes from freedom. Many a martyr's body has been shackled into submission while his spirit remained free. That is true power, and it comes from the wisdom of God.

Wisdom to Deal with the Pitfalls We Escape

And I find more bitter than death
The woman whose heart is snares and nets,
Whose hands are fetters.
He who pleases God shall escape from her,
But the sinner shall be trapped by her.

"Here is what I have found," says the Preacher,
"Adding one thing to the other to find out the reason,
Which my soul still seeks but I cannot find:
One man among a thousand I have found,
But a woman among all these I have not found.
Truly, this only I have found:
That God made man upright,
But they have sought out many schemes."
—Ecclesiastes 7:26–29

Wisdom can give us the power to steer clear of illicit relationships. *The Living Bible* brings this out clearly: "A prostitute is more bitter than death. May it please God that you escape from her, but sinners don't evade her snares" (Ecclesiastes 7:26).

A marital affair leaves incredible destruction in its wake— emotional destruction both in the marriage and in the illicit relationship.

An affair is not real—it is only an illusion of real love. It's a sham—a pitiful misrepresentation of what God designed marriage to be. In this illusion, lovers can only imitate marital intimacy, because the beauty of the commitment of one man to one woman is lost. The delight of ongoing discovery between two people totally dedicated to one another cannot be attained, because one or both unmarried partners are painfully aware of the third person, who is being damaged by their affair. The end result is emotional confusion in the hearts and lives of all concerned.

Solomon addresses the issue of wisdom and immorality extensively in the book of Proverbs. In Proverbs 2:1–10, he talks about acquiring wisdom by listening to instruction, asking for it, searching for it like buried treasure. Then, when wisdom enters your heart, "discretion will preserve you; understanding will keep you" (Proverbs 2:11). Preserve and keep you from what?

From the immoral woman,

From the seductress who flatters with her words,

Who forsakes the companion of her youth,

And forgets the covenant of her God.

For her house leads down to death,

And her paths to the dead;

None who go to her return,

Nor do they regain the paths of life. (Proverbs 2:16–19)

To put it plainly, wisdom gives us the power to resist sexual immorality, as Solomon himself should know. Ray Stedman writes:

Solomon was trapped by sexual seductions. He went looking for love and thought he would find it in a relationship with a woman. He went looking for that which would support him, strengthen, and make him feel life was worth the living. But what he found was nothing but a fleeting sexual thrill. He found himself involved with a woman who did not give what he was looking for at all; he still felt the same empty loneliness as before.[1]

Solomon made his choices, suffered heartbreak, paid the price, and lived to tell the tale. He wants that tale to serve as our warning. "Think!" he exhorts us. "Don't get caught up in the 'greener grass' myth. All that you need, all that can give you joy, is on your side of the fence. Follow the wisdom from above."

That wisdom from above, as James tells us in the New Testament, is "first pure, then peaceable, gentle, willing to yield, full of mercy and good fruits, without partiality and without hypocrisy" (James 3:17). In other words, wisdom flows from a rich, daily walk with God. It is like a cool stream emerging from the heights of a mountain, plunging delightfully to earth, where people come from many villages to enjoy its richness and beauty. As a wise believer, you will have that same effect on people. Who wouldn't be attracted to the person James describes?

George Washington Carver, born in slavery, became a famous agricultural chemist and scientist. He is especially known for his work with the peanut. Once he was invited to testify before a senate committee, and there he was asked, "Dr. Carver, how did you learn all these things?"

"From an old Book," he replied.

"What book?"

"The Bible."

"Does the Bible talk about peanuts?" asked the senator.

"No, Mr. Senator," replied the great scientist, "but it tells me about God who made the peanut. I asked Him to show me what to do with the peanut, and He did."[2]

"In [Christ] are hidden all the treasures of wisdom and knowledge" (Colossians 2:3). When you are facing difficult issues and you don't know what to do, remember that you know Jesus Christ, the wisdom of God. The particulars of your daily decision may not be found in God's Word, but Christ will always be found abiding there. And He will give you what you need through His Holy Spirit, who brings God's Word and our hearts together. The least of the saints has more wisdom in Christ than the most ingenious scientist possesses without Christ.

How, indeed, does that scientist or anyone else make it through a day without the hand of God on his shoulder and the voice of the Spirit in his soul? Imagine taking a walk through the world's greatest and largest technology facility with the president of that company. He gives you an orderly tour, pointing out all the intriguing processes and principles and people involved in the busy work of the factory. Now imagine walking through those vast corridors without the president. You would be lost and confused. I need God to walk with me. So do you.

One of Christianity's oldest hymns comes from the sixth century, written in Latin by an unknown believer. The title is "O Boundless Wisdom, God Most High."

> O boundless Wisdom, God most high,
> O Maker of the earth and sky,
> Who bid'st the parted waters flow
> In heaven above, on earth below:
>
> The streams on earth, the clouds in heaven,
> By thee their ordered bounds were given,
> Lest 'neath the untempered fires of day
> The parched soil should waste away.
>
> E'en so on us who seek thy face,
> Pour forth the waters of thy grace;
> Renew the fount of life within,
> And quench the wasting fires of sin.[3]

Grant us wisdom, O Lord. Grant us courage. As we seek to find what really matters in life, we need wisdom. And the more of it we have, the smaller we feel and the more wisdom we realize we need. Someday, when we feel the smallest and need your wisdom the most desperately, we will find the great object of our quest—and we will know You are there, walking joyfully inside us, eager to share the intricacies of Your wondrous kingdom.

23

Hard to Be Humble

Ecclesiastes 8:1–17

Rags to riches, back to rags, riches again, rags—that is the short answer if you ask quarterback Kurt Warner about his career.

Warner was an all-state high school football player from Iowa who tried out for the Green Bay Packers in 1994, but he was summarily cut. There were no more options for him, athletically speaking, so he took a job in Cedar Falls stocking grocery-store shelves.

Warner's attitude and ambition might have gone south at that point; instead, he grew in humility and redoubled his ambition to make it in football. It wasn't long before he found a niche in the Arena Football League, calling signals for the Iowa Barnstormers. It was fun, but no NFL scouts came calling. So Warner headed for Europe, where he played in Amsterdam. An outstanding season made the St. Louis Rams take notice, and he earned a contract backing up Trent Green for the Rams.

Green went down with a knee injury before the 1999 season, and Rams fans were in misery; all they had in reserve was a former grocery-store stocker. Surely the team would finish in last place. The rest, as they say, is history.

Warner set eight team records, won the NFL's Most Valuable Player award, and led the Rams to their first world championship as the Super Bowl MVP.

Warner climbed the mountain, but he still had not reached the top.

In 2001, Warner led the NFL in multiple categories on the way back to the Super Bowl, and he was league MVP for the second time in two years. *That* was the mountaintop. He had written his name across the NFL record book, as well as in the hearts of the fans.

But in 2002, Warner started down the other side of the mountain. A broken finger and broken hand cramped his style. His record for the first six starts: 0–6. Then came backup quarterback Marc Bulger, who went 6–0.

The 2003 season looked like a potential comeback year for Warner, but his disappointing performance in the opening game relegated him to the bench. Here came Bulger again, leading the Rams to a 12–4 record and the NFC West title.

A *Sports Illustrated* piece focused on Warner at the mountaintop. His game was unsurpassed, he won a Super Bowl, he was a talk-show staple, he nailed down the highest passing rating in NFL history, he wrote a book, and he enjoyed life immensely. Then he was sliding back down that steep slope toward obscurity.[1]

How would you have handled such a life?

In one game, when Bulger was struggling as a starter, the coach called for Warner. Here was his chance. But Warner advised the coach to give the kid a chance to fight through his problems. Bulger came back to win that game.

When asked in the locker room about supporting his competitor, Warner shrugged and said he wouldn't have liked to have been pulled, and he cited the golden rule. He treated Bulger as he himself would have wanted to be treated.

The mountaintop is our destination, but it is on the downward slopes that life takes its measure of us. Tom Selleck said, "Whenever I get full of myself, I remember that nice couple who approached me with a camera on a street in Honolulu one day. When I struck a pose for them, the man said, 'No, no. We want you to take a picture of us.'"

Humility puts us in our proper place; it strips away the coat of pride that collects on our surface as we travel through life's more successful moments.

Most of us are like former secretary of state Dean Acheson, a brilliant man who did not like being humbled in the presence of his boss, President Franklin D. Roosevelt. Acheson once bitterly complained to his friend, Clark Clifford, "Roosevelt made you feel like one of the peasants being called in by the lord of the castle."

Clifford related that conversation and added, "It was ironic that Acheson felt this way about Roosevelt, since so many people felt something similar when in the presence of Dean Acheson."[2]

The eighth chapter of Ecclesiastes defines humility in five ways: knowing how much you don't know, living with what you don't like, accepting what you can't change, enjoying what you can't explain, and discovering what you can't discover.

Humility Is Knowing How Much You Don't Know

Who is like a wise man?
And who knows the interpretation of a thing?
A man's wisdom makes his face shine,
And the sternness of his face is changed.

—ECCLESIASTES 8:1

Proverbs warns us consistently about being wise in our own eyes (Proverbs 3:7; 12:15; 26:5, 12; 28:11). The prophet Isaiah also writes, "Woe to those who are wise in their own eyes, and prudent in their own sight!" (Isaiah 5:21). Solomon, the author of both Proverbs and Ecclesiastes, speaks to the way true wisdom affects a man. A man who is truly wise is changed by the wisdom of God; even his countenance reflects his humility. He knows how much he doesn't know because he knows whom he does know. He has access to God's wisdom, and that is enough.

Paul wrote these words to the Corinthian believers: "And if anyone thinks that he knows anything, he knows nothing yet as he ought to know" (1 Corinthians 8:2). Researchers tell us that the world's knowledge base is replaced every thirty-eight years. More and more quickly, we upgrade or replace what we know, and any good scientist will tell you how often the scientific community has discovered that everything they thought they knew was wrong!

Solomon tells us that a wise man knows his own boundaries of knowledge. This kind of humility, he writes, makes a person's face shine and removes the harsh edges of sternness from his countenance. Perhaps you need to spend less time with cosmetics and more time making your face shine through God's wisdom. William L. Stridger said, "A person's face is the signature of his soul."

It was said about missionary Henry Martyn:

His features were not regular; but the expression was so luminous, so intellectual, so affectionate, so beaming with Divine charity, that no one could have looked at his features and thought of their shape or form—the outbeaming of his soul would absorb the attention of every observer.[3]

Just as Moses came down from the mountain with a shining face, you and I will glow with supernatural beauty from walking down the slope with the Master of our wisdom.

Humility Is Living with What You Don't Like

I say, "Keep the king's commandment for the sake of your oath to God. Do not be hasty to go from his presence. Do not take your stand for an evil thing, for he does whatever pleases him."

> Where the word of a king is, there is power;
> And who may say to him, "What are you doing?"
> He who keeps his command will experience nothing harmful;
> And a wise man's heart discerns both time and judgment,
> Because for every matter there is a time and judgment,
> Though the misery of man increases greatly.
> For he does not know what will happen;
> So who can tell him when it will occur?
> —ECCLESIASTES 8:2–7

What about our feeling of being out of control? In verses 2–7, Solomon uses the illustration of a king whose authority no one would dare question: "And who may say to him, 'What are you doing?'" (verse 4). Solomon has an answer for the person who is forced to live contrary to his desires: "Keep the king's commandment for the sake of your oath to God" (verse 2). Humility is knowing when to submit and obey, even in circumstances where you lack understanding.

We must submit to bosses we do not always respect. We must study textbooks whose assumptions we question. The church may make a decision or two that does not sit well with us. At what point do we quit the job or leave the church? It is hard to know; we feel humbled, and we move closer to God for guidance. There is much we cannot change and must simply trust to Him.

Humility Is Accepting What You Can't Change

Are you a control freak? Maybe you have been in a place where someone else was in control, and it drove you crazy. Or perhaps you lost your control of a work, health, or family situation. Some people are deserted by their spouses or have divorce forced upon them, and the prevailing sense is an outrage at having no control over something so personal and profound.

Impotent anger fills us when others control our lives. But in situations we cannot change, the only healthy response is humility. Though it may sound trite or ineffectual, we must leave it all to God, knowing He will care for us.

I read a very telling headline a few years ago: "Controlled Burn Goes Out of Control." It was about forestry experts whose carefully planned brush fires got away from them. Have you ever experienced that feeling of helplessness? In Ecclesiastes 8:8–14, Solomon suggests four categories we cannot control.

1. DEATH

No one has power over the spirit to retain the spirit,
And no one has power in the day of death.
There is no release from that war,
And wickedness will not deliver those who are given to it.
—ECCLESIASTES 8:8

The day of your death is out of your hands. Comedian Redd Foxx once said, "Health nuts are going to feel stupid someday, lying in hospitals dying of nothing." There are health-conscious people who work out daily, eat a disciplined diet, take their vitamins, and then suffer a heart attack while jogging. We can and should care for our bodies, but there is nothing we can do to be in total control. It is particularly difficult for those in our modern culture to grasp that there could be anything at all out of their control, even death. We are a country of control freaks. The whole message of our society is to be independent, to take control of everything, to be your own boss. But God did not design us that way.

During her lifetime, Queen Elizabeth I was considered the most powerful woman on earth. But as she was dying, she said, "Oh my God! It is over. I have come to the end of it—the end, the end. To have only one life, and to have done with it! To have lived, and loved, and triumphed; and now to know it is over! One may defy everything else but this."[4]

We have to accept this. Perhaps you have lost loved ones recently, and you have mourned deeply. But after a period of mourning, we have to go on with our lives; for Solomon told us that true humility is realizing that "no one has power over the spirit to retain the spirit, and no one has power in the day of death." For Christians, of course, that's not such a bad thing after all, for to die is gain; it is better by far (Philippians 1:21, 23).

2. DISTRESS

All this I have seen, and applied my heart to every work that is done under the sun: There is a time in which one man rules over another to his own hurt.

—ECCLESIASTES 8:9

Solomon says that everyone under the sun gets hurt. That's life. But it is hard to accept the pain that is imposed on us. We want to do something, whether strike back, hurt someone "smaller," or simply sit around and feel sorry for ourselves. We cannot live in a world filled with people without some of them stepping on our feet.

As we think of all the things that worry us, we must ask, "Which of these things can I change?" If you can change some of them, do so; but if you cannot, accept them, trust God with them, and do not let them ruin your life. Jesus said, "Which of you by worrying can add one cubit to his stature?" (Matthew 6:27).

Ruth Bell Graham wrote extensively along these lines. After her two sons had spent a frightening season in the "far country," she wrote a book for worried parents. In *Prodigals and Those Who Love Them*, Ruth writes:

> We mothers must take care of the possible and trust God for the impossible. We are to love, affirm, encourage, teach, listen, and care for the physical needs of the family.
>
> We cannot convict of sin, create hunger and thirst after God, or convert. These are miracles, and miracles are not in our department.[5]

That is a good rule for all of life. We must trust God with what we cannot control. That includes those who want to hurt or distress us—along with all the other unavoidable, unalterable troubles of life.

3. DECEPTION

> Then I saw the wicked buried, who had come and gone from the place of holiness, and they were forgotten in the city where they had so done. This also is vanity.
>
> —ECCLESIASTES 8:10

Warren Wiersbe paints this picture:

> In verse 10, Solomon reports on a funeral he had attended. The deceased was a man who had frequented the temple ("the place of the holy") and had received much praise from the people, but he had not lived a godly life. Yet he was given a magnificent funeral, and an eloquent eulogy, while the truly godly people of the city were ignored and forgotten.[6]

Oh, how we see the same phenomenon. Television shows us a godless celebrity whose death is mourned by the entire world. A successful millionaire is ushered to his grave with great fanfare. But the simple, humble, godly man or woman isn't even afforded an inch on the obituary page. The memory of all their deeds of love and kindness appears to be swiftly forgotten, blown away like the particles of the wind.

This is one more item on which God does not ask our advice. It just happens, fair or not. We reflect that if we were in control, we would make things fair—but to be sure, we would make a huge mess in trying. God has a perfect plan, and if people get more praise than they deserve, let them, for it is little enough reward in the big picture, and they still have to stand before God. If you see someone receiving too little praise, take the initiative and call a celebration. But know that this one, too, will stand before God and receive his or her crown of glory.

4. DEFIANCE

> Because the sentence against an evil work is not executed speedily, therefore the heart of the sons of men is fully set in them to do evil. Though a sinner does evil a hundred times, and his days are prolonged, yet I surely know that

it will be well with those who fear God, who fear before Him. But it will not be well with the wicked; nor will he prolong his days, which are as a shadow, because he does not fear before God.

There is a vanity which occurs on earth, that there are just men to whom it happens according to the work of the wicked; again, there are wicked men to whom it happens according to the work of the righteous. I said that this also is vanity.

—ECCLESIASTES 8:11–14

In his book *Can Man Live Without God?* Ravi Zacharias relates a conversation he had with British journalist Malcolm Muggeridge. Svetlana Stalin, daughter of the evil Soviet dictator Josef Stalin, spent some time in the Muggeridge home. According to Svetlana, as Stalin lay dying, plagued with terrifying hallucinations, he suddenly sat halfway up in bed, clenched his fist toward heaven, and fell back on his pillow, dead.[7]

Defiance! Would you shake your fist at God? Many do so, even if figuratively. "I've done it my way," they boast. "Nothing's happened to me yet, and nothing is going to happen to me. I am the master of my soul, the captain of my fate, and the lord of my life." We live in a generation that wants to go its own way, thinking it knows better than the ancient wisdom of God and His people. We think money, popularity, pleasure, and many of Solomon's "vanities" have suddenly become wise choices.

But the Bible says, "For what profit is it to a man if he gains the whole world, and loses his own soul? Or what will a man give in exchange for his soul? For the Son of Man will come in the glory of His Father with His angels, and then He will reward each according to his works" (Matthew 16:26–27).

When we don't see God sending the lightning rod upon the

neighborhood hedonist, we assume He is asleep at the wheel. He is not. There will be a reckoning for all who have strayed between the cradle and the crypt.

Humility Is Enjoying What You Can't Explain

So I commended enjoyment, because a man has nothing
better under the sun than to eat, drink, and be merry; for
this will remain with him in his labor all the days of his life
which God gives him under the sun.
—Ecclesiastes 8:15

My great surprise in Ecclesiastes is the number of times Solomon tells us to enjoy life. He reminds us that we can't control death, distress, defiance, and deception—and then he tells us to go out and have a good time?

Yes, that is exactly the point! If you can accept that which is unacceptable—not be ignorant of it but know it and acknowledge it and simply trust everything to God—you will not be ruled by misery or anxiety. You will have the power to enjoy life.

This life is difficult but abundant. Goodness and mercy will follow us all our days, but often we will be walking through the valley of the shadow of death when they follow us. The secret of life, the power of finding happiness, is embracing heaven while accepting earth. We change what we can, we accept what we cannot, and we walk on with the joy of God's companionship. Yes, that job is difficult—but God is with each of us, teaching humility and competence and patience. Yes, that marriage has been on the rocks—but God is teaching us so much about Himself as it heals and strengthens in His grace.

Every mountain has an uphill and a downhill, and they are the same. It depends upon which way you are facing.

Humility Is Discovering What You Can't Discover

When I applied my heart to know wisdom and to see the business that is done on earth, even though one sees no sleep day or night, then I saw all the work of God, that a man cannot find out the work that is done under the sun. For though a man labors to discover it, yet he will not find it; moreover, though a wise man attempts to know it, he will not be able to find it.

—ECCLESIASTES 8:16–17

We upgrade our knowledge base every year, yet there is so much we will never discover. The pursuit for knowledge will never reach its goal. French philosopher Blaise Pascal wrote this in his famous *Pensées* (#446):

If there were no obscurity man would not feel his corruption; if there were no light man could not hope for a cure. Thus it is not only right but useful for us that God should be partly concealed and partly revealed, since it is equally dangerous for man to know God without knowing his own wretchedness as to know his wretchedness without knowing God.[8]

God did not forget to tell us anything important. There are things too great for our comprehension and others too dangerous for our grasp. Perhaps we will discover the cure for cancer. Perhaps we will invent a spaceship capable of taking us to other galaxies. But we will only ever know what God permits us to know. As the guardian of all knowledge, He holds every secret. Our response is to bow in humility, then to look up toward the peak of the mountain and get on with the journey.

24

Dropping the "D" Word

Ecclesiastes 9:1–10

The gambler did everything with style—and I mean everything. One day, with all his friends gathered around, he sat at the steering wheel of a brand-new, custom-equipped Cadillac Seville, loaded with luxuries. He wore a hot pink suit and had five hundred-dollar bills clutched between his thumb and forefinger. He looked so natural—almost alive.

Yes, he happened to be embalmed at that time. He was ready to be lowered into the ground, buried in the manner of his choosing. He appeared ready to cruise to the pearly gates on brand-new wheels. (That may have been his biggest gamble!)

A friend walked around the car, studying the silver spokes, the vanity plate, and all the other fine custom details. "Man," he whispered. "That's *living*!"

Funerals come in many flavors. The possibilities are nearly endless if you have enough money to spend. There is only one requirement: all the living must be over.

Death is one of those subjects we do not like to discuss. That is why it is the subject of so many euphemisms. Instead of using the word *dead*, we say, "passed away," "gone to a better place," "sleeping in Jesus," "returned home," or "went to be with the Lord." At least, we use those terms around the sanctuary and the funeral home. In less guarded moments, the same people speak of "kicking the bucket," "buying the farm," "cashing in chips," "biting the dust," or the ever-popular "croaked."

Whether we lean to the reverent right or the flippant left, we shy away from speaking directly of the ultimate enemy.

In his poem "Churchyards," Sir John Betjeman, the late poet laureate of England, wrote,

> Oh, why do people waste their breath
> Inventing dainty names for death?[1]

Solomon was facing his own mortality when he wrote the book of Ecclesiastes during his final years. He tackled the subject head-on, discussing its reality and our responses.

The Reality of Death

For I considered all this in my heart, so that I could declare it all: that the righteous and the wise and their works are in the hand of God. People know neither love nor hatred by anything they see before them. All things come alike to all:

> One event happens to the righteous and the wicked;
> To the good, the clean, and the unclean;
> To him who sacrifices and him who does not sacrifice.

As is the good, so is the sinner;
He who takes an oath as he who fears an oath.

—ECCLESIASTES 9:1–2

On February 1, 2003, the space shuttle *Columbia* broke up over Texas just minutes before its scheduled landing in Florida. What a terrible moment in our collective memory. The seven-member crew was returning home after a successful sixteen-day mission. The burning capsule streaked across the sky of the southern United States, dropping flaming debris and burning reminders of the suddenness of death. We wondered silently, *What would it be like to take that final ride, knowing the end was imminent?*

But for all of us who ride on spaceship Earth, the end is imminent. Every human being lives out a death sentence—the important matter is what we do with the *lives out* part of that phrase. Nineteenth-century Anglican bishop J. C. Ryle wrote,

> Death is the mighty leveler. He spares no one. He will not tarry till you are ready. He will not be kept out by moats, and doors, and bars, and bolts. The Englishman boasts that his home is his castle, but with all his boasting, he cannot exclude death. An Austrian nobleman forbade death and the smallpox to be named in his presence. But, named or not named, it matters little, in God's appointed hour death will come.[2]

You've played the board game Monopoly. You buy railroads and place hotels on Park Place and Boardwalk. You pass "Go" and collect two hundred dollars. Everyone has fun. Then the game ends, and all the hotels, all the colorful tokens, and all the funny money go back into the box. Solomon, who held an empire much less plastic, would tell us that whether you build in plastic or gold, it is all the same. Build a temple, extend a dynasty, even write three God-inspired books—in the end, it all goes back in the box.

Even the righteous and the wicked, Solomon tells us, are cemetery neighbors. Many things set them apart and determine their eternal standing—but in the end, they all die. As Hebrews 9:27 puts it, "It is appointed for men to die once, but after this the judgment." When relatives are on their way, you prepare a room. Death is the cousin everyone shares and no one has met; we only know he will get around to see every relative sooner or later. Are you squirming yet? Stay with me—it's not morbid to discuss what is so inevitable, so universal, and so profoundly important to the soul.

The late pastor Ray Stedman wrote,

> I have noticed that some people . . . are very uncomfortable at funerals. They are nervous and edgy; they want to get it over quickly and get back to their local bar, their comfortable living room, or whatever. In observing that phenomenon, I have asked myself what it is about funerals that makes them so nervous. The answer I came to is that a funeral is one event where one can no longer escape ultimate reality. A funeral is proof that we are not in control of our own lives. . . . This is what makes people uncomfortable and anxious to get back to the comfortable illusions of life.[3]

The Responses to Death

Even as a young seminary student, I dealt daily with death as a hospital chaplain. As I watched the family members and friends of the deceased, I saw some fall into absolute despair. Others grieved, but not as those having no hope.

In *None of These Diseases* Dr. David E. Stern relates some of his experiences as a medical doctor who dealt with dying patients. He told of Matt, who wouldn't see a pastor and even discarded his room's Gideon Bible. In his case there was no physical pain, but he suddenly sat up in bed, eyes blazing, and screamed, "No! No!" Then he expired. His wife suffered grief-driven trauma for many months.

Yet that same week Dr. Stern also sat with a woman dying of breast cancer. In her case there was terrible physical pain, but she passed away whispering to her husband, "I love you, John. See you soon." He kissed her cheek as the pastor read the words of Psalm 23, and one could almost feel the presence of angels coming to bear away a heavenly traveler.

The good doctor never forgot the contrast of the two rooms: "One, a terrified man dropping into the unknown. The other, a restful soul passing through heaven's gate."[4]

How, then, shall we face death?

Don't Deny It

This is an evil in all that is done under the sun: that one thing happens to all. Truly the hearts of the sons of men are full of evil; madness is in their hearts while they live, and after that they go to the dead.

—Ecclesiastes 9:3

I have always liked the legend of the merchant in Baghdad who sent his servant to the market. When the servant returned he was as white as a sheet, trembling all over. He told his master, "When I was at the market I was bumped by someone in the crowd. When I turned around, I saw it was Death who jostled me and made a threatening gesture toward me. Master, please, lend me your horse so I may flee to Samarra and hide where Death cannot find me."

The merchant lent him his horse, and the servant galloped off in great haste. Later that day, the merchant himself was at the market and saw Death standing in the crowd. He approached her and asked, "Why did you threaten my servant this morning?"

"I did not threaten him," Death replied. "I was only surprised to see him in the market in Baghdad, for I have an appointment tonight to see him in Samarra."[5]

We can run from death, but we cannot hide from it. "It is appointed for men to die once, but after this the judgment" (Hebrews 9:27). David, the psalmist, wrote that our days were written in God's book before we were even born (Psalm 139:16).

As a young pastor in Fort Wayne, Indiana, I was asked to conduct the funeral of someone I'd never met. I was told only that he had been a godly individual. As I was returning to my car after the service, a young woman came running across the parking lot toward me, screaming at the top of her lungs. She cursed me in words I'd not heard in a long time. She was furious that I had mentioned her sister's name in the service without mentioning hers as well.

The family was unfamiliar to me, and I had not purposefully omitted her name. But there was her dad, lying in a casket, and she turned her wrath to something smaller, more trivial, more manageable to the emotions. It was her way of denying death and deflecting the intensity of what was inside her. Unprepared to grieve, she vented toward me.

Don't Ignore It

But for him who is joined to all the living there is hope, for a living dog is better than a dead lion.

For the living know that they will die;

> But the dead know nothing,
> And they have no more reward,
> For the memory of them is forgotten.
> Also their love, their hatred, and their envy have now perished;
> Nevermore will they have a share
> In anything done under the sun.
>
> —ECCLESIASTES 9:4–6

Unbelievers live sad half-lives. In a sense, they are already dead. There is no reward, no motivation, no future, no genuine love or even hate. When the end comes, they finish their time under the sun and face only a darkness. Believers, however, can live now in the fullest sense. We can do good things, enjoy life, and embrace hope under the sun.

When Ted Koppel interviewed David Letterman about his heart bypass surgery, Koppel asked, "Do you think about death a lot? I mean, is death something that bothers you?"

Here is Letterman's response:

No, no. I mean, always before, I knew I was going to drop dead of a heart attack. I just knew it. You know, I've seen it in my family. I had the genetic tendency. My cholesterol—it didn't make any difference what I was doing—was always sky high. I could eat pocket lint, and it would be 800. But after the surgery, no, I don't think about it anymore.[6]

Letterman seems to think that since he has had heart surgery, he isn't going to die. At least, not soon. So he isn't going to think about it. With his heart repaired, he thinks he can ignore death.

But who knows?

Have you heard the phrase, "Where there's life there's hope?" It comes from Ecclesiastes 9:4: "But for him who is joined to all the living there is hope." Solomon said that it's better to be a living dog (a despised animal in biblical times) than a dead lion (the king of the jungle).

Solomon was warning us that we cannot successfully deal with death by whistling past the graveyard. It is not enough to shrug and say, "Hey, I'm still standing. As long as there's life there's hope."

Hope is only valid when it is reality based—and our hope is based on the ultimate reality. We are citizens of heaven, ambassadors from a better country whose joys make the pale pleasures of earth look sad indeed. We can, therefore, keep heaven on earth—in our hearts.

Life, As If!

Solomon's message is, if you like ice cream, have a second helping while you can. If you enjoy travel, see the world as soon as possible. You know the number of minutes in an hour and the number of hours in a day, but you do not know the number of days in a lifetime. There could be seven more or seven thousand.

Solomon does *not* say, "Eat, drink, and be merry for we're going to die." But he does give some advice for life.

1. Eat Every Meal As If at a Banquet

> Go, eat your bread with joy,
> And drink your wine with a merry heart;
> For God has already accepted your works.
> —Ecclesiastes 9:7

We are surprised to see how many verses in the Bible tell us to simply enjoy our meals. In the Jewish culture the meal was a very important time. In Solomon's day the evening meal occurred after a grueling day of work. It was a time of joy. Today we rarely eat a meal together. We share a meal with the television or eat on the run as we drive. We have lost the ancient art and pleasure of a shared meal.

Most cultures have recognized something sacred in the idea of a meal shared in fellowship. In warring cultures peace is often made when the chieftains sit down and eat together. Food is strength, and while we have the strength to live on this earth, we celebrate the gardens and pastures and rivers, seas, and skies all filled with good things to eat, furnished by our Lord for our enjoyment.

2. Celebrate Every Day As If at a Party

> Let your garments always be white,
> And let your head lack no oil.
>
> —Ecclesiastes 9:8

Births, weddings, and harvest festivals were special occasions in Solomon's day. He tells us to dress every day as if we are on the way to a celebration of life.

Paul joins the chorus: "Rejoice in the Lord always. Again I will say, rejoice!" (Philippians 4:4). And "rejoice always" (1 Thessalonians 5:16).

Some would say, "What do I have to rejoice about? I could die anytime."

Exactly! That is a great reason to let every waking moment be a celebration of God's gift of life. Get dressed. Eat out with a friend. Why? You can! And God enjoys your enjoyment.

3. Enjoy Marriage As If on Your Honeymoon

> Live joyfully with the wife whom you love all the days of
> your vain life which He has given you under the sun, all your

days of vanity; for that is your portion in life, and in the
labor which you perform under the sun.

—ECCLESIASTES 9:9

Solomon had many honeys and many honeymoons—to the
debasement of his kingdom. He treated himself to hundreds of wives
and concubines. Now, at the end of his life, he wishes he had lavished
all his love on the wife of his youth. A man who had hundreds of
wives now speaks in the singular rather than the plural. One partner,
one heart.

Your husband or wife should be looked upon as a treasure from
heaven, prepared for your joy, to serve and to be served. There are
moments of irritation and seasons of discontent, but remember those
are days and seasons we have but once. Why not let each day be as
joyful as your honeymoon? Marital fulfillment is a choice, so choose
to live and love joyfully.

4. WORK AS IF IT WERE YOUR FINAL WORKDAY

Whatever your hand finds to do, do it with your might; for
there is no work or device or knowledge or wisdom in the
grave where you are going.

—ECCLESIASTES 9:10

I've read that a man or woman of fifty, having worked consistently since school, will have put in fifty-six thousand hours of work.
Imagine, if you will, fifty-six thousand hours of boredom and resentment. Who would come through such an ordeal with a sound mind?
Yet a poor attitude toward one's job creates that environment.

Now imagine someone rising in the morning to say, "Thank
You, Lord! Another day to use the gifts and the strength and the

mind You have given me—to apply them to fruitful enterprise. What a gift You have given me, that I may work and serve." That mind-set will add years to your life and life to your years. It will also bring you success, promotions, and glory for God.

Note the change in the worldview of prize-winning Irish poet Evangeline Paterson: "I was brought up in a Christian environment where, because God had to be given preeminence, nothing else was allowed to be important. I have broken through to the position that because God exists, everything is important."[7]

Work, therefore, as if today were your final workday, for it may be; work as if God is inspecting your work, for He is. "For he will not dwell unduly on the days of his life, because God keeps him busy with the joy of his heart" (Ecclesiastes 5:20).

Why worry about the span of your life? I would rather be like Solomon and stay busy with the joy of my heart. Once again, this is heaven on earth, paradise in our hands, delivery from dread and drudgery—for this is the day the Lord has made, and we can rejoice and be glad in it.

25

Life Cheats!

Ecclesiastes 9:11–18

E cclesiastes 9 covers the ground of life and death—a pretty nice
section of intellectual acreage to plow in one chapter. Solomon's
short answer would read something like this: "Death plays to
win; life plays unfairly."

The long answer? Well, you have to read the chapter. We already
have moved through the first ten verses, and we have seen how death
wins. It comes for the just and the unjust, the rich and the poor, the
child and the ancient.

But *life*? Now things get complicated.

The Best Man Isn't Always Rewarded

I returned and saw under the sun that—

> The race is not to the swift,
> Nor the battle to the strong,

Nor bread to the wise,
Nor riches to men of understanding,
Nor favor to men of skill;
But time and chance happen to them all.
For man also does not know his time:
Like fish taken in a cruel net,
Like birds caught in a snare,
So the sons of men are snared in an evil time,
When it falls suddenly upon them.

—ECCLESIASTES 9:11–12

Life is unfair. Being the best is not the same as winning the contest.

Olympic swimmer Ian Thorpe knows it is true. Widely hailed as the world's fastest swimmer, Thorpe was expected to be the 2004 Olympic champion in the 400-meter freestyle, his best event. Then at the trials in Sydney, he was getting into starting position just before the race when a terrible thing happened: he tumbled off the blocks into the pool.

Thorpe was disqualified. That's the way it works; the rules are written very clearly. The distraught swimmer appealed his case, but a referee and a three-person competition jury refused the hearing. Ian Thorpe, Australia's certain gold medal winner, wouldn't even be in the water for his best event. An uproar ensued, and Australians were furious with the judges. No one likes cruel technicalities, but rules are rules.

Ian Thorpe, the world's fastest swimmer, calmed his nation by saying, "It hurts if you let it but after the initial disappointment, you have to get over it. I've accepted that I won't swim it. I think now everyone else has to accept that as well."[1]

The young man had more wisdom in his grasp than he knew. It

is not a matter of *luck* or *fortune*, whatever dubious providential philosophy those terms may signify.

We have seen this particular little drama played out many times before. A young athlete spends a lifetime preparing for this golden moment in time. The athlete makes every sacrifice imaginable, sacrificing a normal life and many of the joys of a more ordinary childhood and adolescence for this one chance to be the best in the world.

Then something happens: a twisted ankle, an inopportune tumble, even a political crisis such as the United States pulling out of the Olympics in 1980—and the former Soviet Union doing the same in 1984.

Just like that, our stomachs turn upside down as we see the tears of some young man or woman who has given up so much to come away with so little—other than one more lesson in the proposition that *life isn't fair*. The race isn't always to the swift.

But this doesn't sit well with us. Things are *supposed* to be fair, aren't they? Everyone would agree that life—and the people in it—should play by the rules. As C. S. Lewis points out in *Mere Christianity*, every human being appeals to a common law of fair play: "That's my seat—I was there first," or "Give me a bite of that orange; I gave you a bite of mine." Fairness is a kind of natural instinct we carry inside. Lewis shows that no one ever questions that standard of basic fairness; it seems to be implanted within us at birth.

Why? Animals do not live by standards of fairness and justice. Earthquakes and bolts of lightning certainly are impartial when they pick their victims. But regardless of 100 percent of our history and personal experience, we humans cannot get beyond this idea of the way things are *supposed* to run.

Why do we have that idea? Why are we so transfixed by the book of Job, in which the worst happens to the best? It is so because we have our Father's eyes. We are made in the image of a God of justice, created for a heaven of pure rightness. As Solomon has already told us, we have eternity stamped upon our hearts. We are made for heaven, where life is fair; but we must settle for earth, where life deals from the bottom of the deck.

Solomon expands on this idea to tell us that hardly anything on this upside-down planet comes out the way it seems it should. This is why the race isn't to the swift. Who was the toughest? Goliath, but he was defeated by a flimsy shepherd. Who was the wisest? Solomon, who was brought down by the foolishness of love. Who was the most handsome? Absalom, who was brought down by ugly behavior. And oddly enough, who was the man after God's own heart? It was the covetous, lying, murdering adulterer David. Life is complicated; so is godliness.

When our youngest son, Daniel, played college football, he competed for starting quarterback. Even allowing for a proud dad's bias, I will say that nearly everyone thought my son had won the job. Daniel had worked hard during the off-season, hustled during spring practice and fall camp, and had done all that he could to ensure the job. All the same, it went to someone else.

That disappointment was hard on Daniel; it may have been even harder on that proud dad. But my son and I talked about the fact that here it was, case in point: life isn't fair. The race isn't always to the swift, nor the quarterback position to the best arm. "Learn it now when you're young," I told him, "lest you learn it much more painfully down the road."

As we have seen over and over again, this is an amazing book before us. Solomon gives us every reason under the sun to be gloomy. He tells us that death always wins, and life always cheats. He tells us that the best effort we can put forth guarantees exactly nothing. Then, as always, he tells us to be joyful.

Solomon's message is not to candy-coat life but to tell us that life does not need candy-coating. Life is unfair, and death is unstoppable, but we have what we have, and it happens to be this day before us—a gift from God, filled with pleasures, beauty, the satisfying enterprise of work, and the precious presence of God overseeing it all.

Life is smelly, noisy, cruel, and uncaring. How much more glorious is the God who can be seen through the darkness, felt in the cold, and embraced in the valley of the shadow of death! He triumphs over the gloomiest observations you or Solomon could dish out. How shall we then live? Joyfully!

The Good Man Isn't Always Remembered

This wisdom I have also seen under the sun, and it seemed great to me: There was a little city with few men in it; and a great king came against it, besieged it, and built great snares around it. Now there was found in it a poor wise man, and he by his wisdom delivered the city. Yet no one remembered that same poor man.

Then I said:

"Wisdom is better than strength.
Nevertheless the poor man's wisdom is despised,
And his words are not heard.
Words of the wise, spoken quietly, should be heard
Rather than the shout of a ruler of fools.
Wisdom is better than weapons of war;
But one sinner destroys much good."

—Ecclesiastes 9:13–18

Another paradox: wise words are often ignored even as foolishness is given the blue ribbon. Solomon shares a little parable—almost a fairy tale—to make his point.

Once upon a time, he tells us, a great army was smashing its way through the countryside. It found in its path a small, unassuming town. The town wasn't even worth taking a detour around; burning through it would be child's play. The general surrounded the town, placed it under siege, deployed all his heavy artillery, and sent in his messenger to demand surrender and the spoils of war.

The terrified little village was in need of a few good men, but this was a single-stoplight-and-convenience-store kind of town. There wasn't any army, but there was a single pauper who rose to the occasion. Yes, he was just a beggar by the street side, someone everyone had seen and no one had noticed. But he had some spark of hidden genius just waiting for its special moment. The pauper showed up in the war room with an outside-the-box idea that saved the day. What that idea was is a story for another day. Suffice it to say that his clever stroke ended the siege and relegated the attackers to Plan B, the detour.

Now Solomon asks, wouldn't you expect that little man to have a few books written about him? A few songs sung in his honor? You would think the town would place his statue out in front of City Hall and he would never go hungry again.

But, somehow, in the midst of the weeklong celebration, all the medals are handed out to the clueless characters who carried out the plan while the pauper is overlooked. Next week he is back on the sidewalk, begging for bread as the "heroes" walk by, followed by worshipful girls. They don't even stop to throw a nickel in his cup.

Life is unfair, and people have short memories. The people who do the most heavy lifting on church committees get the least credit. We say we have no heroes, but we have a million unsung ones like the little man in the town. In the end we do not value wisdom very highly. We do not appreciate the people who deserve the credit. We all have experienced this painful truth.

But Solomon says, "Get used to it. Life takes what you have to give, forgets all about you, and moves on." You may try to have a biblical perspective on death by being realistic and responding to it by focusing on life—and then life sticks it to you.

So what is the solution? What are we supposed to do, given the unfairness of life? The secret is to remember that this life is just a preparation for the real life that is to come. We are foolish if we think we will ever find heaven on earth.

Remember what Jesus told His disciples on the eve of the most unfair several days in the history of the world:

> Let not your heart be troubled; you believe in God, believe also in Me. In My Father's house are many mansions; if it were not so, I would have told you. I go to prepare a place for you. And if I go and prepare a place for you, I will come again and receive you to Myself; that where I am, there you may be also. (John 14:1–3)

Jesus' Crucifixion—the Ultimate Unfairness

The unfairness of life reached its wretched culmination in the life of Jesus Christ. Here was a man who never hurt anyone, went about doing good, was gentle and humble, and had every reason to be received and accepted for what He was trying to accomplish; a man who is today considered the centerpiece of human history, more influential than all the governments and armies that have tried to hold sway over mankind. Yet Jesus and His disciples after Him were attacked and treated as criminals. Jesus was beaten, scourged, crucified, and killed after a mockery of a trial on trumped-up charges. And each of His disciples was put to death in a similarly unjust way, except John, who died of natural causes while in exile at Patmos.

Jesus understood the unfairness of life. On the night before His arrest, He told His disciples not to put their hope or trust in this world. Though we may keep seeking heaven on earth, our true home is with Him, and He will return for us and take us there someday.

The unfairness of this world, along with death itself, will be swallowed up in the great victory of Jesus Christ over death and this world (1 Corinthians 15:54). And when we know that, when we claim the victory that we cannot see with our eyes but can feel with our hearts, then we can do something remarkable and unexpected and wonderful—something therefore miraculous. We can create those heaven-on-earth moments that occur when, against all odds, people let themselves become channels for the searing, white-hot grace and love of God in a world cold and darkened by evil. In those grace moments we reveal our true birthright as creatures of another world, a world where life is infinitely better than simply "fair."

We can be like Elisabeth Elliot and Steve Saint, two family members left behind by martyred missionaries. Jim Elliot, Nate Saint, and four other men committed their very lives to bringing the gospel to the Auca Indians of Ecuador—and they gave their lives in so doing. They would fly in food, gifts, and supplies to their primitive friends, preparing to tell the news of the much greater gift that is Jesus.

But on January 8, 1956, as the missionaries landed their plane, they were unaccountably met by rage rather than friendly welcome. The spears of the Aucas killed every one of them.

The widows and orphans of the martyred men grieved for a time. For decades no one understood why the attack had happened. I am certain it crossed the families' minds more than once that not only is life unfair, but it is savagely and viciously cruel to those who are the least deserving.

Yet they also knew that Jesus said, "Blessed are you when they revile and persecute you, and say all kinds of evil against you falsely for My sake. Rejoice and be exceedingly glad, for great is your reward in heaven, for so they persecuted the prophets who were before you" (Matthew 5:11–12).

After a time the widows went to the jungle to finish the job their husbands had begun. They worked patiently among the Aucas until a great many of them became followers of Jesus Christ. Their message: death always wins; life plays unfairly; *love conquers all.*

Years later, Steve Saint came across a few Aucas (now known as Huaorani) who had been present at the massacre by the stream in 1956. All his life he had wondered what that horrible moment was like. How did his father greet death? Why did this senseless mass murder happen? Now he would find some answers.

The story of the tragedy unfolded from the accounts of Indians who had been eyewitnesses. One man in the tribe had committed some sexual misdeed. His life was on the line, so to divert the anger of the people, he said all manner of evil against the missionaries. He claimed that the six white men were planning to eat the Aucas. This was why the ambush occurred. But there was more to the story.

Dawa, a young woman, hid in the brush during the tragedy. From the bushes by the pool of water where the men died, she heard the whole event. But as the men were killed, she and others who were present heard an odd kind of music peculiar to their ears. They looked up and saw *cowodi* (foreign visitors) singing above the treetops in flashes of bright color.

Only later, when Dawa heard choral music on phonograph records for the first time, did she identify the treetop music as being very similar to what was on the record.[2]

Could it be that angels ushered the martyrs to the reward that awaited them? The story is compelling, but there is no way for us to know for sure. We can only be certain that heaven is very close during such moments. When God's heartbreaking goodness intersects with human barbarity, the lights of heaven break through the trees.

For just a moment, the intense darkness flees in the presence of that eternal light. All the unfairness and injustice is momentarily forgotten in the face of the obvious truth that our God is near, He is in control, and He will make all things right.

Then we can shrug away the insistence of death and the injustice of life and stand to sing a chorus with yet another missionary. Amy Carmichael, Christ's servant in India, prayed she might bring the light of heaven to the earth—the greatest goal life offers us, the ultimate joy, the Rosetta stone that deciphers every one of life's imponderables.

Here is Amy's prayer:

> Before the winds that blow do cease,
> Teach me to dwell within Thy calm;
> Before the pain has passed in peace,
> Give me, my God, to sing a psalm.
> Let me not lose the chance to prove
> The fullness of enabling love,
> *O Love of God, do this for me:*
> *Maintain a constant victory.*
>
> Before I leave the desert land
> For meadows of immortal flowers,
> Lead me where streams at Thy command
> Flow by the borders of the hours,
> That when the thirsty come, I may
> Show them the fountains in the way.
> *O Love of God, do this for me:*
> *Maintain a constant victory.*[3]

26

Foolishness in Little Things

Ecclesiastes 10:1–3

Life rolls along. It's another slow news day, and we each grind through our own daily rituals—work, eat, sleep, play—with reassuring predictability. We nod and smile at familiar faces on the street. We see neighbors at the grocery store and pause for a moment of superficial chatter. The world turns one more revolution, the sun retreats, the moon rises, and all is calm on the western front.

Then, abruptly, something jars us awake from the trance of regularity. News of a terrorist attack, a misfortune in some relative's life, a scandal at church, a lost job, a broken leg, a tearful child. That's when we find out about people.

Exhibit A: a series of devastating California wildfires that broke out in our community. Residents responded in a variety of ways, all revealing. Here I was, typing away, immersed in the ancient wisdom of Solomon—and just like that, his observations are played out before me in the reactions of the community.

Two dozen people tragically lost their lives. Many of our friends lost their homes. The flames spread faster than people could flee.

Many folks complained about lack of warning. Sgt. Conrad Grayson commented, "We're begging people to leave, and they don't take us seriously. They want to pack some clothes, or fight it in the backyard with a garden hose. They don't seem to understand that this is unlike any fire we've seen. If people don't move fast, they're going to become charcoal briquettes."

Jon Smalldridge sounded the alarm like Paul Revere, only to be received like Chicken Little. People either ignored him or took things casually—you know, the California way. They spent time unhooking their home theater systems, computers, and other equipment as the fires raged ever closer. "They looked like they were packing for a trip," said Smalldridge. "The ones who listened to me and left the area, lived. The ones who didn't, died."[1]

A fool is traditionally a comic figure, but foolishness can be as serious as wildfire.

Wisdom and Folly

> Dead flies putrefy the perfumer's ointment,
> And cause it to give off a foul odor;
> So does a little folly to one respected for wisdom and honor.
> A wise man's heart is at his right hand,
> But a fool's heart at his left.
> Even when a fool walks along the way,
> He lacks wisdom,
> And he shows everyone that he is a fool.
>
> —ECCLESIASTES 10:1–3

Solomon spent a lifetime dealing in wisdom—accepting it, nurturing it, exercising it, brooding upon it, and eventually betraying it. Wisdom was the one shining gift he asked of God, when any gift in the world could have been his. Solomon knew that God's wisdom was his in a way that no other man or woman would ever be able to claim. He wrote a section of the Bible—Proverbs, Song of Solomon, and Ecclesiastes—that we refer to now as the Books of Wisdom. So this king had a keen eye for the wise stroke, and therefore the foolish joke as well.

If wisdom is your highest reference point, then you see foolishness as the bane of existence. Solomon saw it everywhere, and it galled him. In his three books he uses the words *fool*, *fools*, *foolish*, and *folly* a staggering total of 128 times. In Ecclesiastes 10, he uses these words nine times. The word *fool* occurs in verses 2, 3, 12, 13, 14, and 15.

A sharp dividing line is drawn between the ways of the wise and the follies of the foolish. Not surprisingly, criminals often turn up on the wrong side of that line. The often hilarious misdeeds of the world's most inept crooks have been documented in books and on websites. We find that, unlike the suave, ingenious criminal masterminds of the movies, real-life hoodlums are often little more than common fools. And for the chronically inept, a life of crime can be highly stressful.

Rafiq Abdul Mortland simply was not cut out for a life of crime. The thirty-eight-year-old found that robbery made him a nervous wreck. Mortland committed a string of robberies in Hennepin County, Minnesota. Eventually he was taken into custody and received a sentence of eight to ten years in prison for holding up eight local businesses.

Mortland was known in law enforcement as "The Rolaids Robber." Apparently his signature calling card was demanding antacid tablets from store clerks while the crimes were in progress. He explained that the job was too stressful; robbery gave him a bad case of indigestion.[2]

It is true, of course. Crime and foolishness are known causes of both heartburn and heartache. Wisdom, on the other hand, is healthy, has no ill side effects, and is recommended by 100 percent of doctors. Solomon knows there is more than a dividing line between wisdom and folly—there is a canyon. He warns us to stay away from the edge. He seeks to provide us with mile markers and signposts that help us stay on the safe side of life. Ecclesiastes 10, like a lost chapter of Proverbs, dispenses short nuggets of wisdom to keep us on the wise side. He warns us about foolishness in four prominent areas of life: in little things, in leadership, in labor, and in language.

A Fly in the Ointment

To illustrate his point that little things can create big problems, Solomon uses a rather unusual illustration about perfume. The wealthy king had access to the rarest and costliest perfumes of his day. In Proverbs 7:17, he speaks of the seductive power of perfume in the arsenal of the prostitute. In Proverbs 27:9, he notes the legitimate power of perfume and ointment to delight the heart. Twice in Song of Solomon, he mentions perfume's power to enhance a married couple's relationship. But without question, his strangest reference to perfume is this one: "Dead flies putrefy the perfumer's ointment, and cause it to give off a foul odor; so does a little folly to one respected for wisdom and honor" (Ecclesiastes 10:1).

Suppose you purchased a small vial of expensive perfume, took it home, and put it in a safe spot. Sometime later, you opened the vial and discovered a dead horsefly floating on top. The insect, now partially decayed, had putrefied the precious perfume. This is the source of the well-known phrase, a fly in the ointment. It is Solomon's vivid way of illustrating how a tiny bit of foolishness can destroy the powerful fragrance of a person's dignity and reputation.

They say the devil is in the details, and that can be very true. On the big days and big events of life, we are more likely to be on our guard. It is the details that trip us up. We witness the downfall of this politician or that well-known Christian and wonder how such a little thing, something so avoidable, brought down a big man.

Think of the enormous impact of little things in the realm of politics. All it took was the perspiration on Richard Nixon's lip to ruin his televised debate with John F. Kennedy. All it took to make a difference was a few tears in the eyes of Edmund Muskie, Michael Dukakis riding in a tank, Al Gore sighing and moaning during his debate with George W. Bush, Jimmy Carter talking about malaise, Howard Dean screaming into a microphone.

Over and over, giants are slain by the details. In 1 Corinthians 5:6 we read that "a little leaven leavens the whole lump." If you have ever baked homemade rolls, you know it does not take much yeast to have an impact on dough.

Song of Solomon 2:15 warns about the "little foxes that spoil the vines." James 3:5 warns that although the tongue is a small part of the body, it can produce a spark that kindles a forest fire.

"Little sins are not like an inch of candle, which soon expires," said a seventeenth-century British clergyman named William Secker, "but they resemble a train of powder, which takes the fire from corn to corn, till at last the barrel be burst asunder."[3]

In 1859, Charles Haddon Spurgeon (at the time only twenty-four years old) preached a sermon entitled "Little Sins." Here is part of what he said:

> The best of men have always been afraid of little sins. . . . Men, with their eyes well opened by divine grace, have seen a whole hell slumbering in the [smallest] sin. Gifted with a microscopic power, their eyes have seen a world of iniquity hidden in a single act, or

thought, or imagination of sin; and hence they have avoided it with horror—have passed by and would have nothing to do with it. . . . Little sins lead to great ones. . . . Nay, stand back! Little though the temptation be, I dread thee, for thy little temptation leads to something greater, and thy small sin makes way for something worse.

Years ago there was not a single thistle in the whole of Australia. Some Scotsman who very much admired thistles—rather more than I do—thought it was a pity that a great island like Australia should be without that marvelous and glorious symbol of his great nation. He, therefore, collected a packet of thistle-seeds, and sent it over to one of his friends in Australia. Well, when it was landed, the officers might have said, "Oh, let it in; is it not a little one? Here is but a handful of thistle-down, oh, let it come in; it will be but sown in a garden—the Scotch will grow it in their gardens; they think it a fine flower, no doubt—let them have it, it is but meant for their amusement." Ah, yes, it was but a little one; but now whole districts of country are covered with it and it has become the farmer's pest and plague. It was a little one; but all the worse for that, it multiplied and grew. If it had been a great evil, all men would have set to work to crush it. . . . Take heed of the thistle-seed, little sins are like it. Take care they are not admitted into your heart.[4]

Thistle seeds are all over the place, everywhere we go. They are like the little burrs that stick to your socks as you walk through a meadow. As Spurgeon points out, the whole town rallies to fight the barbarian at the gate, so the enemy is more likely to send a spy who can more easily penetrate the castle walls.

No big deal, we think. *It's just a little thing.* A "little" relationship, a "little" flirtation at the office," a "little" edge in the tone of voice, a "little" padding on the expense account, a "little" experimentation in the wrong area—*just a little thing.*

Obedience in Little Things

French priest Jean Nicolas Grou, who died in 1803, said,

> Little things come daily, hourly, within our reach, and they are
> not less calculated to set forward our growth in holiness, than are
> the greater occasions which occur but rarely. Moreover, fidelity in
> trifles, and an earnest seeking to please God in little matters, is a
> real test of devotion and love. Let your aim be to please our dear
> Lord perfectly in little things.[5]

Solomon adds an interesting thought to his reasoning: "A
wise man's heart is at his right hand, but a fool's heart at his left"
(Ecclesiastes 10:2). Now, this has nothing to do with being right-
handed or left-handed. In biblical times, a person's right hand was
perceived to be the place of power. The adviser who stood or sat to the
king's right was his most trusted official.

Obedience in little things implies that we are standing in a place
of wisdom and power. When we keep slipping up in little things, it
indicates we are standing in a place of foolishness, and our power and
influence are diluted.

On January 12, 1997, Swiss men Bertrand Piccard and William
Verstraeten set out on a venture to be the first to circle the earth in
a hot-air balloon. Their aircraft, the *Breitling Orbiter*, was a picture
of high-tech perfection, complete with solar panels for power and a
pressurized cabin allowing them to fly at high altitudes. Their plan
was to float high enough to enter the jet stream, which would carry
them around the globe at two hundred miles per hour. The price tag
for their venture was a lofty $1.5 million.

Not long after takeoff, however, disaster struck. Inside their
sealed and pressurized cabin, the two men noticed a strong kerosene

smell—and it got worse by the minute. They tried tightening all the connections on the lines carrying the kerosene fuel, to no avail. They e-mailed their support crew of technicians on the ground seeking advice and, hopefully, a solution. They were told to descend to an altitude at which it would be safe to depressurize the cabin so they could get fresh air, and try to hold on until they reached the northern coast of Africa. However, the fumes proved to be overwhelming, and they were forced to ditch their craft in the Mediterranean Sea.

Upon inspection, they discovered what ended the $1.5 million epic voyage: a defective hose clamp, like those that secure an automobile radiator hose. Cost of the clamp? $1.16. A small, seemingly insignificant defect can ruin an otherwise noble venture.[6]

Small Decisions Affect Big Outcomes

I'm certain you are familiar with this old saying:

> For want of a nail, the shoe was lost;
> For want of the shoe, the horse was lost;
> For want of the horse, the rider was lost;
> For want of the rider, the battle was lost;
> For want of the battle, the kingdom was lost;
> And all for the want of a horseshoe nail.

Think about that. For want of a nail, a kingdom was lost. You would think that would be impossible, but every detail of life sets in motion a chain of events we cannot predict. We have talked about that desert sojourn, when Jesus prepared for the ministry upon which all of human history would turn. The devil's very first suggestion involved no more than a crust of bread. Jesus was hungry; He was fasting so that His spiritual perception and unity with the Father would be fully optimized.

"If You are the Son of God, why not just command these stones to become bread?" the devil asked. Why not indeed? It was no big deal, just a little thing. Here is how "little":

> For want of abstaining from a crust of bread, a fast would be lost.
>
> For want of a fast, a prayer would be lost.
>
> For want of a prayer, a vision would be lost.
>
> For want of a vision, a mission would be lost.
>
> For want of a mission, a sacrifice would be lost.
>
> For want of a sacrifice, an eternal kingdom would be lost.

If Jesus had yielded to the lure of the little thing at that moment, all that followed would have been impossible. The spotless Lamb could not have been slain, the atonement could not have been achieved, the sin could not have been forgiven; and you and I would be without any hope for this life or the one to come.

What about your life? What are the little horseshoe nails, the little crusts of bread, the tiny temptations that affect the direction of your life? According to Solomon, the one who pays the terrible price for the tiny bait is the fool.

Saintly Scottish preacher Horatius Bonar wrote:

> A holy life is made up of a multitude of small things. It is the little things of the hour, and not the great things of the age, that fill up a life like that of [the apostles] Paul or John, like that of . . . [David] Brainerd, or [Henry] Martyn. Little words, not eloquent speeches or sermons, little deeds, not miracles, nor battles, nor one great heroic act or mighty martyrdom, make up the true Christian life.[7]

Another new day faces you. Ask God, through the loving grace and overcoming power of His Holy Spirit, to afford you the wisdom to choose light at every turn. I believe that as you connect the dots of wise choices, a great haze will drop away from your vision. A dark cloud may have followed you for so long that you have ceased to be aware of it. But that haze is a barrier that can keep you from seeing the City of God that lies ahead. It can make an eleven-day journey turn into thirty-eight years of wandering in the wilderness. It can make you stop believing in your God or yourself after a while. It is just the kind of cloud the enemy wants to keep you wrapped up in, all the better to deliver you to the destiny of his choosing.

But as you make wise choices, live the godly way, and keep the vision of Christ before you, the light will begin to disperse the darkness. You will see the very image of heaven on earth. And that sight, my friend, is *not* a little thing.

27

Foolishness in Leadership

Ecclesiastes 10:4–7, 16–19

Among those who enjoy the activity of rock climbing, *Trail* magazine is a popular periodical. The February 2004 issue provided directions for climbers descending Britain's highest peak, Ben Nevis. The summit is 4,409 feet high, and coming down in bad weather can be tricky. *Trail* offered detailed instructions for the descent—but the instructions were wrong.

Roger Wild of the Mountaineering Council of Scotland caught the error and immediately contacted the magazine to point it out. *Trail* admitted that a crucial step in the instructions was somehow left out.

It's a good thing nobody had followed the plan. In poor visibility, climbers would have walked off the edge of a cliff into Gardyloo Gully. The one-thousand-foot drop is one of the longest in Britain.

Guy Procter, editor of *Trail*, apologized for the missing sentence that made the potentially tragic difference. He pointed out that *Trail* advises all climbers to use an Ordnance Survey map and a good compass.[1]

A deleted sentence is a "little" thing with large consequences. So is the issue of leadership. What if we find out, all too late, that it's all been a case of the blind leading the blind? We have to be careful who we follow, because it's a long way to the bottom. Solomon now turns to the topic of foolish leadership, providing sound advice for all of us who lead in church, in business, in government, and at home (Ecclesiastes 10:4–7, 16–19).

In tough times we look to our leaders. Families, churches, businesses, cities, states, and nations all need strong leadership, or the future will be bleak for those who follow. Just look at the sons and successors of Solomon, the kings who followed in his wake on the throne of Judah. The books of 1 and 2 Kings are studies in wise and foolish leadership. When the king was a morally upright man and a wise manager, the nation prospered. When the king was careless, heartless, ruthless, and godless, the entire nation slid toward abysmal ruin.

In a 1954 speech Winston Churchill reflected on his leadership during World War II when he rallied the British Isles to withstand the Nazi threat. He said, "I have never accepted what many people have kindly said—namely, that I inspired the nation. . . . It was the nation and the race dwelling around the globe that had the lion heart. I had the luck to be called upon to give the roar."[2]

Ego-Driven Leaders

If the spirit of the ruler rises against you,
Do not leave your post;
For conciliation pacifies great offenses.
—ECCLESIASTES 10:4

This is a picture of a leader who shouts and screams at everyone around him. This leader verbally abuses those who want to serve him.

He thinks he is above everyone else, giving him the right to oppress them with cruel language.

Woodrow Wilson once wrote that every man who takes office in Washington either grows or swells. He said, "When I give a man an office, I watch him carefully to see whether he is swelling or growing."[3] The ego-driven leader swells, and he often bursts out in anger. Sound like your boss?

Solomon has ideas for dealing with the ego-driven leader. He says, "If the spirit of the ruler rises against you, do not leave your post; for conciliation pacifies great offenses."

When we see a boss or a leader of any kind abuse power, our first impulse is to just walk away. At least, it is a better strategy than staying and doing something foolish. But Solomon says there is a better way still. Do not panic, do not quit your job, and do not leave your post. Do not overreact to an overreaction. Just hang in there, and deal with the person.

In the book of Proverbs, Solomon gives similar advice:

> A soft answer turns away wrath,
> But a harsh word stirs up anger. (Proverbs 15:1)

> As messengers of death is the king's wrath,
> But a wise man will appease it. (Proverbs 16:14)

> By long forbearance a ruler is persuaded,
> And a gentle tongue breaks a bone. (Proverbs 25:15)

The apostle Paul says much the same thing in Romans 12:18: "If it is possible, as much as depends on you, live peaceably with all men" (with all women too!).

King Solomon is saying that we may find ourselves in the

workplace dealing with obnoxious, temperamental, ego-driven leaders. Stay calm in the face of their tirades. Follow the Scripture. Try underreacting. Remember that a soft answer turns away wrath. We are often surprised at what happens when we try that.

In his book *At Ease: Stories I Tell to Friends*, President Dwight Eisenhower tells how he learned this lesson. When he was ten, he became so angry at someone that he beat his fists into an old apple tree until his knuckles were bleeding. That night his mother came into his bedroom. He was sobbing into the pillow, and she sat in the rocking chair by the bed and said nothing for a long time. Then she began to talk about anger, quoting Proverbs 16:32: "He who is slow to anger is better than the mighty, and he who rules his spirit than he who takes a city."

There was little to be gained in hating another person, she told him as she put salve on his injured hands. We hurt only ourselves.

Eisenhower considered that conversation one of the most valuable moments of his life, and it led to his developing a curious habit as an adult. Whenever someone angered him, he would write the person's name on a piece of scrap paper, drop it into the lowest drawer in his desk, and say to himself, "That finishes the incident."[4]

In other words, there is a time to stay at our post with unruffled spirits even when others are ranting and raving around us. As Rudyard Kipling said, "If you can keep your head when all about you are losing theirs and blaming it on you. . . . you'll be a man, my son."[5] That's true, even when facing egomaniacal tyrants and swaggering rulers.

Missionary-author Isobel Kuhn discovered this at a critical moment. She was serving in China with her husband, John, and their little son, Danny, who was six. John was in a distant location, so Isobel found herself virtually alone and in horrible danger. Dreaded bands of local thugs, the Lo-zi-lo-pa, had been bribed by the Communists to terrorize the area in advance of a full-fledged invasion.

Friends and national Christians encouraged Isobel to flee with her little son because her status as a foreign Christian would put her at special risk. Isobel was paralyzed with uncertainty. She had no way of sending word to John that she was fleeing, and he might well lose his life trying to get to her. In addition, escaping from China across the rugged Pienma Pass would involve grave danger and hardship.

In her fascinating book *In the Arena*, she wrote,

> I use a Scripture calendar and the verse that morning was, "Do not leave your post!" (Ecclesiastes 10:4). Very appropriate. Just like an answer. . . . On this occasion, with the threat of the ruthless Lo-zi-lo-pa descending on us, I felt the verse was from Him. And after deciding not to flee I had perfect peace—another sign it was His voice. . . . And so it proved. Day after day passed with quietness.[6]

Conditions improved just long enough for Isobel's husband, John, to reach his family, and they were able to begin planning a safer evacuation from the area.

Robert Greenleaf coined the term *servant-leader* to refer to leaders who choose as their highest priority to serve those under them. Here is how he describes the servant-leader:

> The servant-leader *is* servant first. . . . It begins with the natural feeling that one wants to serve, to serve *first*. Then conscious choice brings one to aspire to lead. He or she is sharply different from the person who is *leader* first, perhaps because of the need to assuage an unusual power drive or to acquire material possessions. For such it will be a later choice to serve—after leadership is established. The leader-first and the servant-first are two extreme types. Between them there are shadings and blends that are part of the infinite variety of human nature.

The difference manifests itself in the care taken by the servant-first to make sure that other people's highest priority needs are being served. The best test, and difficult to administer, is this: Do those served grow as persons? Do they, *while being served,* become healthier, wiser, freer, more autonomous, more likely themselves to become servants? *And,* what is the effect on the least privileged in society? Will they benefit, or, at least, will they not be further deprived?[7]

Greenleaf says servant-leaders may or may not be in formal positions of leadership. That means anyone can be a servant-leader. I believe Solomon would say there is wisdom in being a servant-leader when you are being abused by an ego-driven leader. By using conciliation, servant-leaders may well change the hearts of the abusive leaders over them.

Easygoing Leaders

There is an evil I have seen under the sun,
As an error proceeding from the ruler:
Folly is set in great dignity,
While the rich sit in a lowly place.
I have seen servants on horses,
While princes walk on the ground like servants.
—ECCLESIASTES 10:5–7

Solomon next warns against easygoing leaders. Easygoing leaders put unqualified people in office while ignoring those who should be serving under them. Often strong leaders put strong people around them, but weak leaders surround themselves with weak people. Often these so-called leaders are insecure; sometimes they are just lazy. In any event, they are not effective.

It happens all the time in our society that seasoned veterans—those who have served for years with loyalty—are passed over. Has it happened to you? Have you been in an environment where the most qualified people were replaced or sidelined while unqualified people assumed the reins? You could see disaster in the making, yet there was little you could do about it.

Leaders without strength are not leaders but mere puppets. James Truslow Adams, in his book *The Adams Family*, describes what set many of America's colonial leaders apart:

> As we look over the list of the early leaders of the republic, Washington, John Adams, Hamilton, and others, we discern that they were all men who insisted upon being themselves and who refused to truckle to the people. With each succeeding generation, the growing demand of the people that its elective officials shall not lead but merely register the popular will has steadily undermined the independence of those who derive their power from popular election. The persistent refusal of the Adamses to sacrifice the integrity of their own intellectual and moral standards and values for the sake of winning public office or popular favor is another of the measuring rods by which we may measure the divergence of American life from its starting point.[8]

Winston Churchill was beside himself in the years leading up to World War II because England's easygoing, peace-at-any-cost leaders were naive about the rising Nazi threat on the Continent. To Churchill's exasperation, Britain's ruling class continued to maintain a relaxed schedule, adhering to antiquated customs of leisurely weekends in country estates away from London. Churchill bitterly complained that Parliament "takes its weekends in the country" while "Hitler takes his countries in the weekends."[9]

One of America's foremost leadership gurus, Peter Drucker, once observed there is little correlation between a leader's effectiveness and his or her intelligence, imagination, or knowledge. Brilliant people are often strikingly ineffectual, he said. "They never have learned that insights become effectiveness only through hard systematic work."[10]

The Engineered Leader

Woe to you, O land, when your king is a child,
And your princes feast in the morning!
Blessed are you, O land, when your king is the son of nobles,
And your princes feast at the proper time—
For strength and not for drunkenness!

—ECCLESIASTES 10:16–17

Solomon speaks of inexperienced leaders who acquire office by the help of family and friends. Their leadership is orchestrated, arranged, or negotiated. They often haven't a clue as to what they are doing; consequently, they do little at all. In the morning, when they should be caring for the matters of work, home, state, or government, they are feasting and drinking, enjoying the perks of their roles without investing the passion or perseverance needed for success. Woe to you when your king is childish, wrote Solomon, and when your leader is immature.

Childish leaders are a terrible problem today. We seem to have plenty of them in the sports world. They should be role models, but instead they are moral disasters. Ditto for many of our politicians, entertainers, and business and financial leaders.

Do you know how to identify mature leaders? They are the ones who take the blame when things go wrong but share the credit when things go well. In his book on leadership, *The Winner Within*, Coach Pat Riley tells of pulling Magic Johnson aside one afternoon during the summer of 1980 and telling him that in more than twenty years of playing and coaching basketball, he had never seen such a complete package—great skills combined with great attitude. Riley asked Magic point-blank to explain his success.

Magic Johnson said that when he was a little boy, playing youth league basketball in East Lansing, Michigan, his coach had told him, "You're the biggest. You're our best player. You should shoot the ball all the time."

Magic did as he was told, but it was not satisfying to him. Even though he scored the most points and his team won consistently, the other players seemed miserable. They felt like nobodies. Magic did not like it that way, especially because it was driving a wedge between him and his friends. So he changed his style. Instead of scoring all the points, he would draw the defenders then pass to whomever was open. His unselfishness enhanced others' skills, and his team began to experience the same kind of enthusiasm that he enjoyed.[11]

The engineered leader, however, never understands that. He thinks it is all about him.

The Evil Leader

Because of laziness the building decays,
And through idleness of hands the house leaks.
A feast is made for laughter,
And wine makes merry;
But money answers everything.

—ECCLESIASTES 10:18–19

Picture a guy sitting at home with a bottle of beer in his hand, watching television. He is supposed to be doing work, taking care of things, providing for those for whom he is responsible. He is supposed to be a steward of the tasks entrusted to him. But the house is falling down. The roof is leaking. The bills are stacking up. The beer belly is growing larger.

Solomon offers no excuses for such a person. He is just an evil man who cares nothing about his responsibilities. Through his laziness, his leadership is dissipated, and his kingdom is destroyed.

Solomon has strong views on this subject—and remember that this book of Ecclesiastes was inspired by the Holy Spirit, so it reflects God's views. How does God view laziness? Take your Bible sometime and read through Proverbs, underlining the verses that talk about being slothful, lazy, diligent, or hardworking. You will come away with a whole new perspective on ambition and energy in your life.

If we want to be wise leaders, what should we do? How should we live? The following is from the private diary of William E. Sangster, a great Methodist leader who helped London endure the Battle of Britain during World War II. After his death this journal entry was found in which Sangster expressed his growing conviction that he should take a more active part in the leadership of the Methodist Church in England. His attitude is a shining example of what we find inside a true leader:

> This is the will of God for me. I did not choose it. I sought to escape it. But it has come. Something else has come too. A sense of certainty that God does not want me only for a preacher. He wants me also for a leader. . . . I feel a commissioning to work for God for the revival of this branch of His church—careless of my own reputation, indifferent to the comments of older and jealous men.

I am thirty-six. If I am to serve God in this way, I must no longer shrink from the task, but do it.[12]

In what field of life are you a leader? In the home? At work? In a Sunday school class? If you are wise, you will realize that you never stand alone before God; with you stand the souls of those you lead. Your stewardship of these souls is an issue with eternal consequences— a heaven-on-earth issue. Remember that a good leader walks ahead of his people, to point the way; beside his people, to share in their journey; and behind his people, to protect them and cover their mistakes. In other words, he leads in the same way Christ leads us. So as Christ covers us, and we cover those we lead, we make our way forward in wisdom and eagerness for all that God has in store.

28

Labor, Language, and Lunacy

Ecclesiastes 10:8–15, 20

Not too long ago the book *Working Smart* by Michael Leboeuf was all the rage in management circles. The author demonstrated that the key to better production is not longer hours but more effective ones. And we all know the truth of that proposition. There is no substitute for putting in the time, but it does not mean much if you are not working as wisely as possible. It pays to work smart.

This chapter in Ecclesiastes might be called "Working Dumb." Solomon paints a slightly amusing picture of the ignorant and ineffective laborer. He gives us five illustrations of the errors we make on the job.

Foolishness in Labor

He who digs a pit will fall into it,
And whoever breaks through a wall will be bitten by a serpent.

He who quarries stones may be hurt by them,
And he who splits wood may be endangered by it.
If the ax is dull,
And one does not sharpen the edge,
Then he must use more strength;
But wisdom brings success.

—Ecclesiastes 10:8–10

It is the weekend, and you are out in the backyard digging a pit. You have decided to put in a swimming pool, so you make the hole nice and deep. You are really sweating, and the shovel is putting calluses on your hands. But you start thinking about a nice, cool swim—and in the midst of your reverie, you are swimming in loose dirt. You have fallen into your own hole. Calling for help, you know you will never live this one down.

This kind of thing actually happens, even in worse settings. My friend the mortician once told me of the time people were walking to put a casket down, and one of the pall bearers fell into the grave. It was a double hole where two people are buried, one on top of the other. The poor man fell all the way down and landed with a thump on the casket that was already there.

It is important to watch where you are walking and to make sure the hole you are digging isn't your own grave.

While Solomon is in outdoor-project mode, he moves to a second example: knocking out a section of wall. The worker forgets that snakes love to live in the cold caverns of walls, and when he reaches into the wall he just breached, he is bitten by a snake. Serpents of one sort or another are always lurking nearby, and the wise laborer keeps an eye out for them.

A third man labors in a stone quarry. He becomes careless and brings a great stone down on himself. I am certain Solomon was thinking of a specific case here because he had eighty thousand men who quarried stone in the mountains for the great public-works projects he initiated.

> And the king commanded them to quarry large stones, costly stones, and hewn stones, to lay the foundation of the temple. So Solomon's builders, Hiram's builders, and the Gebalites quarried them; and they prepared timber and stones to build the temple.
> (1 Kings 5:17–18)

There weren't any construction firms that specialized in world-class temples, so Solomon must have been exposed to his share of foolish laborers. One of the eighty thousand was a careless soul, and the sad news came to the throne. We can imagine the supervisor reporting to the king. "We lost another one down in the quarry," he says. Solomon wants to know how. "Just some stupid mistake. The guy dug out a small stone that turned out to be the only thing keeping a five-ton one from rolling out."

Our fourth witless worker is splitting wood. He, too, becomes careless, and someone is hurt. Moses had anticipated this kind of thing, for we read in Deuteronomy 19:5:

> When a man goes to the woods with his neighbor to cut timber, and his hand swings a stroke with the ax to cut down the tree, and the head slips from the handle and strikes his neighbor so that he dies—he shall flee to one of these cities [of refuge] and live.

Numbskull number five is another one who failed Woodshop 101 in high school—or at least he was out sick on the day when tool maintenance was covered. This fellow does not stop to sharpen his ax, so he works twice as hard, twice as long, and sees half the results. If he were wise, he would take time to sharpen his ax and thus save himself a lot of time and energy. As it is, he is working harder when he should be working smarter.

The world is filled with ineffective workers. For example, did you read about the fellow who was killed when a Coke machine toppled on him as he was attempting to tip a soda out of it? Or the Toronto lawyer named Garry Hoy who was demonstrating the safety of windows in a downtown Toronto skyscraper? He crashed through a pane with his shoulder and plunged twenty-four floors into the courtyard of the Toronto Dominion Bank Tower. He had been explaining the strength of the building's windows to visiting law students. Peter Lauwers, managing partner of the firm Holden Day Wilson, told a Toronto newspaper that Hoy was "one of the best and brightest" members of the two-hundred-man association.

Then there was Ken Charles Barger, who accidentally shot himself to death in Newton, North Carolina. He was in bed when the phone rang, and when he reached for it he grabbed instead a Smith & Wesson .38, which discharged when he drew it to his ear.

Another news report told of six people who drowned while trying to rescue a chicken that had fallen into a well in southern Egypt. An eighteen-year-old farmer was the first to descend into the sixty-foot well. He drowned after an undercurrent in the water apparently pulled him down. His sister and two brothers, none of whom could swim well, went in one by one to help him, but they also drowned. Two elderly farmers then came to help, but they apparently were pulled by the same undercurrent. The bodies of the six were later pulled out of a well in the village of Nazlat Imara, south of Cairo. The chicken was also pulled out. It survived.[1]

All of which makes Solomon's point. When you are using your hands, use your head. The best power tool you have is the one whirring away between your ears. We need to learn to use that wonderful thing called *common sense*, although it seems more and more uncommon to find people with good sense. Work in wisdom.

Foolishness in Language

Poet Robert Frost once gave this commentary about the tongue: "Half the world is composed of people who have something to say and can't, and the other half who have nothing to say and keep on saying it."[2]

Another writer quipped, "Nothing is more frequently opened by mistake than the human mouth."

Foolishness and the Tongue

How appropriate for Solomon to conclude Ecclesiastes 10 with a discussion about the tongue. I have observed in studying the wisdom literature of Scripture that there is seldom a discussion about foolishness without some reference to a person's use of the tongue.

Jesus says, "A good man out of the good treasure of his heart brings forth good things, and an evil man out of the evil treasure brings forth evil things" (Matthew 12:35).

If there is one place where we can spot foolishness, it is in the way people use their tongues. Solomon shows us five ways misuse of the tongue reveals a foolish heart.

1. The Untamed Tongue

> A serpent may bite when it is not charmed;
> The babbler is no different.
>
> —Ecclesiastes 10:11

In Solomon's colorful court there were charmers purported to hypnotize snakes. Many of these snakes were cobras, with their flickering tongues and beady eyes. The snake would rise and sway to the plaintive tones of the charmer's flute. People would marvel at the obedience of such a sly and powerful creature—until the cobra showed he was even slyer than they thought.

The charmer, it seemed, was not quite charming enough. It works just the same way with the "babbler"—the person with the gift of gab. Solomon points out that this person's tongue is much less charming than expected, and at the least predictable moment . . . it *bites*. We have all been victims of biting comments, and we recognize the universality of this principle. Solomon does well in comparing the tongue to a cobra.

In Ecclesiastes 3, Solomon says there is a time to speak and a time to be silent. Babblers forget the latter part of that advice. They always have an opinion or an answer. The tongue is the rudder with which they navigate their way through life (an analogy James uses in the New Testament), and it is a far less trustworthy implement than they think.

Occasionally I will find myself determined to say something when I know in my heart I should be silent. *Jeremiah, just keep your big mouth shut. Don't say anything,* whispers the Spirit. I am always wise when I listen to that counsel, and never wise when I ignore it. Whatever you do, do not be a babbler because you might get hurt in the process.

This is the question no one wants to answer, so take a deep breath. Just between you and me, do you have a tendency to talk too much? Have you seen it in people's eyes during your conversations? A young man known for his incessant talking once approached Socrates for speech lessons. The great orator agreed but warned, "I will have to charge you double my usual fee. I can show you how to use your tongue, but first you must learn how to hold it."

The ancient philosopher Zeno said, "We have two ears and one mouth; therefore we should listen twice as much as we talk." A good rule of tongue.

2. The Unkind Tongue

> The words of a wise man's mouth are gracious,
> But the lips of a fool shall swallow him up.
>
> —Ecclesiastes 10:12

Compare Ecclesiastes 10:12 with Proverbs 10:32, which says, "The lips of the righteous know what is acceptable, but the mouth of the wicked what is perverse."

I am sure you will agree that some of the worst problems of your life have been instigated by your tongue—or someone else's. Ill-chosen words are like the evil spirits released from Pandora's Box. Once loose, they never again can be contained. You cannot unsay something you have said any more than you can "unring" a bell. James says you can control a horse or rudder a ship more easily than you can guide the weapon that lurks behind your teeth.

What is fascinating about the tongue is that as evil as it can be, it is capable of amazing goodness as well. Solomon says the words of the wise are filled with grace. Robert Webber grew up on the mission field, where his parents served with Africa Inland Mission. Once, on furlough, the family settled in Montgomery, Pennsylvania, in a small home near a farm. Robert was nine, and he loved blackberries. One day he grabbed a bucket and started picking from the nearby bushes. Without thinking, he strayed onto the neighbor's property and started picking the farmer's crop.

Suddenly the neighbor burst out the front door, waving his fist. "Get out of my field!" he shouted. "And don't let me catch you on my property ever again! Do you understand me?"

Robert was terrified, and he quickly ran to tell his father. Mr. Webber said, "Give me that pail of blackberries. We're going next door to talk to that man."

The two marched across the yard, Robert thinking to himself, *Good! My dad will show him a thing or two!*

"Mr. Farmer," said Robert's dad, "I'm sorry my son was on your property. Here, I want you to have these blackberries."

The neighbor was completely disarmed. "Hey," he said, "I'm sorry I yelled at the boy. I don't want the blackberries. I don't even like blackberries. You keep them. And you can pick all the berries you want from my field."[3]

"The words of a wise man's mouth are gracious," says Solomon, "but the lips of a fool shall swallow him up" (Ecclesiastes 10:12).

3. THE UNWISE TONGUE

The words of his mouth begin with foolishness,
And the end of his talk is raving madness.
A fool also multiplies words.

—ECCLESIASTES 10:13–14

Some people are simply enamored with the sound of their own voices. I am certain you know someone like this. There may be nothing in the world to say, but these people say it anyway; then they say it again. Few things in the world test our patience more grievously. Proverbs 10:19 tells us, "In the multitude of words sin is not lacking, but he who restrains his lips is wise."

Students who talk excessively are one of the biggest disciplinary challenges schoolteachers face, and entire seminars are devoted to managing children who are incessant talkers. When it is an adult, it's even more vexing.

Roxanne Lulofs labels an undisciplined talker as "HARM," for Hit-and-Run Mouth. She says that people with hit-and-run mouths, for whatever reason, feel compelled to tell you just what they think of you and your actions, regardless of how well they know you. Their desire is to be heard without hearing, to be known without knowing. They do not care about getting their facts straight. They want attention.[4]

Here is the epitaph of a hit-and-run mouth:

> Beneath this stone, a lump of clay,
> Lies Arrabella Young,
> Who on the 24th of May
> Began to hold her tongue.[5]

4. THE UNREASONABLE TONGUE

> No man knows what is to be;
> Who can tell him what will be after him?
> The labor of fools wearies them,
> For they do not even know how to go to the city!
> —ECCLESIASTES 10:14–15

Solomon tells us about the man who is always forecasting what roads lie ahead then gets lost on his way to the office. Here are people with little sense of direction in life, yet they are always talking about what they are planning to do in the future, how the future is going to be played out, and what they intend to accomplish. Solomon refers to this phenomenon several other times in Ecclesiastes:

For who can bring him to see what will happen after him? (3:22)

Who can tell a man what will happen after him under the sun? (6:12)

For he does not know what will happen;
So who can tell him when it will occur? (8:7)

The same point comes up in Solomon's book of Proverbs: "Do not boast about tomorrow, for you do not know what a day may bring forth" (27:1).

In the evening of his life, Solomon must have wondered about the future of the kingdom he had built. Due to the king's unfaithfulness, God had determined that Israel would become a house divided against itself. Solomon knew that the judgment had to come and that he bore primary responsibility. This lends a touch of poignancy to Solomon's fascination with a future no one knew—except for the ill forebodings in his heart.

5. The Unfaithful Tongue

Do not curse the king, even in your thought;
Do not curse the rich, even in your bedroom;
For a bird of the air may carry your voice,
And a bird in flight may tell the matter.

—Ecclesiastes 10:20

This is the origin of the little expression: "A little bird told me." Birds don't talk, of course, but Solomon is reminding us with this illustration that a wise person does not say something in private that he would not want someone to hear in public.

Zig Ziglar was playing golf with a young associate. At the beginning of the game, he looked at the youth with amusement. The young man was about six foot three and weighed about 220 pounds. He was uncomfortable as he approached the tee in an unorthodox way. He picked up his club, wiggled it a few times, laid it down, then repeated the whole process. Zig whispered to someone nearby, "That young man is obviously not a golfer." A moment later the young man drove the ball about 240 yards right down the middle of the fairway. So much for Ziglar's opinion!

After the fellow hit the ball, he walked over to Zig, looked him in the eye, and said, "Mr. Ziglar, I heard what you said."

Zig wanted to disappear. He wished he could evaporate into thin air. But the young man continued, "I heard what you said when you spoke in my hometown three years ago, and it completely changed my life. I want you to know, Mr. Ziglar, that it is an honor for me to even be on the same golf course with you."

Writing in his book *Top Performance*, Ziglar said that he breathed a sigh of relief and made a new resolution that day to be far more careful in uttering his comments—especially negative ones—about another person.[6]

So we must guard our own tongues, not allowing them to be untamed, unkind, unwise, unreasonable, or unfaithful. Our language, like our labor, is part of the "little things" that guide the well-being of our lives.

Perhaps the best way to end this chapter is to give you an assignment. Before going to the next chapter, take a few moments to memorize a verse of Scripture that will be of constant help to you in all areas of life.

Here it is—the greatest treasure I could give you: "If any of you lacks wisdom, let him ask of God, who gives to all liberally and without reproach, and it will be given to him" (James 1:5).

That verse has meant a great deal in my life. I make it my "Solomon prayer" every morning as I ask God for His wisdom, just as the young king did. I record the request in my prayer journal like this: "My Lord and my God, I am a rudderless ship without You. I cannot work; I cannot speak; I cannot live or love as I should unless

Your wisdom lights my path. Protect me from my own foolishness and teach me Thy way."

> Teach me Thy way, O Lord, teach me Thy way!
> Thy guiding grace afford, teach me Thy way!
> Help me to walk aright, more by faith, less by sight;
> Lead me with heav'nly light, teach me Thy way![7]

29

Life Is Uncertain: Embrace It!

Ecclesiastes 11:1–6

Newspaper columnist Rosemary Smith wrote about where she finds her daily encouragement: "When I need cheering up, I read my paper towels." Her favorite brand comes imprinted with sayings, jokes, and proverbs. One day, on the verge of tears, she tore off a sheet to wipe up some coffee and read, "When the chips are down, switch to popcorn." Something about that gave her a needed uplift.

When paper towels fail her, Smith looks for encouraging words on church signs. Sometimes she finds inspiration from bumper stickers or billboards or even on the sides of trucks. If all else fails, she keeps an assortment of little books full of pithy advice. One of her favorite sayings is "Life is uncertain. Eat dessert first."[1]

That saying actually comes from the title of a book published several years ago, based on the story of a lady who loved dessert but who, one day, put off eating her favorite treat until later that evening. The problem was that she was aboard the *Titanic*.

The Bible is a far better source of inspiration than paper towels or church signs, but as Solomon ends his book of Ecclesiastes, his message is one the columnist would embrace—life is uncertain.

Solomon began this journal of Ecclesiastes by giving us a conclusion about life: all is vanity. Arriving at the end of the book he returns to the same conclusion: "Vanity of vanities," says the Preacher, "all is vanity."

In his vast wisdom, Solomon understands that life under the sun, without God, is a meaningless experience. It is life on the treadmill—you get your exercise, but you don't go anywhere.

Solomon employs many metaphors to describe the vanity of life. Chasing the breeze. A puff of smoke. Dust in the wind. The laughter of fools or a forgotten memory. Life without God, as Solomon has demonstrated in many ways, is utterly meaningless.

Now, toward the end, Solomon resolves all the questions he has raised, and he gives us his ultimate conclusion. In preparing for this climactic finish, Solomon articulates some overarching principles on which we should base our lives. These are his final admonitions—four of them:

1. Life is uncertain: embrace it! (Ecclesiastes 11:1–6)
2. Life is short: enjoy it! (11:7–12:8)
3. Life is mysterious: examine it! (12:9–12)
4. Life is obedience: express it! (12:13–14)

Have You Hugged Your Life Today?

Solomon's first point about life is that it's uncertain; therefore, it is to be embraced. Have you hugged your life today?

A few years ago, the newspaper of Camden, Maine, the *Herald*, ran two photos on the same page. The first was a picture of Camden's board of selectmen and town manager huddled around a table, hard at work. The second photograph showed a healthy flock of sheep.

As often happens in the hurried world of newspaper deadlines, someone reversed the captions. The caption under the picture of the sheep identified them left to right as town officials. The first picture, however, had a caption that read, "The Sheep Fold—naive and vulnerable, they huddle for security against the uncertainties of the outside world."[2]

Who is to say whether both pictures might not have wound up with more informative captions than were originally intended?

After all, we often feel like those selectmen are purported to feel: naive and vulnerable, huddled together against the uncertainties of the outside world. That's exactly the problem Solomon addresses in these verses. We are like helpless sheep in a dangerous world, given all that we do not know about the way the world works. Four times in Ecclesiastes 11:1–6, Solomon reminds us of what we do not and cannot know:

- You do not know what evil will be on the earth.
- You do not know what is the way of the winds.
- You do not know the works of God.
- You do not know which will prosper.

Consider the variables. Because men are evil, we do not know what will happen. We must not leave our houses unlocked. We must not trust a stranger on the phone with our credit card numbers. We must not leave our wallets and pocketbooks unattended in public. People are evil, and that invites uncertainty into the world.

Because the winds are unaccountable, we do not know what will happen. We will say more about this later, but the earth itself reflects the fallen state of humanity. A tornado never announces its schedule in advance. A wildfire may come along and destroy neighborhoods. The wind blows where it will, and that invites uncertainty into the world.

Because God's plans are hidden, we do not know what will happen. We trust Him, we love Him, and we obey Him; but we do not know His timetables. He may call us home at any instant—or He may send us on some new earthly mission. God moves in mysterious ways, and that invites uncertainty into the world.

Because we cannot foretell the future, we do not know what will happen. We work hard and seek prosperity, but the economy and the company and even our ability to work are all intangibles. We do not know what the future holds, and that, too, invites uncertainty into the world.

Solomon does not tell us to eat dessert first, but he gives us two much more practical, much more useful scraps of advice.

Be Diversified in Your Investments

> Cast your bread upon the waters,
> For you will find it after many days.
> Give a serving to seven, and also to eight,
> For you do not know what evil will be on the earth.
>
> —Ecclesiastes 11:1–2

Did you read that heading right? The last thing you expected from Solomon was advice about a diversified investment portfolio. Had I been Solomon, I would have advised, "Since life is so uncertain, make sure your spiritual foundation is strong. Make sure your hope of heaven is secure. Make sure your faith is in Christ, the unchanging Rock."

Solomon will come to such considerations in due time. But part of the charm and uniqueness of Ecclesiastes is that it is so surprisingly grounded in everyday life on Planet Earth. And who can deny that finance is a considerable part of that everyday life? Not only that, but economic issues are as uncertain as everything else in life. If you have ever followed the Dow Jones Industrial Average, you understand perfectly.

Actually, Paul was not above a little investment tip himself. In 1 Timothy 6:17 he warns, "Command those who are rich in this present age not to be haughty, nor to trust in uncertain riches." Guard your investments with humility.

Solomon was one of the richest men in history, and his legendary wisdom encompassed money management. To this day some of the best financial advice ever written is contained in the book of Proverbs. And here, in this passage in Ecclesiastes, we see the invention and advancement of the widely lauded strategy of financial diversification.

Notice verse 1: "Cast your bread upon the waters, for you will find it after many days." This is one of the most quoted verses in Ecclesiastes, but what does it mean?

As it happens, Solomon had quite a fleet of ships. "King Solomon also built a fleet of ships at Ezion Geber, which is near Elath on the shore of the Red Sea, in the land of Edom" (1 Kings 9:26).

The next chapter talks about ships transporting gold, precious stones, and expensive woods (1 Kings 10:11). We read of his traveling merchants, his income from international trade, and of yet more ships bringing in the wealth of the world, including "gold, silver, ivory, apes, and monkeys" (verses 15, 22).

Then as now, one of the main trade commodities was grain. The merchants of Solomon's day would load their grain ships and send them off. The Israelites were "casting [their] bread upon the water." But notice that with Solomon, the word is plural: "cast your bread on the waters." In other words, don't put all your grain in one ship. Put your wheat in several ships, and send it out in a diversified way so that if one of the ships should sink, you will not be ruined.

Grandma called this not putting all your eggs in one basket; we call it diversifying our portfolio. Solomon is telling us that since life is so uncertain, we should spread out our investments. In fact, he goes so far as to recommend that we diversify using seven or eight different places. Look at Ecclesiastes 11:2: "Give a serving to seven, and also to eight, for you do not know what evil will be on the earth."

That is God's counsel regarding our financial investments. Spread them out because life is uncertain.

Be Diligent in Your Involvement

If the clouds are full of rain,
They empty themselves upon the earth;
And if a tree falls to the south or the north,
In the place where the tree falls, there it shall lie.
He who observes the wind will not sow,
And he who regards the clouds will not reap.

As you do not know what is the way of the wind,
Or how the bones grow in the womb of her who is with child,
So you do not know the works of God who makes everything.
In the morning sow your seed,
And in the evening do not withhold your hand;
For you do not know which will prosper,
Either this or that,
Or whether both alike will be good.

—ECCLESIASTES 11:3–6

Some people are paralyzed by uncertainty. Like a soldier who suddenly becomes aware that he has run into the middle of a mine-field, every step is uncertain, and you tend to freeze. When the Allied troops landed on the beach at Normandy on June 6, 1944, they found the shore well-fortified by German machine guns. Many of the men crouched behind the great wood-and-iron mines, shaped as crosses and protruding from the water. Those who hunkered down in fear inevitably died; those who kept moving, even into the cascade of gun-fire, had much greater hopes of surviving.

Solomon's advice is to keep moving forward; the more uncertainty, the more determined we should be. When he heard people say, "Life is uncertain, so let's give up," he replied, "Life is uncertain, so let's roll up our sleeves."

Prepare for the worst, and work for the best. Over and over, the Bible tells us to work, to be faithful, to be diligent, to be strong, and to use our gifts and resources wisely. "[Redeem] the time," says Ephesians 5:16, "because the days are evil."

After all, the king asserts, we are surrounded by intangibles and variables. Solomon stands in the field between the sky and the dust and the waters, and he knows that greater forces surround him. Overpowering natural forces were not given to our control. No one under the sun can know when the rain will fall, yet it holds within its capricious course the future of all that we grow, all that we eat.

Solomon rests upon a fallen tree and observes that this solid wood, at least, is no mystery; it is tangible, sturdy, and we know its seasons of bloom and decay. But the rain, the clouds, and their inscru-table timetables—these are beyond our mastery.

The king feels the breeze in his hair and broadens his observation. He comments that the wind, too, is a furtive stranger among us. It moves and ceases moving without regard to the affairs of God's chil-dren. It respects no kings, neither does it hold contempt for peasants.

It glides among them all, heralding its presence by the tossing of leaves and the rippling of wheat, before moving on to some destination we cannot know.

That wind carries the distant laughter of a child to Solomon's ears, and again he reflects on the mystery of the world—not just around us, but within us. Greatest of all riddles, perhaps, is the living one that lies within the mother's womb. From the tiniest seed springs all the complexity of the human spirit.

Solomon smiles faintly, and the years show themselves around the corners of his eyes. With all his godly and world-renowned wisdom, with all his years and experience and authority and international relations—he still does not possess the tiniest mustard seed of comprehension of this miracle. All Solomon can do is look beyond the sky—there is the One who harnesses the wind, who dispenses the rain, who hand-forms the child.

Solomon rises from the fallen tree and offers his response. To the wisest man in the world—fully as much as to the most outrageous fool—the world is like the wind, uncertain and inscrutable. The only One who knows is the only One who controls, and that is a hopeful thought. It remains for us to sow our seeds vigorously and trust in the rain even if it isn't trustworthy, to count on the wind whether it tosses the hair or topples the barn, to embrace the newborn child for what he is: a creation of and gift from God.

The world is a mystery and life but a vapor, Solomon tells us; but hard work, wise living, and joyful countenance are not. They are the best chance for those who would make the most of earth on their way to heaven. Life is uncertain—embrace it with joy.

More than two hundred years ago, the Connecticut House of Representatives was in session on a bright, sunny springtime day. Suddenly, the sky grew dark and ominous shadows flooded across the chamber. The representatives grew alarmed as they looked out the windows in puzzlement. This was an age that lacked the science to foretell solar eclipses. No one could have expected or understood the sudden blanket of darkness.

A clamor arose among the representatives. "Adjourn! Let us hurry from this House to get our own houses in order!" was the consensus. Some legislators believed the second coming of Christ was surely at hand.

But the Speaker of the House, a devout believer himself, rose to speak. He gently acknowledged that the House was upset by the darkness and that some were afraid. "But the Day of the Lord is either approaching or it is not," he said. "If it is not, there is no cause for adjournment. And if the Lord is returning, I, for one, choose to be found doing my duty. I therefore ask that candles be brought."[3]

In these days of uncertainty, we can ask for no better course. Even as the darkness falls, the light is certain to overcome it. So bring the candles. Lift them aloft to spread their light for as long as the wax holds out, for as long as our strength holds out. The Lord could come today, or He could come in a thousand years. In either case, let us be about our Father's business.

Let us seize the day, raise His flag, and set our thoughts on things eternal.

> Tomorrow, Lord, is Thine
> Lodged in Thy sovereign hand;
> And if its sun arise and shine,
> It shines by Thy command.

> The present moment flies,
> And bears our life away;
> O make Thy servants truly wise,
> That they may live today.[4]

30

Life Is Short: Enjoy It!

Ecclesiastes 11:7–12:8

D r. Benjamin Elijah Mays, a great Christian educator and sixth president of Morehouse College, wrote a classic poem that is worth memorizing. It is entitled "Life Is Just a Minute."

I have only just a minute
Only sixty seconds in it
Forced upon me—can't refuse it
Didn't seek it—didn't choose it,
But it's up to me to use it.
I must suffer if I lose it.
Give account if I abuse it.
Just a tiny, little minute—
But eternity is in it![1]

Dr. Mays must have been reading Ecclesiastes when he wrote that, for it captures the theme of the last two chapters. Life is uncertain, so we should embrace it. Life is short, so we should enjoy it.

How do we enjoy life? Solomon is going to suggest four specific ways for our consideration.

Each Day Totally

Truly the light is sweet,
And it is pleasant for the eyes to behold the sun;
But if a man lives many years
And rejoices in them all,
Yet let him remember the days of darkness,
For they will be many.
All that is coming is vanity.

—ECCLESIASTES 11:7–8

We do not know how long we have to live, so we should live every day with gusto.

I love the sunshine. I love to see the sun peeking through the window when I get up in the morning. The psalmist said, "From the rising of the sun to its going down the LORD's name is to be praised" (Psalm 113:3).

That is the theme behind the anonymous hymn "When Morning Gilds the Skies." There are many, many stanzas—far more than I can quote here. But here are a few:

When morning gilds the skies my heart awaking cries:
May Jesus Christ be praised!
Alike at work and prayer, to Jesus I repair:
May Jesus Christ be praised!

When you begin the day, O never fail to say,
May Jesus Christ be praised!

And at your work rejoice, to sing with heart and voice,
May Jesus Christ be praised!

Sing, suns and stars of space, sing, ye that see His face,
Sing, Jesus Christ be praised!
God's whole creation o'er, for aye and evermore
Shall Jesus Christ be praised![2]

We praise God because it is right, because it is appropriate, and because it is commanded. But praising God also has a radical effect on us. I dare you to begin the next seven days with intense, heartfelt praise and worship. Read a praise psalm each day, and reflect on a thoughtful hymn like the one above. Praise Him for the sunshine or the rain—whichever blessing comes that day. Exalt Him for the sheer goodness of a life that features His presence. Sit at His feet for just a few moments, and then watch the effect on your day.

Sigmund Freud suffered from a horrible cancer in his mouth. In 1926, he also developed heart trouble and spent time in a sanitarium. He returned to Vienna with a yearning for morning drives, and for the first time he experienced the glories of springtime in Vienna. "What a pity," he wrote, "that one has to grow old and ill before making this discovery."

Keith LeClair was one of America's youngest and brightest baseball stars. As a twenty-five-year-old head coach, he took Western Carolina University to within one game of the College World Series. LeClair was named the Southern Conference coach of the year three times before leaving to take over the East Carolina program in 1998. He continued his success with the Pirates and turned the program into a perennial contender. Suddenly, his career came to a dramatic stop when he was diagnosed with ALS, amyotrophic lateral sclerosis, more commonly called Lou Gehrig's disease.

"Not long ago, baseball absorbed my life 365 days a year," LeClair said. "I gave the profession of coaching everything I had until after the 2002 season, [when] a doctor said, 'I'm sorry, but you have ALS and there is nothing I can do to help.' All of a sudden, baseball seemed to not matter a whole lot to me anymore. Instead, my thoughts were focused on God and my family."

LeClair now begins each day in the Scriptures, and he has gained a new appreciation for the beauties of each morning. "It astounds me to think of all the help God has provided for our family, and that keeps me going to see another day," LeClair said.[3]

I'm glad I can make this discovery anew every morning. Were you to peek inside my journal, you'd find that almost every entry says in one way or another: "Thank You, Lord, for this day, for a good night's rest, and for the privilege of being alive one more day on this earth to serve You."

Robert Louis Stevenson said, "The man who forgets to be grateful has fallen asleep in life."[4] Develop the attitude of totally experiencing each day.

Enjoy Your Youth Thoroughly

Rejoice, O young man, in your youth,
And let your heart cheer you in the days of your youth;
Walk in the ways of your heart,
And in the sight of your eyes;
But know that for all these
God will bring you into judgment.
Therefore remove sorrow from your heart,
And put away evil from your flesh,
For childhood and youth are vanity.

—ECCLESIASTES 11:9–10

By now you have realized that Solomon has a favorite string on his violin, and it is *the enjoyment of life*. Here he tells young people to live it up. He encourages those who are young to live with adventure and excitement because these are some of their best days.

As I have watched the young people in my church and community, it seems that they are always eager to be older. Sixteen-year-olds want to be eighteen, and eighteen-year-olds can't wait to be twenty-one.

Somewhere along the way that process starts to reverse itself.

We ought to be telling our kids to enjoy themselves. Youth has many advantages: less responsibility, lots of energy, many good friends, and boatloads of opportunity. I have watched my own children and grandchildren over the years. One day after football practice my sons and I were talking about how much fun it was to play football in college, yet we all agreed it was even more fun in high school. College football is a pressure-packed business, but in high school there is camaraderie, school spirit, family, friends, and the brisk aura of Friday nights on the field.

While young people face many challenges and difficulties today, it is also true that life tends to become harder and heavier as we grow older. Solomon counsels us to rejoice in our youth.

But there is a warning. Sow joyfully, but sow healthy seeds and not wild oats. Youth is no excuse for exploits that do not honor Him.

If I were a young person, I would look at my life as a bowl of premium chocolate ice cream. I would savor every bite. It would be foolish to hurry through it when there is only so much in the bowl. I would take a moment to thank God before digging in and be grateful that He designed this treat to melt so delightfully on the tongue. He would be ever in my grateful thoughts. Youth is to be enjoyed and dedicated to the One who planned it for us.

If I were a new parent, I would let my kids be kids. I would not want them to grow up too quickly, and when they stumble along the learning path, I would gently help them up and show them how to walk upright. Kids have lots of energy and crazy imaginations, but I would see God's joy in that rather than shushing them and imposing unnatural restraint on their natural vitality.

Express Your Faith Thoughtfully

Remember now your Creator in the days of your youth,
Before the difficult days come,
And the years draw near when you say,
"I have no pleasure in them":
While the sun and the light,
The moon and the stars,
Are not darkened,
And the clouds do not return after the rain.
—ECCLESIASTES 12:1–2

I think of Solomon, sitting in the courtyard of the palace and watching the children romp beneath the trees. With all the weight of the empire on his shoulders, the presence of children must have made him feel young again.

A teenager sits at the king's feet. Perhaps it is a grandchild, a pretty young girl. Solomon is struck by how fast she is growing up. He smiles and begins telling her why she should take care not to lose God in all the commotion of adolescence. The king knows how easy it is for young people to say, "I've got a lot of living to do; the whole world is out there waiting for me! And the Lord will always be there for me later."

He can already see the patronizing look in the eyes of this young girl before him. He says, "Really, hear me out! *Now* is the very time to draw near to your God. The longer you wait, the less you will desire Him, and the more elusive He will prove to be. *Now* is the time when you will make the pivotal decisions on which your whole future will turn. Please don't make them without your Lord."

"Remember" is about memories for us. But as Solomon uses the word—remember your Creator—the term signifies commitment and involvement. Get with God. Get with Him daily as you spend time together. Get with Him through His Word. Get with Him in service and with His other children. Get with Him and honor Him.

It is traditional for kids to be criticized by ex-kids.

Grumpy old [former kid] Martin Luther [said about the teens of his day]: "The young people of today are utterly dissolute and disorderly."

Plato, [philosopher and past child,] agreed. "The youth are rebellious, pleasure-seeking, and irresponsible," he wrote. "They have no respect for their elders."

Socrates, [a one-time juvenile, sniped], "Children now love luxury. They have bad manners, contempt for authority. They show disrespect for elders and love chatter."[5]

There is also the Egyptian from six thousand years ago—anonymous but presumably a previous youngster—who carved this inscription on a tomb:

"We live in a decadent age. Young people no longer respect their parents. They are rude and impatient. They inhabit taverns and have no self-control."

The next time you think the "modern generation" is going from bad to worse, remember that God always has a rich handful of teenage heroes ready to change the world. [In the Bible] we read of

Joseph the dreamer, Daniel in Babylon, David the giant killer, and the virgin Mary (likely still a teen [when she gave birth to Jesus]).

As a teenager, Charles Spurgeon preached to great crowds, but when they referred to his youthfulness, he replied, "Never mind my age. Think of the Lord Jesus Christ and His preciousness."

In our own day we've been deeply moved by young people like 17-year-old Cassie Bernall of Littleton, Colorado, who was [gunned down] for her faith during the Columbine tragedy.[6]

Let us encourage our young people and pray for them. God's going to use them to change the world, and they need a head start. They need to remember their Creator in the days of their youth.

Embrace Your Aging Thankfully

In the day when the keepers of the house tremble,
And the strong men bow down;
When the grinders cease because they are few,
And those that look through the windows grow dim;
When the doors are shut in the streets,
And the sound of grinding is low;
When one rises up at the sound of a bird,
And all the daughters of music are brought low.
Also they are afraid of height,
And of terrors in the way;
When the almond tree blossoms,
The grasshopper is a burden,
And desire fails.
For man goes to his eternal home,
And the mourners go about the streets.

Remember your Creator before the silver cord is loosed,
Or the golden bowl is broken,
Or the pitcher shattered at the fountain,
Or the wheel broken at the well.
Then the dust will return to the earth as it was,
And the spirit will return to God who gave it.

"Vanity of vanities," says the Preacher,
"All is vanity."

—ECCLESIASTES 12:3–8

Life can only be enjoyed day by day, bite by bite. We enjoy our youth thoroughly, express our faith thoughtfully, and finally we learn to embrace the aging process thankfully.

Notice how wonderfully clever God is as He inspires Solomon to write these pages. He knows our smiles might fade a bit as He brings up this particular subject. But Solomon keeps a heavy subject light—and downright funny. Isn't that just what we need when we fret about fresh wrinkles? We need to take ourselves a little less seriously. We need a good laugh.

Solomon gives us a poetic picture of getting older. Let's work our way through this passage looking at the phrases he chooses:

The day when the keepers of the house tremble. Those are your arms and hands. As we get older, they begin to shake and tremble more.

And the strong men bow down. Knees and shoulders grow weaker, more frail as we age, bending and bowing and slumping.

When the grinders cease because they are few. What are "grinders"? Your teeth, of course! We can be thankful for improved dental care, but we still lose a tooth every now and then.

And those that look through the windows grow dim. Are you getting the idea? Our eyes, the windows of mind and body. No one had spectacles in Solomon's time; they had to live with blurry vision.

When the doors are shut in the streets, and the sound of grinding is low. Our ears and our hearing begin to fail. We can't hear the old street sounds or the mills grinding away.

When one rises up at the sound of a bird. Teenagers can sleep until noon, but that is a skill we lose as we age. We old-timers are up with the chickens. My parents used to stay at our house. No matter what time I got up in the morning, my dad was sitting at the kitchen table. I would ask him, "Dad, did you go to bed last night?" Sure—he just liked those early hours.

And all the daughters of music are brought low. Your voice starts to quiver and weaken. You don't sing as loudly or clearly as you once did.

Also they are afraid of height, and of terrors in the way. We become much less eager to climb ladders and stairways as we grow older. We don't even like a high curb.

When the almond tree blossoms. What tree blossoms as you grow older? Your hair puts forth white shoots! Rather than informing your spouse you have spotted another gray hair, why not say, "Nice almond tree, honey!"

The grasshopper is a burden. By summer's end, grasshoppers lose their hop. They are more like "grass-limpers."

And desire fails. You can work this one out for yourself. Hint: there are several lines of pharmaceuticals to help.

For man goes to his eternal home, and the mourners go about the streets. This is referring to the unavoidable funeral and funeral procession.

This description of aging in the Bible reminds me of the couple in Florida who wanted to get married. Jacob was ninety-two and Rebecca was eighty-nine. As they discussed their wedding, they passed a drugstore, and Jacob suggested they go in. Addressing the man behind the counter, Jacob said, "We're getting married. Do you sell heart medication?"

"Yes, of course we do," said the pharmacist.

"How about medicine for circulation?"

"All kinds."

"Medicine for rheumatism, scoliosis?"

"Definitely."

"Medicine for memory problems, arthritis, jaundice?"

"Yes, a large variety," said the pharmacist. "Whatever the doctor orders."

"What about vitamins, sleeping pills, Geritol?"

"Absolutely."

"And wheelchairs and walkers?"

"All speeds and sizes."

"Great!" said Jacob, "We'd like to use this store as our bridal registry."

Live long enough and, upon hearing that one, you won't laugh but say, "Hmm, good idea." Regardless of whether you have been hatched recently or you are soon to be dispatched, why not enjoy life to the fullest?

Solomon goes on in verse 6 to give us four images of what it is like to die.

- It's like a silver cord that loosens and falls away.
- It's like a golden bowl that plummets to the floor and crashes.
- It's like a pitcher shattered at the fountain.
- It's like a wheel broken at the well.

Fallen. Crashed. Shattered. Broken. These are all images of lost beauty. Together their picture is heartbreaking.

Then again, Art Linkletter once said that it is better to be over the hill than under it. Whatever life is for us, wherever we find ourselves in age or stage, every moment is a gift of God—brightly wrapped, waiting to be opened, admired, and delighted in. The bittersweet nature of loss makes the present more precious; knowing that the silver cord will one day slip away, we cherish it all the more while it is in our hands.

We must not spend too much time brooding over life's transience, for that defeats the very purpose. The time is to be used, to be invested in joy and meaning.

That includes *today*. Go ye therefore and have fun!

31

Life Is Mysterious: Examine It!

Ecclesiastes 12:9–12

So you finish the course. What happens? Final exam!

There is King Solomon at the front of the classroom, passing everyone a copy of the exam. "Let's test your wisdom," he intones. "Use a number two pencil, and keep your eyes on your own scroll."

The test is going to cover all twelve chapters of Ecclesiastes. You will be asked about life, death, pleasure, suffering, food, work, money, poverty, wisdom, foolishness—pretty much everything under the sun.

"That's a lot of material!" you whisper in panic to the fellow in the next seat. "What if I don't have a clue?"

"Whenever you don't know one, the probable answer is 'vanity,'" your friend whispers back. "Works every time. When I'm stumped I just write, 'Life is filled with such questions that can't be answered. This too is vanity.' Teacher likes that one."

You mutter, "I hope he was serious when he said that true wisdom is realizing how much we *don't* know. If he sticks to that one, I'll get an A."

Solomon comes to the exam in these final verses, but, characteristically, he reverses the formula. For Solomon it is exam first, lessons later. It is a bit like the scene in Lewis Carroll's *Alice in Wonderland* when the king asks the jury to consider its verdict. "No, no," objects the queen. "Sentence first—verdict afterwards."[1]

In school we study and then take an exam. Solomon claims that in the real world we face the exam, and then we study. He tells us that wisdom comes through instruction, through insight, and through inspiration.

This world desperately needs wise people. In the late 1700s in France, a young man named Jean-Baptiste Vianney wanted to become a preacher. His family was very poor, and his studies were hindered by lack of funds. When he finally came up with a way to attend school, his studies were interrupted by the terrors of the French Revolution, then by the wars of Napoleon.

As it turned out, Jean-Baptiste was not a particularly bright student, and when he was finally ordained at age twenty-nine, he was described by his superiors as being academically underqualified. He was sent to the small, obscure village of Ars-en-Dombes, where, to everyone's surprise, he became a powerful preacher whose sermons forcefully impacted the everyday lives of his parishioners.

Jean-Baptiste was especially skilled in individual counseling, and he seemed to be blessed with extraordinary psychological insight. He possessed a knack for helping people know how to apply the Word of God to their daily lives so as to find freedom for real living. Some people became convinced he was a mind reader; and as his fame spread, people came from hundreds of miles to hear him preach and to seek his counsel. During the last year of his life, one hundred thousand people traveled from all over Europe to hear him. He was a kind of eighteenth-century Solomon.[2]

Couldn't we use a few people like him today? If you agree, then why not volunteer? You can be a Solomon. You can be wise. You can acquire the biblical, spiritual, and mental skills to help people.

Wisdom Comes Through Instruction

And moreover, because the Preacher was wise, he still taught the people knowledge; yes, he pondered and sought out and set in order many proverbs.

—ECCLESIASTES 12:9

Solomon taught the people knowledge through the use of proverbs. A proverb is an earthly saying containing heavenly truth. It is the wisdom of God wrapped in a pretty package. It is distilled wisdom, a practical word for a complicated world. Proverbs are God's "sound bites." The preamble to Solomon's book of Proverbs reads:

The purpose of these proverbs is to teach people wisdom and discipline, and to help them understand wise sayings. Through these proverbs, people will receive instruction in discipline, good conduct, and doing what is right, just, and fair. These proverbs will make the simpleminded clever. They will give knowledge and purpose to young people.

Let those who are wise listen to these proverbs and become even wiser. And let those who understand receive guidance by exploring the depth of meaning in these proverbs, parables, wise sayings, and riddles. (Proverbs 1:2–6 NLT)

Some define *wisdom* as "seeing life from God's point of view." I prefer to say that wisdom is the ability to apply biblical truth to real-life situations.

Without the Bible, no one can be wise, for wisdom is the ability to see more than things as they are "under the sun." It is the ability to perceive how the God of heaven sees a situation and apply His divine wisdom to it.

As we study the proverbs of Solomon, we'll grow in wisdom. And sometimes a simple sentence of truth—one Spirit-inspired sentence—can change a person's whole attitude and life.

Wisdom Comes Through Insight

The Preacher sought to find acceptable words; and what was written was upright—words of truth.

—ECCLESIASTES 12:10

Solomon's teaching was like that of Jesus, who (being God incarnate) possessed an infinite magnification of the wisdom of Solomon. Christ's words were acceptable, full of grace and truth.

Do you ever struggle to find just the right words to say to someone? Well, remember God's offer in James 1:5: "If any of you lacks wisdom, let him ask of God, who gives to all liberally and without reproach, and it will be given to him."

How often I have been in a crisis or tense situation and claimed this truth. I have been with my children, my parishioners, or with someone needing my help, and I have whispered a prayer to God: "Lord, give me wisdom!" If you have been abiding in the Scriptures, it is amazing and inspiring how just the right word rolls off your tongue. You may have little or no education, but you have access to the greatest wisdom of the universe.

Alexander Grigolia immigrated to America from Soviet Georgia, learned English, earned three doctoral degrees, and became a successful professor at the University of Pennsylvania. Despite his freedom and achievements, there was a deep shadow in his heart—a misery he could not remove.

One day while getting a shoeshine, he noticed that the bootblack went about his work with a sense of joy, scrubbing and buffing and smiling and talking. Finally Dr. Grigolia could stand it no longer. With his Russian accent he asked, "Why are you so happy?"

Looking up, the bootblack paused and replied, "Jesus. He loves me. He died so God could forgive my badness. He makes me happy."

The professor snapped his newspaper back in front of his face, and the bootblack went back to work. But Dr. Grigolia never escaped those words, and they brought him eventually to the Savior. He later became a professor of anthropology at Wheaton College, where he taught a young student named Billy Graham. An accomplished professor had to bow to the wisdom of a simple, unlearned bootblack.[3]

Wisdom Comes Through Inspiration

The words of the wise are like goads, and the words of
scholars are like well-driven nails, given by one Shepherd.
And further, my son, be admonished by these. Of making
many books there is no end, and much study is wearisome to
the flesh.

—Ecclesiastes 12:11–12

Wisdom comes through instruction, insight, and inspiration. The best, deepest, finest, and most lasting wisdom is that which comes from "one Shepherd." Notice the word *Shepherd* is capitalized. That Shepherd is God. The wisdom He gives is like nails that drive truth into the walls of our hearts by the Holy Spirit. Elsewhere the Word of

God is likened to a sharp, two-edged sword and is like a hammer that breaks rocks to pieces.

In verse 12, Solomon warns us against studying too many books to the exclusion of the Bible. "Of making many books there is no end, and much study is wearisome to the flesh." That is a favorite verse for college students, but Solomon is not telling us *not* to love and appreciate books. He is warning us that we should not study other books to the exclusion of Holy Scripture. Other books were given for our information, but the Bible was given for our transformation. Ruth Bell Graham was once asked the best way to become wise. Her reply, "Read, read, read—but use the Bible as home base." She's right.

In one of his remarkable sermons, Charles Spurgeon thundered:

> Ah! You know more about your ledgers than your Bible; you know more about your daybooks than what God has written; many of you will read a novel from beginning to end, and what have you got? A mouthful of froth when you have done. But you cannot read the Bible; that solid, lasting, substantial, and satisfying food goes uneaten, locked up in the cupboard of neglect.[4]

The Bible is an every-single-day book for me. It has been for many years, and it will be until the day I die. To go through a day without immersing myself in its freshness would be like going through a day without bathing—or breathing, for that matter. As D. L. Moody said, "Those who read the Bible most find it ever new." The Bible that is falling apart, it has been said, usually belongs to someone who isn't.

I try to read the Bible every day, but I also read whatever assists me in grasping it. I read newspapers, journals, and sometimes bestsellers. I try to read the classics of the ages. But I use the Shepherd's words as the grid on which I chart all other information since I believe that the Bible gives us the final answers to life. What Solomon is saying, I believe, is that our faith is not primarily about searching; it is about finding. It's not about questions; it's about answers.

In C. S. Lewis's *The Great Divorce*, there is a scene in which the main characters are on the borders of heaven, and a lifelong searcher outside of heaven is being told to come in. The person called the White Spirit meets him at the borders and says, "The only thing I can give you when you come in is forgiveness for having perverted all of your values and all of your brain and all of your intelligence. There is no atmosphere in this place called Heaven for inquiry. I am going to bring you to the land, not of questions but of answers, and you will see the face of God."

The man answers, "Ah, but we must interpret those beautiful words in our own way!"

The White Spirit replies, "Once you were a child. Once you knew what inquiry was for. There was a time when you asked questions because you wanted answers, and you were glad when you had found them. Become that child again, even now."

"Ah," said the inquirer, "but when I became a man I put away childish things."

The encounter ends when the inquirer mentions he has an appointment, and he makes his apologies, leaving the borders of heaven and hurrying off to his discussion group in hell. Here was a character exposed to the answer, but because he thought reality was in the quest, he wouldn't accept the fact that *answers are available.*[5]

We often wonder whether those in the no-absolutes camp—who claim one person's "truth" is as good as another's—really *want* to find the final Truth. If they could stand on the very borders of heaven, would they embrace the final answers, or would they turn and walk away to keep playing the game of unending speculation?

There is one truth from one Shepherd. Jesus said, "Your word is truth" (John 17:17). We must not get so caught up in postmodern inquiry as to forget that questions are for answers, and the answers are available in God's Word.

Conclusion

Life Is Obedience: Express It!

Ecclesiastes 12:13–14

Let us hear the conclusion of the whole matter:

> Fear God and keep His commandments,
> For this is man's all.
> For God will bring every work into judgment,
> Including every secret thing,
> Whether good or evil.
>
> —ECCLESIASTES 12:13–14

Old Solomon sits in his private chamber—the place where he studies and thinks the deep thoughts; the place where his path intersects with the path of the Shepherd who has herded him for so many years of obedience, grazing, growing, and wandering—and not a few wolf bites.

As Solomon ponders "the conclusion of the whole matter," he thinks not simply of the end of a book nor of the end of a king's life but the beginning of wisdom in life before the King. All of it comes together here. Solomon thinks of childhood at the elbow of his beloved father, King David. He thinks of that evening when he made his great request of God, the years of building and conquest and prosperity, the advisors, the too-many wives—all of it blurs together, and he feels smaller than ever before the God of his fathers.

Having held the world's greatest jewels, built the world's greatest temple, and led the world's greatest nation, Solomon seeks the final treasure—no less than the meaning of life itself. He has hungered for happiness, the foretaste of heaven divine.

So much flashes before him: the world's great libraries, wise men from around the world, priests and princes and prophets, ships from exotic lands previously unknown. And all of it comes down to . . . *nothing.*

Never was there the brief hint of heaven on earth. But there was something Solomon's father taught him, something known to Abraham and Isaac and Jacob, to Joseph and all the brothers and their tribes, some simple little thing you might hear on the tongue of the poorest peddler down in the street. And somehow this brief word trumps all the wisdom and learning of the world.

And the word is this:

> Fear God, and keep His commandments,
> For this is man's all. (Ecclesiastes 12:13)

All indeed.

> For God will bring every work into judgment,
> Including every secret thing,
> Whether good or evil. (12:14)

You could have no riches, no power, no glory, none of life's ordinary pleasure, and if you knew that *one thing*—simple enough for any child—you would have the map to finding happiness. Eternity is fixed in our hearts; light calls to light; deep calls to deep. Therefore, we must travel or be forever wretched, miserable creatures.

Fear God: that is the point of departure. *Keep His commandments*: that is the path. Travel it seriously, eyes fixed ahead as you walk the narrow way, and you will indeed see glimpses of the Eternal City.

And thus Solomon comes to his journey's end, a rest for his soul. It is as if the final installment of that gift he requested so many years ago has just been made. Surely this is the end point of all wisdom.

A single tear wells up in the eye of the world's wealthiest, wisest, and most powerful man. In his journal he scribbles in blunt letters, jagged with a hand trembling from age and emotion: "Fear God." To fear God means to be struck with awe in His all-consuming, holy presence; to stand always and forever in breathless exaltation of who He is and what He has done and how vastly and infinitely His greatness overshadows our brief, vaporous existence.

Just beneath that, Solomon scrawls, "Keep His commandments." Yes, Solomon nods, it is the only way. Find out what God wants done, and *go do it*, regardless of the cost. All the rest is vanity, heartache, wandering blind.

In 1866, D. L. Moody was conducting a series of evangelistic meetings in Brockton, Massachusetts. Daniel B. Towner, director of the music department at Moody Bible Institute in Chicago, was leading the music for those meetings.

A young man rose to give his testimony of following Christ, and he included in his remarks these words: "I am not quite sure—but I am going to trust, and I am going to obey."

Mr. Towner was so touched by these words that he jotted them down and sent them to the Reverend J. H. Sammis, a Presbyterian minister and later a teacher at Moody Institute. Reverend Sammis expanded those words into the stanzas and chorus of the beloved

319

hymn, "Trust and Obey." We could inscribe those words right beneath the ones Solomon has written:

> When we walk with the Lord in the light of His Word
> What a glory He sheds on our way!
> While we do His good will, He abides with us still,
> And with all who will trust and obey.
> Trust and obey for there's no other way
> To be happy in Jesus, but to trust and obey.[1]

God created you with a place in your heart that only He can fill. He has set eternity in your heart. Life for you and for me is like a trip to the mall on Christmas Eve. There is color and music and mingled fragrances everywhere, all sensuous, all seductive, all competing for our attention—all the vanities and pursuits that come up empty. Solomon tried every one of them.

Then, in the back corner, we see the narrow door. It is quiet, plain, unmarked, and largely ignored as people rush by. But we know that our Savior has left this door ajar for us and that it leads us to the place where we will find all that our hearts have desired.

The door is open just a crack, as if in invitation, and we see a brilliant light trying to break through. We know instantly it is the light of another world. It is the light of heaven on earth.

The Good Shepherd said, "I have come that they may have life, and that they may have it more abundantly" (John 10:10). The door may be plain, but the world behind it is rich indeed. Rich and joyful, filled with pleasures. As a matter of fact, all the vain things that charmed us most in this earthly life—the pleasures and pursuits that felt and tasted so empty—are now as wonderful as they always should have been. The Shepherd makes the very sunshine itself feel brighter.

My friend, open that door. Begin the adventure that will be the greatest of your life and the joy that will be the richest. If you do not know my Lord Jesus Christ, I ask you to meet Him this very moment by praying:

> Lord, I realize now that my whole life has been a search for heaven on earth. I long to know, to taste, to feel the truth that is true, the love that is genuine, the Master who will never let me down. You died for me so many years ago on a painful cross, and I realize now that You took the payment for all my sins—every one of them. How I long to be relieved of their burden! Just as You rose from the dead, conquering death forever, I choose right now to accept eternal life—to know that death will have no hold on me. And I will pursue You down that path toward the Eternal City with every breath I breathe for the rest of this life until the day You and I meet face to face. Amen.

Notes

PREFACE

1. Hole, vocal performance of "Celebrity Skin," by Courtney Love, Eric Erlandson, and Billy Corgan, on *Celebrity Skin*, David Geffin Company DGC25194, 1998, CD.

INTRODUCTION

1. John Berryman, quoted in John Leax, "'Grace Soften My Dreams'—John Berryman," *Christianity Today*, April 1, 1977, 25–26.
2. Victor E. Frankl, *Man's Search for Meaning* (New York: Pocket Books, 1984), 122.
3. Carl Jung, *Modern Man in Search of a Soul* (New York: Harvest Books, 1955), 70.
4. Frankl, Ibid., 128.
5. Rick Warren, *The Purpose Driven Life* (Grand Rapids: Zondervan, 2002), 19–20.
6. Jack Higgins, "What's Missing?" *Our Daily Bread*, July 9, 1994.
7. Abba Eban, *Abba Eban: An Autobiography* (New York: Random House, 1977), 609.
8. Jon Krakauer, *Into Thin Air* (New York: Doubleday/Anchor Books, 1997), 3–4.
9. Peggy Lee, vocal performance of "Is That All There Is?" by Jerry Lieber and Mike Stoller, on *Is That All There Is?*, Capitol Records, Capitol ST-386, 1969, 33 1/3 rpm.

CHAPTER 1: WILL THE CIRCLE BE UNBROKEN?

1. Thomas Toivi Blatt, *From the Ashes of Sobibor* (Evanston, IL: Northwestern University Press, 1997).

2. Bertrand Russell, *Autobiography* (London: Routledge, 2000), 237.

3. Harold Kushner, *When All You've Wanted Isn't Enough* (Random House, 1988), 20.

4. Ernest Hemingway, "A Citation Report," *Look*, September 4, 1956.

5. C. Douglas Caffey, "Brevity of Life," International War Veterans' Poetry Archives, January 20, 2002, http://iwvpa.net/caffeycd/zz -brevity-.php. © 2002. All rights reserved. Used by permission.

6. Kansas, vocal performance of "Dust in the Wind," words and music by Kerry Livgren, on *Dust in the Wind*, Kirshner ZS8 4274, 1977, 45 rpm.

7. James S. Hewett, *Illustrations Unlimited* (Wheaton, IL: Tyndale House Publishers, 1988), 291–92.

CHAPTER 2: BORED TO DEATH

1. Paula Guran, OMNI Online, January 1998, reposted as "Kathe Koja: Transcendence and Transformation," Dark Echo, http:// www.darkecho.com/darkecho/archives/koja.html.

2. Michael Crichton, *Timeline* (New York: Ballantine Books, 1999), 443.

3. Victor E. Frankl, *Man's Search for Meaning* (New York: Pocket Books, 1984), 129.

4. Clifton Fadiman and Andre Bernard, eds., *Bartlett's Book of Anecdotes* (Boston: Little, Brown & Co., 2000), 146.

5. Rudyard Kipling, "The Holy War," *The Years Between* (London: Methuen, 1919), 39.

6. Chris Ross, *Jacksonville Daily Progress*, November 2, 2003.

7. Johnson Oatman, Jr., "Higher Ground," 1898; music by Charles H. Gabriel, 1892.

8. Howard Mumma, "Conversations with Camus," *Christian Century* 117, no. 18 (June 7, 2000): 644.

9. Information on Pascal taken from www.gospelcom.net; Emile Caillet and John C. Blankenagel, trans., *Great Shorter Works of Pascal* (Philadelphia: Westminster Press, 1948); and Bill Tsamis, "Blaise Pascal," C. S. Lewis Society, http://www.apologetics.org /BlaisePascal/tabid/81/Default.aspx.

CHAPTER 3: TRIVIAL PURSUITS

1. Lawrence Taylor and Steve Serby, *LT: Over the Edge* (New York: HarperCollins, 2003), i.
2. Jim Sami, "L. T. Comments Rile TV Analysts," *Smith Florida Sun-Sentinel*, December 1, 2003.
3. James Dobson, monthly newsletter, May 1996.
4. T. S. Eliot, "Choruses from *The Rock*," in *Collected Poems: 1909-1962* (New York: Harcourt Brace, 1963), 147.
5. *The Star*, Johannesburg, South Africa, December 13, 2003, 1.
6. Vance Havner, *The Secret of Christian Joy* (Old Tappan, NJ: Fleming H. Revell, 1938), 40.
7. David W. Henderson, *Culture Shift: Communicating God's Truth to Our Changing World* (Grand Rapids, MI: Baker, 1998), 186.
8. David Kidner, *A Time to Mourn, and a Time to Dance* (Downers Grove, IL: InterVarsity Press, 1976), 35.
9. "Nigeria No. 1 in Happiness, U.S. Ranks 16th," CNN.com, October 2, 2003.
10. C. S. Lewis, "The Weight of Glory," *The Weight of Glory and Other Essays* (New York: Macmillan, 1980), 7.

CHAPTER 4: CAREENING CAREERS

1. Mart De Haan, "Winning Big," http://odb.org/1999/08/27/winning-big.
2. Derek Ratcliffe, "Image and Reality: More Reflections on TV Natural History," *ECOS* (a publication of the British Association of Natural Conservationists), vol. 21, NU, July 1, 2000, 5.
3. Mark Bennett, "Diesler Prompts Depression Talk," UEFA.com, December 9, 2003, http://www.uefa.com/news/newsid=131979.html.
4. Norman Vasquez, testimonial on "What People Are Saying About Mission Control," Mission Control India, http://www.mission controlindia.com/customer-testimonial.html.
5. Andrew Curry, "Why We Work," *U.S. News and World Report*, February 24, 2003.
6. James Shirley, "Death the Leveler," *The Oxford Book of English Verse, 1250-1900*, comp. and ed. Arthur Thomas Quiller-Couch (Oxford: Clarendon, 1919), http://www.bartleby.com/101/288.html.
7. William Lane Craig, *Reasonable Faith* (Wheaton, IL: Crossway Books, 1994), 58-59.

8. "Like Smoke and Cotton Candy," *Generation Magazine* 2, no. 3, http://www.gogeneration.com/v2iss3/likesmoke.htm.
9. Clara T. Williams, "Satisfied," 1875.

CHAPTER 5: IMPRESSIONS ABOUT LIFE
1. Pete Seeger, vocal performance of "Turn! Turn! Turn (To Everything There Is a Season)" by Pete Seeger, 1962, on *The Bitter and the Sweet*, Columbia CS 8716, 1962, 33 1/3 rpm.
2. David Jeremiah, *A Bend in the Road* (Nashville: Word Publishing, 2000).
3. Harold S. Kushner, *When Bad Things Happen to Good People* (New York: HarperCollins, 1982).
4. Donald Regan, *For the Record: From Wall Street to Washington* (San Diego: Harcourt Brace Jovanovich Publishers, 1988), 232.
5. Robert J. Morgan, *From This Verse: 365 Inspiring Stories About the Power of God's Word* (Nashville: Thomas Nelson, 1998), 54.
6. Thomas O. Chisholm & William Runyan, "Great Is Thy Faithfulness" (Carol Stream, IL: Hope Publishing Co., 1951).

CHAPTER 6: INSIGHTS ABOUT GOD
1. Waldemar Januszczak, "Philip Guston—Exposing a Futile Existence," *Times Online*, January 25, 2004, http://www.thesundaytimes.co.uk/sto/culture/article248381.ece.
2. William Shakespeare, *Macbeth*, act 5, scene 5, lines 19–28.
3. Brother Lawrence, *The Practice of the Presence of God* (Grand Rapids: Spire Books, repr. 1999).
4. Diane Ball, "In His Time," 1978. © 1978 Maranatha! Music, ASCAP.
5. Malcolm Muggeridge, *A Twentieth Century Testimony* (Nashville: Thomas Nelson, 1978), 18.
6. Allan C. Emery, *Turtle on a Fencepost* (Nashville: Thomas Nelson, 1980), 110–11.
7. Frederick W. Faber, *Jesus and Mary* (London: Richardson and Son, 1852).
8. Tommy Nelson, *The Problem of Life with God—Living with a Perfect God in an Imperfect World* (Nashville: Broadman & Holman, 2002), 49.
9. C. S. Lewis, *Mere Christianity* (New York: Macmillan Publishing, 1952), 120.

10. St. Augustine, *Confessions of St. Augustine*, book 1, chapter 1, trans. Albert Outler, http://www.fordham.edu/halsall/basis/confessions-bod.asp.
11. C. S. Lewis, quoted in Ray C. Stedman, *Is This All There Is in Life?* (Grand Rapids: Discovery House Books, 1999), 51.
12. Tom Bisset, *Good News About Prodigals* (Grand Rapids: Discovery House Publishers, 1997), 127–30.

CHAPTER 7: READ THE INSTRUCTIONS
1. William Cowper, "God Moves in a Mysterious Way," 1774.
2. Jim McGuiggan, *The Irish Papers: Lessons from Life* (Fort Worth, TX: Star Bible & Tract Corporation, 1992), 42.
3. *Westminster Larger Catechism* (Phillipsburg, NJ: P & R Publishing, 2002), 3.
4. Taken from "Ma Sunday Still Speaks: A transcription of the tape recording she made shortly before her death," published by Winona Lake Christian Assembly, Winona Lake, IN, 1957.

CHAPTER 8: WHEN JUSTICE ISN'T JUST
1. Bob Woffinden, "Ear-print Landed Innocent Man in Jail for Murder," *The Guardian Unlimited*, January 23, 2004, http://www.guardian.co.uk/uk/2004/jan/23/ukcrime1.
2. Connie Cass, "Report: 1 of Every 75 U.S. Men in Prison," Associated Press, May 28, 2004.
3. Paul Harvey Jr., ed., *Paul Harvey's For What It's Worth* (New York: Bantam Books, 1991), 129.
4. James Russell Lowell, "The Present Crisis," *Boston Courier*, December 11, 1845.
5. William Wadsworth Longfellow, *Poems and Other Writings* (New York: Library of America, 2000), 697.
6. Maurice S. Rawlings, *To Hell and Back* (Nashville: Thomas Nelson, 1993), 20.
7. John Parker, "God Holds the Key of All Unknown," *Poems with Power to Strengthen the Soul*, comp. and ed. James Mudge (New York: Eaton & Mains, 1907), 208.

CHAPTER 9: FROM OPPRESSION TO OBSESSION
1. Tommy Nelson, *The Problem of Life with God: Living with a Perfect*

God in an Imperfect World (Nashville: Broadman & Holman Publishers, 2002), 59–60.

2. Mark Sidwell, *Free Indeed: Heroes of Black Christian History* (Greenville, SC: Bob Jones University Press, 2001), 83.

3. Charles A. Tindley, "We'll Understand It Better By and By." © 1905 Tindley Music Company. BMI.

4. Robert J. Morgan, *Real Stories for the Soul* (Nashville: Thomas Nelson, 2001), 20–22.

5. Michael Millar, "Professional Jealousy Grips the Nation," *Personnel Today*, February 2, 2004, http://www.personneltoday.com/articles /02/02/2004/22184/professional-jealousy-grips-the-nation.htm.

6. J. I. Packer, *Knowing God Through the Year* (Downers Grove, IL: InterVarsity Press, 2004), 222.

7. Martha Irvine, "Young Adults Yearning for the Simple Life," *Salt Lake Tribune*, January 26, 2004.

CHAPTER 10: WHEN 1 + 1 > 2

1. T. S. Eliot, "The Cocktail Party," *Complete Poems and Plays* (New York: Harcourt, Brace, & Co., 1952), 364.

2. Warren Wiersbe, *An Old Testament Study: Ecclesiastes: Be Satisfied—Looking for the Answer to the Meaning of Life* (Wheaton, IL: Victor Books, 1990), 58–59.

3. Charles Wesley, "Two Are Better Far Than One," in John Wesley, *A Collection of Hymns, for the Use of People Called Methodists* (London: Wesleyan-Methodist Book-Room, 1889), 487.

4. Steve Campbell, "What Players Really Want Is the Hardware," *Houston Chronicle*, January 28, 2004, http://www.chron.com/sports/ article/What-players-really-want-is-the-hardware-1973775.php.

CHAPTER 11: A GOD WHO CAN'T BE USED

1. Craig Brian Larson, ed., *750 Engaging Illustrations for Pastors, Teachers, and Writers* (Grand Rapids, MI: Baker Books, 2002), 51.

2. Julie Juola-Exline, "When God Disappoints: Difficulty in Forgiving God and Its Role in Negative Emotions," *Journal of Health Psychology* 4, no. 3 (1999).

3. Aaron Sorkin, "Two Cathedrals," *The West Wing*, season 2, episode 22, directed by Thomas Schlamme, aired May 16, 2001 (Warner Bros. Television), DVD.

4. Eva J. Alexander, "Rescuing Women," *Decision*, October 1997, 4–5.

CHAPTER 12: GOVERNMENTS NEVER CHANGE

1. Fred Kaplan, *1959: The Year Everything Changed* (Hoboken, NJ: John Wiley & Sons, 2009), 273 n. 108.
2. The Who, vocal performance of "Won't Get Fooled Again," by Pete Townshend, on *Who's Next*, MCA Records DL 79182, 1971, 33 1/3 rpm.
3. Aleksandr Solzhenitsyn, *The Gulag Archipelago*, vol. 2, trans. Thomas P. Whitney (New York: Harper & Row, 1975), 615.
4. Rev. John Rusk, *The Authentic Life of T. DeWitt Talmage* (n.p.: L. G. Stahl, 1902), 371.
5. John R. Vile, *The Constitutional Convention of 1787: A Comprehensive Encyclopedia of America's Founding* (Santa Barbara, CA: ABC-CLIO, 2005), 593.
6. Will Durant, quoted in Robert Andrews, ed., *The Columbia Dictionary of Quotations* (New York: Columbia University Press, 1993), 155.

CHAPTER 13: DOLLARS AND SENSE

1. "Hundreds of Coins Found in French Patient's Belly," Associated Press, February 18, 2004, http://www.nbcnews.com/id/4304525/#.UW2q6bWfi6O.
2. Quoted in Doug Rehberg, "How to Die" (sermon), January 12, 2003, Hebron Church, Pittsburgh, PA.
3. William MacDonald, *Changing the Wind* (Chicago: Moody Press, 1975), 47.
4. Peter Collier and David Horowitz, *The Rockefellers, an American Dynasty* (New York: Holt, Rinehart and Winston, 1976), 48.

CHAPTER 14: MONEY WITHOUT MEANING

1. "Lottery Winner Dies in Accident Hours After Show," Associated Press, January 24, 2004; http://www.creditinfocenter.com/community/topic/222988-lottery-winner-dies-in-accident-hours-after-show.
2. Chuck Rasmussen, untitled sermon illustration, www.christianglobe.com/illustrations/a-z/m/money_love_of.htm.
3. "A Year Later, $315 Million Powerball Winner Wishes He'd Been Quieter," Associated Press, December 24, 2003, http://www.wave3

.com/story/1576965/a-year-later-315-million-powerball-winner
-wishes-hed-been-quieter?clienttype=printable.

4. Jerry White, *The Power of Commitment* (Colorado Springs: NavPress, 1985), 46.

5. Warren Wiersbe, *An Old Testament Study: Ecclesiastes: Be Satisfied—Looking for the Answer to the Meaning of Life* (Wheaton, IL: Victor Books, 1990), 74–75.

6. John Woodbridge, ed., *More Than Conquerors* (Chicago: Moody Press, 1992), 340–43.

CHAPTER 15: EMPLOYMENT WITHOUT ENJOYMENT

1. Barbara Davies, "'Depressed' Colly Books into Priory," Mirror.co.uk, March 3, 2004, http://www.thefreelibrary.com/'DEPRESSED'+COL LY+BOOKS+INTO+PRIORY%3B+Dogging+shock+star+seeks+help .-a0113834743.

2. Marvin Lubenow, *Bones of Contention: A Creationist's Assessment of Human Fossils* (Grand Rapids: Baker Book House, 1992), 44.

3. George A. Young, "God Leads His Dear Children Along," 1903.

4. Robert J. Morgan, *Then Sings My Soul 2* (Nashville: Thomas Nelson, 2004), 245.

CHAPTER 17: THE JOY OF MISERY

1. Warren Wiersbe, *An Old Testament Study: Ecclesiastes: Be Satisfied—Looking for the Answer to the Meaning of Life* (Wheaton, IL: Victor Books, 1990), 84.

2. Bill Bright, quoted in Michael Richardson, *Amazing Faith: The Authorized Biography of Bill Bright* (Colorado Springs: Waterbrook, 2000), 51.

3. Hudson Taylor, *To China with Love* (Grand Rapids, MI: Baker Books, 1972), 62–63.

4. *Our Daily Bread*, published by Radio Bible Class, date unknown.

CHAPTER 18: THE PLEASURE OF REBUKE

1. Mark Twain, quoted in Robert Andrews, *The Concise Columbia Dictionary of Quotations* (New York: Columbia University Press, 1987; repr. 1992), 56.

2. Conrad Hilton, *Be My Guest* (New York: Simon & Schuster, 1994), 76–77.

3. Gordon MacDonald, *Ordering Your Private World* (Nashville: Thomas Nelson, 1984), 115–16.

4. Moody Bible Institute Stewardship Department, *Today in the Word*, November 9, 1995, 16.

5. J. Oswald Sanders, *Spiritual Leadership* (Chicago: Moody Press, 1967), 143.

6. Gordon MacDonald, *Restoring Your Spiritual Passion* (Nashville: Thomas Nelson, 1986), 192–93.

CHAPTER 19: THE HARD WAY MADE EASY

1. Robert Frost, "A Servant to Servants," *North of Boston* (New York: Henry Holt & Co., 1915), 66.

2. Stephen Covey, *The 7 Habits of Highly Effective People* (Free Press, 1989), 95–144.

3. Andre Castelot, *Napoleon*, trans. Guy Daniels (New York: Harper & Row, 1971), 231.

4. C. S. Lewis, *The Screwtape Letters* (New York: Macmillan Co., 1961), 56.

5. Fanny Crosby, "O Child of God," 1886; music by Ira D. Sankey.

CHAPTER 20: TIME TO MOVE ON

1. W. Michael Cox and Richard Alm, "The Good Old Days Are Now," Reason.com, December 1995, http://reason.com/archives /1995/12/01/the-good-old-days-are-now/1.

2. Paul Simon, vocal performance of "Kodachrome," by Paul Simon and Phil Ramone, on *There Goes Rhymin' Simon*, Columbia, 1973. 45 rpm.

3. Arthur Bennett, "The Valley of Vision," in *The Valley of Vision, A Collection of Puritan Prayers and Devotions*, ed. Arthur Bennett (Edinburgh: Banner of Truth Trust, 1975), xxiv.

CHAPTER 21: THE PERSPECTIVE OF WISDOM

1. Robert J. Morgan, *Nelson's Complete Book of Stories, Illustrations, and Quotes* (Nashville: Thomas Nelson, 2000), 653–54.

2. Dan Jansen and Jack McCallum, *Full Circle: An Olympic Champion Shares His Breakthrough Story* (New York: Villard, 1994).

3. "State of the World 2004: Richer, Fatter, and Not Much Happier," Worldwatch Institute, January 8, 2004, http://www.worldwatch .org/state-world-2004-richer-fatter-and-not-much-happier.

4. Warren Wiersbe, *An Old Testament Study: Ecclesiastes: Be Satisfied: Looking for the Answer to the Meaning of Life* (Wheaton, IL: Victor Books, 1990), 89–90.

Chapter 22: The Power of Wisdom

1. Ray Stedman, "Whoever Said Life Was Fair?" *Discovery Papers*, October 31, 1982 (Palo Alto, CA: Peninsula Bible Church Discovery Publishing, 1982), 3.
2. Michael Guido, *The Michael Guido Story* (Metter, GA: The Guido Evangelistic Association, Inc., 1990), 134.
3. "O Boundless Wisdom, God Most High," trans. Gabriel Gillet, in *The English Hymnal* (London: Oxford, 1906), 50.

Chapter 23: Hard to Be Humble

1. Rick Reilly, "Destiny Frowns on Kurt Warner," *Sports Illustrated*, December 1, 2003.
2. Clark Clifford, *Counsel to the President* (New York: Random House, 1991), 140–41.
3. Constance E. Padwick, *Henry Martyn* (Chicago: Moody Press, 1980), 162.
4. Arthur W. Pink, *The Seven Sayings of the Savior on the Cross* (Grand Rapids: Baker Book House, 1958), 110.
5. Ruth Bell Graham, *Prodigals and Those Who Love Them* (Colorado Springs: Focus on the Family Publishers, 1991), 118.
6. Warren Wiersbe, *An Old Testament Study: Ecclesiastes: Be Satisfied: Looking for the Answer to the Meaning of Life* (Wheaton, IL: Victor Books, 1990), 100.
7. Ravi Zacharias, *Can Man Live Without God?* (Dallas: Word Publishing, 1994), 26.
8. Blaise Pascal, *Pensées*, trans. A. J. Krailscheimer (New York: Penguin, 1995), 139.

Chapter 24: Dropping the "D" Word

1. John Betjeman, "Churchyards," *Faith and Doubt of John Betjeman: An Anthology of His Religious Verse*, ed. Kevin J. Gardner (New York: Continuum, 2005), 77.
2. J. C. Ryle, "A Common End," ChristianBeliefs.org, http://christianbeliefs.org/articles/death.html.

3. Ray C. Stedman, "Ah, Sweet Mystery of Life," RayStedman.org, http://www.raystedman.org/old-testament/ecclesiastes/ah-sweet -mystery-of-life.

4. S. I. McMillen and David Stern, *None of These Diseases* (Grand Rapids: Fleming H. Revell, 2000), 227–28.

5. An ancient fable retold by W. Somerset Maugham in his play *Sheppey* (1933).

6. David Letterman, interview by Ted Koppel, *Nightline*, ABC, July 8, 2002.

7. Mark Noll, *The Scandal of the Evangelical Mind* (Grand Rapids: MI: W. B. Eerdmans, 1994), 245.

CHAPTER 25: LIFE CHEATS!

1. "Thorpe Qualifies for Athens," BBC Sport, March 29, 2004, http://news.bbc.co.uk/sport2/hi/other_sports/3576529.stm.

2. Steve Saint, "Did They Have to Die?" *Christianity Today* 40, no. 10 (September 16, 1996), 20, http://www.christianitytoday.com/ct/1996 /september16/6ta020.html.

3. Amy Carmichael, *Rose from Brier* (Fort Washington, PA: Christian Literature Crusade, 1933; repr. 2012), 16.

CHAPTER 26: FOOLISHNESS IN LITTLE THINGS

1. Scott Bowles, "Hesitation Is a Fatal Mistake As California Firestorm Closes In," *USA Today*, October 30, 2003, http://usatoday30 .usatoday.com/news/nation/2003-10-30-fires-usat_x.htm.

2. Chuck Shepherd, "News of the Weird," *The Reader's Guide*, January 16, 2004.

3. William Secker, *The Nonsuch Professor in His Median Splendor; or, Singular Actions of Sanctified Christians* (New York: Fleming H. Revell, 1888), 302.

4. Charles Haddon Spurgeon, "Little Sins" (sermon, Music Hall, Royal Surrey Gardens, April 17, 1859), http://www.spurgeon.org /sermons/0248.htm.

5. Mary Wilder Tileston, ed., *Daily Strength for Daily Needs* (Boston: Little, Brown, and Company, 1898), 47.

6. Craig Brian Larson, ed., *750 Engaging Illustrations for Pastors, Teachers, and Writers* (Grand Rapids, MI: Baker Books, 2002), 159.

7. Horatius Bonar, *God's Way of Holiness* (Durham, England: Evangelical Press, 1979), eBook, http://gospelpedlar.com/articles /Christian%20Life/GWH_Bonar/ch_8.html.

CHAPTER 27: FOOLISHNESS IN LEADERSHIP

1. Tom Peterkin, "The Quickest Way to Gardyloo Gully," January 22, 2004, http://www.telegraph.co.uk/news/uknews/1452259/The -quickest-way-to-Gardyloo-Gully.html.
2. "1954: Winston Churchill Turns 80," BBC Home, http://news.bbc .co.uk/onthisday/hi/dates/stories/november/30/newsid_3280000 /3280401.stm.
3. Woodrow Wilson, quoted in Robert Andrews, *The Concise Columbia Dictionary of Quotations* (New York: Columbia University Press, 1992), 240.
4. Dwight Eisenhower, *At Ease: Stories I Tell to Friends* (New York: Doubleday, 1967).
5. Rudyard Kipling, *Rudyard Kipling Complete Verse* (New York: Anchor, 1989), 578.
6. Isobel Kuhn, *In the Arena* (Singapore: OMF International, 1995), 189–93.
7. Robert K. Greenleaf, *Servant Leadership: A Journey into the Nature of Legitimate Power & Greatness* (Mahwah, NJ: Paulist Press, 2002), 27. See also http://www.greenleaf.org.
8. James Truslow Adams, quoted in Suzy Platt, ed., *Respectfully Quoted* (New York: Barnes and Noble Books, 1993), 193–94.
9. William Manchester, *The Last Lion: Winston Spencer Churchill: Alone: 1932–1940* (New York: Dell, 1988), 481.
10. Peter F. Drucker, *The Effective Executive* (New York: Harper & Row Publishers, 1967), 1.
11. Pat Riley, *The Winner Within* (New York: Berkley Books, 1994), 36–37.
12. From the private diary of William E. Sangster, quoted in J. Oswald Sanders, *Spiritual Leadership* (Chicago: Moody Press, 1967), 22.

CHAPTER 28: LABOR, LANGUAGE, AND LUNACY

1. Each of these news stories was nominated for the 1995 Darwin Awards, copyright www.DarwinAwards.com.
2. Robert Frost, quoted in Robert I. Fitzhenry, ed., *The Harper Book of Quotations*, 3rd ed. (New York: Collins Reference, 2005), 103.
3. Dr. Robert Webber, "A Father's Influence," Gloria Gaither, ed.,

What My Parents Did Right (Nashville: Starsong Publishing Group, 1991), 207–8.

4. Roxane S. Lulofs, "The Hit-and-Run Mouth," *Christian Herald*, July/August 1986.

5. Quoted in Arthur Wentworth Eaton, ed., *Funny Epitaphs* (Boston: The Mutual Book Company, 1902), 61.

6. Zig Ziglar, *Top Performance* (Grand Rapids, MI: Revell, 2003; repr. 2005), 93–94.

7. Benjamin Ramsey, "Teach Me Thy Way, O Lord," 1919.

CHAPTER 29: LIFE IS UNCERTAIN: EMBRACE IT!

1. Rosemary Smith, "Life Is Proverbs to Eat Along the Way," http://www.news-journalonline.com/NewsJournalOnline/Opinion/Columnists/Close/03ColumnsCLOSE012204.htm.

2. Paul Lee Tan, ed., *Encyclopedia of 7,700 Illustrations: Signs of the Times*, electronic edition, 1996.

3. As retold in "Tahtinen: We Will Prevail," Michigan Tech, http://www.admin.mtu.edu/urel/breaking/2002/911_mem.html.

4. Philip Doddridge, "Tomorrow, Lord, Is Thine," 1755.

CHAPTER 30: LIFE IS SHORT: ENJOY IT!

1. Dr. Benjamin Mays, "God's Minute," quoted in "NAACP Gives 67th Spingarn Medal to Dr. Benjamin E. Mays," *The Crisis*, August/September 1982, 30.

2. Edward Caswall, trans., "When Morning Gilds the Skies," 1744.

3. Chris Kline, "LeClair Speaks About Life After Baseball," Baseball America, April 7, 2004, www.baseballamerica.com/today/features/040407leclair.html.

4. Robert Lewis Stevenson to Trevor Haddon, April 1884, in *New Letters and Miscellanies of Robert Lewis Stevenson*, ed. Sidney Colvin (New York: Charles Scribners' Sons, 1912), 191.

5. Robert J. Morgan, *Then Sings My Soul* (Nashville: Thomas Nelson, 2003), 151.

6. Ibid.

CHAPTER 31: LIFE IS MYSTERIOUS: EXAMINE IT!

1. Lewis Carroll, *The Annotated Alice* (New York: W. W. Norton, 2000), 124.

2. Susan Tracy Otten, "St. Jean-Baptiste-Marie Vianney," *The Catholic Encyclopedia*, vol. 8 (New York: Robert Appleton, 1910), 326–27, http://www.newadvent.org/cathen/08326c.htm.
3. Ruth Bell Graham, *Legacy of a Pack Rat* (Nashville: Thomas Nelson, 1989), 187.
4. Charles Haddon Spurgeon, "The Bible" (sermon, Exeter Hall, Strand, March 18, 1855), www.spurgeon.org/sermons/0015/htm.
5. C. S. Lewis, *The Great Divorce* (New York: Macmillan, 1946), 33–44.

CONCLUSION: LIFE IS OBEDIENCE: EXPRESS IT!

1. John H. Sammis, "Trust and Obey," 1887.

About the Author

D<small>R.</small> D<small>AVID</small> J<small>EREMIAH</small> is the founder of Turning Point, an international ministry committed to providing Christians with sound Bible teaching through radio and television, the Internet, live events, and resource materials and books. He is the author of more than fifty books, including *Is This the End?*, *The Spiritual Warfare Answer Book*, *David Jeremiah Morning and Evening Devotions*, and *Airship Genesis Kids Study Bible*. Dr. Jeremiah serves as the senior pastor of Shadow Mountain Community Church in San Diego, California, where he resides with his wife, Donna. They have four grown children and twelve grandchildren.

Stay connected to the teaching ministry of

DR. DAVID JEREMIAH

Publishing

Radio

Television

Online

FURTHER YOUR STUDY OF THIS BOOK

31 Days to Happiness Resource Materials

To enhance your study on this important topic, we recommend the correlating audio message album, study guide, and DVD messages from the *31 Days to Happiness* series.

Audio Message Album

The material found in this book originated from messages presented by Dr. David Jeremiah at the Shadow Mountain Community Church where he serves as Senior Pastor. These ten messages are conveniently packaged in an accessible audio album.

Study Guide

This 128 page study guide correlates with the *31 Days to Happiness* messages by Dr. Jeremiah. Each lesson includes a chapter summary, outline, overview, and application questions.

DVD Message Presentations

Watch Dr. Jeremiah deliver the ten *31 Days to Happiness* original messages in this special DVD collection.

To order these products, call us at 1-800-947-1993 or visit us online at www.DavidJeremiah.org

with Dr. David Jeremiah

Delivering the
UNCHANGING WORD OF GOD
to an
EVER-CHANGING WORLD

Dr. Jeremiah *on* Radio

Dr. Jeremiah's English radio program, *Turning Point,* was launched in 1982 and is now transmitted over 2,200 stations, with over 6,000 daily broadcasts heard in the United States, Canada, the Caribbean, Central America, the South Pacific, Europe, and Africa. The thirty-minute radio programs are also available worldwide via the Internet.

In addition, *Turning Point's* Spanish programming, *Momento Decisivo,* reaches all 23 Spanish speaking countries with nearly 70 translated series. On any given day there are more than 800 programs airing from 573 transmitters around the world, 85 of which are in the United States.

Turning Point is also broadcasting in China potentially reaching 780 million Mandarin Chinese speakers. Turning Point is currently working toward translating and transmitting radio programs into ten other languages including Punjabi, Tagalog, and Farsi, seeking to deliver biblical truth to people around the world.

For more information, and to find a station in your area that carries *Turning Point,* visit the Turning Point website at www.DavidJeremiah.org/Radio

Dr. Jeremiah *on* Television

Dr. Jeremiah's ministry, Turning Point, also features weekly television programming. Senior Pastor at Shadow Mountain Community Church, Dr. Jeremiah's Sunday sermons are recorded live and adapted for hour and half-hour long telecasts.

Launched nationwide in April of 2000, *Turning Point* Television has grown through partnering with local stations as well as such nationwide networks as Trinity Broadcasting, USA, Lifetime, ION, Daystar and INSP. Today the program can be viewed by virtually every TV household in America. At the same time, Turning Point has spread across the international scene through local stations in other countries as well as worldwide distribution by satellite. It's estimated that over 2.7 billion households throughout the world have access to Turning Point with Dr. David Jeremiah every day.

Turning Point Television continues to grow and expand, reaching into additional local stations in cities across the United States in order to minister more directly to receiving communities.

For more information on *Turning Point* Television, go to www.DavidJeremiah.org/Television

Dr. Jeremiah Online

Dr. Jeremiah's website offers up-to-date information on ministry happenings including current television and radio series, available resources, upcoming live events, and articles by Dr. Jeremiah. You can also read daily devotionals, learn about Turning Point's global outreach, and shop at the online bookstore.

From the Turning Point bookstore you can purchase the resources offered through Turning Point, including books by Dr. Jeremiah, teaching series on CD and DVD, pamphlets, study guides, and many other resources.

Shop today at www.DavidJeremiah.org/Shop

Stay connected to the teaching of

DR. DAVID JEREMIAH

Take advantage of two great ways to let Dr. David Jeremiah give you spiritual direction every day! Both are absolutely FREE.

Turning Points Magazine and Devotional

Receive Dr. Jeremiah's magazine, *Turning Points* each month:

- Thematic study focus
- 48 pages of life-changing reading
- Relevant articles
- Special features
- Humor section
- Family section
- Devotional readings for each day of the month
- Bible study resource offers
- Live event schedule
- Radio & television information

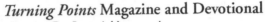

Your Daily Turning Point E-Devotional

Start your day off right! Find words of inspiration and spiritual motivation waiting for you on your computer every morning! You can receive a daily e-devotional from Dr. Jeremiah that will strengthen your walk with God and encourage you to live the authentic Christian life.

There are two easy ways to sign up for these free resources from Turning Point. Visit us online at **www.DavidJeremiah.org** and select "**Subscribe to** *Turning Points* **Magazine**" or visit the home page and find Daily Devotional to subscribe to your daily e-devotional.